Contemporary Apartment Marketing

To the Carneses, great good friends with much affection and appreciation for wonderful times together.

THE HARMONS
Portland
August, 1993

Editorial Consultants
Nancy A. Bishop, CPM®
Natalie D. Brecher, CPM®
Nancy M. Hogan, CPM®

Joseph T. Lannon
Publishing and Curriculum Development Manager

Caroline Scoulas
Senior Editor

Contemporary Apartment Marketing

Strategies and Applications

Kathleen McKenna-Harmon, CPM®
Laurence C. Harmon, CPM®

Institute of Real Estate Management
of the **NATIONAL ASSOCIATION OF REALTORS**®
430 NORTH MICHIGAN AVENUE • CHICAGO, ILLINOIS 60611

© 1993 by the Institute of Real Estate Management
of the NATIONAL ASSOCIATION OF REALTORS®

All rights reserved. This book or any part thereof may not be reproduced, stored in a retrieval system, or transmitted, in any form or by any means, electronic, mechanical, photocopying, recording, or otherwise, without the prior written permission of the publisher.

This publication is designed to provide accurate and authoritative information in regard to the subject matter covered. Forms or other documents included in this book are intended as samples only. Because of changing and varying state and local laws, competent professional advice should be sought prior to the use of any document, form, exhibit, or the like.

This publication is sold with the understanding that the publisher is not engaged in rendering legal, accounting, or any other service. If legal advice or other expert assistance is required, the services of a competent professional should be sought.

The opinions expressed in this book are those of the authors and do not necessarily reflect the policies and positions of the Institute of Real Estate Management. To protect the identities of employees and the interests of the authors' clients, names of people, places, and properties have been changed.

Library of Congress Cataloging-in-Publication Data
McKenna-Harmon, Kathleen, 1946-
    Contemporary apartment marketing : strategies and applications /
Kathleen McKenna-Harmon, Laurence C. Harmon.
      p. cm.
    ISBN 0-944298-77-X
    1. Apartments. 2. Real estate business. 3. Building leases.
4. Advertising—Real estate business. 5. Real estate listings.
I. Harmon, Laurence C., 1943- . II. Institute of Real Estate
Management. III. Title.
HD1390.5.M378   1992
333.33'8--dc20   92–24419
                                                                                     CIP

Printed in the United States of America

                1 2 3 4 5 6 7 8 9 10 Printing/Year 01 00 99 98 97 96 95 94 93 92

To Laura and Blair Harmon and Jeremy and Collin McKenna
who have come to understand—or at least to tolerate—the fact that
their parents' fascination with apartment buildings, market studies,
leasing skills, and all the other things that they included in this book
can sometimes take precedence over on-time dinners, baseball games,
dance recitals, and even summer vacations.

Preface

Marketing is the bringing together of buyers and sellers. In the apartment business, marketing is employed to deliver renters to landlords—and to keep them once they arrive. In fact, some type of marketing is indispensable to the successful performance of every apartment unit in every apartment community in every city in this country. Apartment managers are engaged in creating, implementing, evaluating, and modifying a variety of customer-driven systems, and this full-service concept of contemporary apartment marketing is the subject of this book.

As the 1990s began, investment real estate was experiencing the disastrous consequences of two events—an accumulation of nearly twenty years' worth of reckless overbuilding and enactment of the Tax Reform Act of 1986, which obliterated much of the economic benefit of real estate ownership. This situation was confirmed in a survey of real estate owners conducted by Arthur Andersen and Company for the Institute of Real Estate Management Foundation in 1990. The chief concern of the real estate owners surveyed was the glut of available space and its implications for the future—runaway vacancy was the most pressing concern, exceeding even rising property expenses, spiraling interest and inflation rates, construction costs, financing, and energy expenses. In such a recessionary climate, tenant retention was viewed as the most important task facing property managers. Indeed, property owners considered tenant relations—which includes tenant retention, negotiating leases, obtaining tenants, and handling tenant relations—to be the top priority for management firms. In the 1990s, management companies will stay in business to the extent that they can capture and care for tenants. This book suggests a number of ways to do just that.

Why This Book is Needed

Because they are related to finding and keeping residents, marketing skills are important in apartment management today as never before. Managers and owners are faced, on the one hand, with a market supersaturated with product and, on the other hand, with a consumer base that is shrinking as the population ages. To make the situation worse, the recent collapse of savings and loan institutions has virtually shut down apartment financing, not just for new construction, but for much-needed rehabilitation and operating capital as well. For all these reasons, apartment marketing is serious business. Done well, it can be the salvation of the multifamily housing industry between now and the millennium.

In an imaginary perfect world, apartment marketers might wish to control the behavior of prospective residents so that they would rent apartments at any price, accept rent increases at whatever frequency and in whatever amounts imposed, and live in a property indefinitely, asking in return only that a roof be kept over their heads. However, it is impossible to dictate human behavior to such an extent, and few would argue the desirability of doing so. While marketing makes no claims of such control, it is clear that apartment marketers should use all of the tools available to them to attract prospects to their apartments and, once acquired, to retain their residents.

This book, then, is about the types of tools available for influencing prospects' behavior and their use in impacting, swaying, and guiding it. We believe successful contemporary apartment marketing results from development and implementation of specific strategies, and examples of these are identified in every chapter.

We begin by outlining the components of marketing research. Chapter 1 tells you how to define the market of consumers of rental housing in your area so that you can focus your efforts to market apartments to them. Equally important, it presents methods for evaluating the competitive strength of an apartment community based on its physical condition and its fiscal condition. It goes on to discuss marketing grid analysis as a basis for structuring rents in an apartment property to capitalize on its competitive strengths. Information about the market and the property provides the basis for developing a comprehensive marketing plan, as outlined in chapter 2. There we discuss budgeting issues, the planning process, and responses to changing market conditions.

Adjuncts to marketing success include market research, targeted advertising, and a professional staff. Chapter 3 suggests ways to determine customer preferences using specific market research techniques which should help focus your marketing effort in general and your advertising campaigns in particular. It outlines specific, inexpensive methods that can be used immediately. Chapter 4 addresses issues specific to apartment advertising. It discusses the benefits of using an advertising agency, outlines the array of costs involved, and details specific considerations related to media selection. Chapter 5 presents strategies for hiring and training leasing personnel, including techniques we have used in identifying the best candidates to hire.

The objective of marketing is to obtain signed leases. Your trained staff becomes an extension of advertising and other efforts to bring people to your apartment community. The on-site activities of talking to prospects, showing them apartments, and convincing them to sign leases are viewed as a continuation of marketing. Chapter 6 describes traditional leasing "sales" techniques and suggests ways of improving on them using strategies employed in retailing. Chapter 7 then catalogs the important details of completing the leasing transaction—filling out application forms, qualifying prospective residents, and complying with fair housing laws.

Having once acquired residents, apartment managers are finding it increasingly desirable to retain them. Resident retention is much more efficient and economical than continuous resident turnover. Strategies for achieving this are described in chapter 8. Market research is revisited as a way of measuring resident satisfaction, and application of a "customer service" philosophy is recommended as a means of improving it. Specific examples from retailing and apartment management are cited.

Some Notes About Style

This book is a recollection of our successful (and some not-so-successful) approaches to apartment marketing. Its tone is conversational: The word "we" is used throughout in referring to our personal experiences and opinions; the reader is addressed as "you" when we describe what apartment marketers can do on their own to improve their success rates.

Tenants in apartment properties are often called "residents," and we have used that term consistently, unless the context is specific to a lease. Tenant (or lessee) is more common terminology in legal documents. We have occasionally used the word "landlord" in referring to the other party to a lease (the lessor) because apartment renters commonly perceive the landlord as any person they deal with regarding the leasing arrangement. In actual fact, the owner of the property is the landlord, but real estate managers and others sometimes are empowered to sign leases as the owner's agents, and various management personnel usually interact directly with residents on the owner's behalf. Technical terms that have precise meanings in the fields of marketing, advertising, and real estate are italicized and defined in the text, obviating the need for a separate glossary.

As a point of information, *location* is generally a primary consideration in development, marketing, and leasing of any type of real estate. We do not deny this. However, most of the examples in this book do not emphasize location because it has not been a specific marketing issue for us. (That fact is noted in several contexts.) The apartments we manage offer extensive amenities and resident services, and these factors are emphasized accordingly.

Although we have managed and marketed apartments in several different cities, we currently work in a market area that is unique. The twin cities of Minneapolis and St. Paul, Minnesota, are separated from each other only by a line on a map, and that division is often indistinguishable on the ground. However, the two cities are distinctly different from each other in the makeup of their business districts, their residential neighborhoods, and their surrounding suburbs, and each separately presents very different challenges for marketing apartment communities. The fact of their being separate cities means we have access to a wider array of advertising media and creative people than are available in most markets of the same size, and we have had opportunities to manage and market a variety of interesting and unique apartment properties. Writing *Contemporary Apartment Marketing* has provided us with an opportunity to share what we have learned from our many experiences. Some of these lessons are set apart at the ends of chapters using a heading that begins: A Practical Example—.

We would have preferred to sit down in the same room or across a table from everyone who markets apartments and talk with them about what constitutes successful apartment marketing. We would have liked to discuss the questions they have and explore answers with them. We could all learn more that way. Because such a personal dialogue is not possible, we decided to do the next best thing. In writing this book, we have tried to provide a starting point from which people in the tough, competitive, sometimes seemingly thankless business of marketing apartments can build toward their own success. We hope you will try out those things we have found to be successful, avoid the mistakes we made, and seek ways to improve on what works for you.

ACKNOWLEDGMENTS

Nonfiction is inspired by and grounded in experience. Ideally, an author's own experience will blend with the experiences of others with similar interests and backgrounds to produce an inspired foundation for a written work. Because *Contemporary Apartment Marketing* is nonfiction, its existence quite literally depends on the beneficence of a number of individual and institutional owners—our clients—who hired us over the years and who provided us with the on-the-job training that is the underpinning of this work. We are indebted as well to our professional colleagues and friends who have shared their own insights and experiences with us over the years.

The following people have significantly enriched the content of this book and our lives: John Appert of Great Places in Minneapolis; Bodie J.

Beard, CPM®, of Bodie Beard Interests, Inc., in Houston; Antonio Bernardi of Sentinel Management Company in Minneapolis; Robert S. Bisanz, Terrence E. Troy, Pamela J. George, and Michael J. Semsch, CPM®, of Real Estate Equities, Inc., AMO®, in Saint Paul; Norman P. Bjornnes, Jr., Esq., of Namron Company in Minneapolis; John P. Brandstatter, CPM®, of Mellon Bank, N.A., in Pittsburgh; James F. Collins, CPM®, of Leasing Legends in Davidson, North Carolina; E. Paul Dunn, CPM®, of The Welsh Companies, Inc., in Eden Prairie, Minnesota; Sandra L. R. Durand, CPM®, of Newman, Herfurth & Durand Property Management Company, AMO®, in Minneapolis; Ron Fingerhut of Family Partners, Ltd., in Minneapolis; Charlie Fox of Merrill Lynch Hubbard, Inc., in New York City; Professor Evelyn Franklin of the University of Minnesota in Minneapolis; Michael Gembecki of Marine Midland Bank in New York City; Ed A. Harrington, CAE, and John G. Horner, Esq., of Minnesota Multi Housing Association in Minneapolis; Edward T. LaGrassa and Anthony F. Navarro of Citicorp Real Estate, Inc., in New York City and Chicago; Robert H. McElroy, CPM®, of General Electric Capital Corporation in Boston; Petra A. Marquart of Hennepin Technical College in Minneapolis; Donald Maurus and Nadine Huff of The Phoenix in Hartford, Connecticut; Michael J. Miles, CPM®, of PREMISYS Real Estate Services, Inc., in Chicago; William S. Reiling and Mark W. Reiling of Towle Real Estate Company in Minneapolis; David A. Rivnak, Teachers Insurance & Annuity Association of America in New York City; Susan M. Schnarr, CPM®, of Mid-Continent Management Corporation in Saint Paul; Terrence P. Sullivan of Boston Bay Capital, Inc., in Boston; Karen Walders, CRM, CAPS, of Lang-Nelson Associates, Inc., in Minneapolis; Denise D. Williams of Chemical Bank in New York City; and consultant Joseph L. Yousem, CPM®, of Joseph L. Yousem Company, Inc., AMO®, in Los Angeles.

We also wish to express our appreciation and admiration to Par Shaw Loomis, herself an author and owner of a Minneapolis advertising agency, for her insights about service as a "profit center" for apartment managers as well as advertising. Her many valuable contributions are reflected in chapters 4 and 8.

We acknowledge with thanks our staff, past and present: Elaine "Cookie" Abramson; Linda Fieldman; Jayne Hayes; Katherine Scott Herzig, CPM®; Maureen Kelly; Barbara Mack; Judith Murray; Diane Peterson, and Gwen Hamilton Starr.

While our family, friends, and professional colleagues motivated us to write this book, others were instrumental in its preparation. Barbara L. Holland, CPM®, chairperson of the IREM Publishing Committee, exhorted us to "control the architecture" of our book. Joseph T. Lannon, Publishing and Curriculum Development Manager at IREM, generally allowed us to do so. Caroline Scoulas, our editor, challenged and inspired us with her remarkable writing and editing skills; she understands this book and has come to have the same parental feelings about it that we do.

We also thank the following individuals who kindly critiqued the manuscript and improved several of its sections in significant ways: Nancy A.

Bishop, CPM®, of Howard Bishop & Company in Denver; Natalie D. Brecher, CPM®, of Forest City Management, Inc., in Los Angeles; and Nancy M. Hogan, CPM®, of First Realty Management Corporation in Boston.

Finally, we extend our thanks to Thomas Y. Mandler, Esq., of the Chicago law firm of Schwartz & Freeman, who reviewed the legal aspects of personnel management contained in chapter 5.

Kathleen M. McKenna-Harmon, CPM®
Laurence C. Harmon, CPM®

Contents

Chapter 1   **Understand the Market**................................. 1
Understanding Management Objectives   1
Defining the Market   3
Evaluating the Competition   15
Focusing on the Property   23
Apartment Marketing and Economics   26
A Practical Example—Competing Against Concessions   28

Chapter 2   **Strategize Marketing**................................. 30
Budgeting for Marketing   32
Developing a Marketing Plan   34
The Impact of Market Conditions   53

Chapter 3   **Understand Your Customers**......................... 62
The Concept of Market Research   63
Why Do Market Research on Apartments?   65
Market Research Methods   71
A Practical Example—A Focus Group Session   79

Chapter 4   **Advertise**.. 87
Advertising Objectives   88
Advertising Strategies   90
Budget Considerations   93

Staff Requirements 97
Media Selection 104
Evaluation 108
A Practical Example—Experiments with Media 110

Chapter 5 **Build a Professional Staff** 119
Hiring Leasing Personnel 119
Training Leasing Personnel 129
Motivating Employees 132
Building a Leasing Team 134
Maintaining Staff Morale 136

Chapter 6 **Strategize Leasing Activities** 139
Strategies for Getting Acquainted 140
Strategies for Showing Apartments 147
Strategies for Closing 158
A Practical Example—The Retailing Comparison 163

Chapter 7 **Enhance the Leasing Activities** 176
Qualifying Prospects 177
Documenting the Residential Lease 189
Renewal Strategies 191
Adjunct Issues 193

Chapter 8 **Market to Current Residents** 196
Customer Service in the 1990s 196
Service in the Apartment Industry 200
"Moments of Truth" in Multifamily Housing 207
A Practical Example—Market Research Applications 213

Index 225

Contemporary
Apartment Marketing

CHAPTER

1

Understand the Market

The days of the three-line want ad and the five-minute apartment tour are long gone. Today, real estate managers and apartment marketers must be increasingly creative in attracting new residents to their apartment communities—and getting them to stay once they move in. Rental income can be maximized only if all—or nearly all—the units in an apartment community are occupied and their residents are paying maximum rents. High occupancy levels are the result of successful leasing strategies that capitalize on properly focused marketing campaigns coupled with well-thought-out resident retention programs.

Marketing and leasing are the most exciting and challenging aspects of residential property management. Chances are the "four white walls and a rug" (i.e., the apartments) available in your building are not much different from the "four white walls and a rug" in the building next door. What sets your apartments apart may be mostly intangibles (e.g., a service-oriented staff). That is why it is important to isolate the specific differences and use them in marketing your apartments. You have to convince rental prospects that those differences are important reasons for renting in your building and that they justify any additional rent charged for your apartments. Otherwise, your prospect will rent the "four white walls and a rug" next door. Apartment marketing, when it is successful, makes renting decisions rational rather than random.

Marketing strategies are designed to create specific demand for particular apartments that are part of the total supply of housing in the market. Apartment managers have to do extensive research and analysis before they can develop appropriate marketing strategies. In this chapter, we will describe the different types of information the manager must collect and compare in order to make sound marketing decisions and develop a viable marketing plan that will lead to achievement of ownership's occupancy and other goals for the apartment property.

Understanding Management Objectives

Owners employ professional property managers and others to market their apartments in order to achieve the financial goals established for their properties. They expect these management professionals to pay attention to demographic trends and economic developments as well as more-subtle property-specific factors that can influence the properties' fiscal performance.

The objective of apartment management, which includes marketing and leasing of individual apartments, is to maximize the fiscal performance of the property. This is achieved by maximizing income and minimizing expenses. The gross income of a property can be improved by increasing rents, charging fees for the various ancillary services provided by management, and aggressively collecting delinquent accounts. Expenses can be lowered by controlling maintenance expenditures, pursuing energy-saving alternatives, and purchasing supplies more prudently.

However, there are some major income and expense items over which property managers have little or no control. Market conditions affect income and expenses both directly and indirectly. In "soft" markets, steady rent increases tend to reduce occupancy levels and thus offset the income derived from a rent increase. Property taxes and utility rates are set by others, and they impact operating expenses both currently and in the future. In short, there are significant external factors that can slow down or prevent the realization of the financial goals that have been set for a property.

These factors are maddening, not only because they are external, but because they seem to be unpredictable. They can affect different properties—even properties in the same market—in ways that appear to be random. Property managers often assume, for example, that they cannot reasonably forecast the magnitude of property tax increases, which can have tremendous negative impact on the income generated by their properties. Likewise, they may assert that a sudden downturn in a once-solid market could not possibly have been anticipated. Eventually they may work in a reactive "victim" mode, trying to do their best to manage what they have come to believe is an uncontrollable environment.

Occasionally, such rationalizations turn out to be correct. For example, an oil embargo in a distant part of the world that results in exorbitant energy costs can take even the most sophisticated observer by surprise. On the other hand, what appears to be an overnight decay in an apartment market may actually have been quite foreseeable—the manager may simply have been unaware of subtle changes that had been under way for months. That jump in property taxes might have been anticipated, too; in retrospect, the manager may find that the signs were discernible to anyone reasonably attuned to the local economy and political climate.

While it is a fact that some factors affecting income and expenses are beyond the manager's influence, there are still other factors that the manager can control. In fiscal terms, the essence of effective real estate management is setting rent levels, controlling vacancy losses, collecting delinquent rents, and containing maintenance costs. The first two are especially important because they are marketing issues. Because marketing itself can be controlled by the manager, it is possible through that means to exercise greater control over rents and vacancies.

The key to maximizing property income is improving occupancy levels by implementing productive marketing strategies and resident retention programs. To do this effectively, the manager must first conduct *marketing research* to establish the location and extent of the market for the apartment community. Only then can he or she do a proper analysis of the rents and other characteristics of the managed property as compared to its competition. In other words, the manager must evaluate—and take advantage of—the competitive position of the managed property within its market. (Marketing research is distinguished here from "market research"—determination of consumer preferences—which is the subject of chapter 3.)

Defining the Market

Conditions in the local market drive the short- and long-term performance of the apartment industry as a whole as well as that of individual apartment communities. The overall soundness of the economy within a particular area and the financial strength of local employers, as well as population growth, transportation facilities, educational institutions, cultural activities—even climatic conditions and recreational opportunities—all contribute to the strength of the apartment industry. These and other factors determine whether particular areas are desirable places to live.

The desirability—or undesirability—of an area as a place to live affects the prosperity of apartment properties that compete within it, and it is therefore useful to know, in a general sense, whether that area is itself economically viable and if it is likely to remain so. In the apartment industry, the market of a particular apartment community is defined in terms of its region and its neighborhood. The term *region,* as applied in the apartment industry, is defined as the market area in which changes in economic conditions (e.g., employment, population, income) are likely to affect the fiscal performance of a particular apartment community and thereby determine its value. Similarly, the term *neighborhood* is defined as a section of a larger region or market area, within which apartment buildings generally compete with one another for residents.

Analysis of the vitality of the region and the neighborhood in which an apartment community is situated is the indispensable foundation for a property manager's planning and forecasting efforts. Such an analysis enables those with marketing responsibilities to define the position of the apartment community in its market as well as determine the scope and intensity of the advertising campaign that will be required to attract residents. The acquired knowledge will improve the property manager's ability to anticipate vacancy levels and project rent increases as well as advise owners regarding the desirability of undertaking renovations or selling the property.

The following discussions will address the differences between regions and neighborhoods and their respective importance in characterizing a property's market.

The Region. For apartment marketing purposes, a region is a physical area of indeterminate size that has distinctive economic conditions which affect the property's financial health. Analysis of the region will indicate whether and how much demand exists for rental apartments as well as the supply of available housing.

This concept of a region can be understood by looking at population changes in urban areas and the measurement of those changes by demographers. The proportion of the U.S. population living in cities or urban areas has steadily expanded. The process of people moving to cities or to densely settled areas is one that can be measured and analyzed, and that analysis leads to useful conclusions about regional growth and the demographic characteristics of regions.

Demography is the statistical study of populations. It examines sets of characteristics about people that relate to their behavior as consumers. The most frequently analyzed demographic factors are age, sex, race, marital status, education, and income. However, household size and composition (e.g., number of children and their ages) are other factors that directly impact housing choices. Demographers seek out old and new data—from censuses, surveys, birth and death records, for example—that can be shaped into manageable form through the use of rates and ratios or even raw numbers.

Early demographers faced the challenge of how to fix the boundaries of the geographic areas they wanted to study. They were struck by the startling population growth of cities in these areas, and as early as 1950, they began to focus on what they called standard metropolitan statistical areas or SMSAs. In order to provide a consistent urban definition for government agencies, the United States Office of Management and Budget (OMB) started to designate metropolitan statistical areas (MSAs) in 1983. MSAs are composed of one or more counties, at least one of which includes an urbanized area (UA)—a city with a population of 50,000 or more. UAs consist of a central city (or cities) in a metropolitan area, along with the surrounding closely settled territory constituting its "urban fringe" (a density of at least 1,000 persons per square mile). A UA may include some less densely settled areas within incorporated city limits but typically does not include open rural land that would otherwise be part of an MSA's outlying territory. An MSA may be a single county, or it may contain a number of adjacent counties. Regardless of their composition, the counties in an MSA are economically and socially integrated.

While studying demographic data, the property manager may encounter other terms that have their origins in the SMSA concept. MSAs with populations in excess of one million are often further subdivided, and primary MSAs (PMSAs) within them are identified. A PMSA may comprise one or more large urbanized counties, all of which have strong internal economic and social links, but it may not have a central city as such. MSAs in which such PMSAs are identified are redesignated as consolidated MSAs (CMSAs).

The fact that the government collects, sorts, and analyzes data according to MSAs provides real estate managers with a valuable resource for apartment market studies—the MSAs are defined according to the same interdependent economic indicators that are important to the manager. Whether the region relevant to an apartment community is defined as an MSA or some derivative of the MSA—or by another method altogether—understanding of certain statistical concepts can make the analysis more meaningful. Demographic data are presented in a variety of ways; among the most useful are counts, rates, ratios, proportions, and periodic measures. These will be discussed in the following paragraphs, using hypothetical examples.

A *count* is the absolute number of any population statistic or demographic event occurring in a specified area in a specific time period. Count data, which frequently reflect census figures, are raw numbers that provide the basis for a variety of other statistical refinements and analyses. The size of a population and its distribution among age, income, and other groupings are typically expressed as counts.

Exhibit 1.1 shows examples of count data. The percentages in the top part of the exhibit indicate that unemployment fluctuated somewhat over the period 1988 through 1991, but no specific trends can be discerned. A conclusion regarding trends in unemployment would require examination of factors outside the data that might have influenced the higher or lower percentages. Several major corporations might have entered the region sometime in 1988, and the numbers of employees they hired could have driven the unemployment percentages downward in 1989. Conversely, a substantial number of people might have entered the work force in 1991, and their inability to find employment could have moved the percentage upward.

The housing start counts in exhibit 1.1 indicate an apparent upward trend beginning in 1987, and then an apparent decline beginning in 1990. The figures would encourage the analyst to look for external circumstances that might have affected these numbers beginning in 1990 and continuing more dramatically the following year. Such factors might include federal and local tax policies that made multifamily housing ownership less desirable than in previous years or, perhaps, the beginning of a recessionary period.

EXHIBIT 1.1

Count Data

ANNUAL AVERAGE UNEMPLOYMENT
MSA, 1988–1991

1988	1989	1990	1991
4.3%	3.3%	3.8%	4.4%

HOUSING STARTS BY TYPE
MSA, 1987–1991

Year	Total Units	Single-Family	Multifamily
1987	21,643	12,083	9,560
1988	22,260	12,665	9,595
1989	27,345	16,320	11,025
1990	26,766	16,235	10,531
1991	20,730	13,755	6,975

Conclusions drawn from demographic data have important implications for the economic performance of apartments in the region defined by the MSA. Income levels, employment figures, and other characteristics of commerce in the region (e.g., types of industries, trades, and professions; how consumers spend their incomes; construction permits and housing starts) are indicators of economic activity. The economic condition of the region affects the ability of potential apartment residents to pay rents in general and to pay rents in particular amounts. It is vitally important to express counts and other data as clearly as possible and derive only those conclusions that the data support.

Rates reflect the frequency of demographic events in a population in a specified time period. These may be "crude" measures for an entire population or "specific" rates computed for a specific subgroup. The latter may be age-specific, sex-specific, race-specific, occupation-specific, or the like. Data of this type are useful in comparing numbers or percentages of one indicator to numbers or percentages of other indicators or to an entire field of data.

Exhibit 1.2 is an example of the use of rate data. It shows that older housing (i.e., more than 50 years old) comprises nearly one-half of the housing stock in an urban area. This fact may support the conclusion that additional housing product is needed or that existing older stock should be rehabilitated.

A *ratio* is the relation of one demographic subgroup to another subgroup in the same population—that is, one demographic subgroup divided by another. Analysis by means of ratios is helpful when a demographic sector

EXHIBIT 1.2
Rate Data

AGE OF HOUSING
PERCENT OF TOTAL URBAN AREA
MSA, JANUARY 1, 1991

Year Built	Number	Percent
Pre-1939	146,892	49.3
1940–1959	66,245	22.2
1950–1979	63,365	21.3
1980–1991	21,398	7.2
TOTAL	**297,900**	

EXHIBIT 1.3
Ratio Data

AVERAGE MONTHLY RENTS

	1-Bedroom	2-Bedroom	3-Bedroom
MSA	$552.49	$670.67	$817.53
Suburban	$502.38	$598.82	$702.14
Suburban as % of MSA	90.9	89.3	85.9

is being evaluated against a larger field, as in a comparison of single-person households to the total number of households in a population.

Exhibit 1.3 shows a comparison of suburban rent levels to rents in the entire MSA. Overall, it appears that rents are higher in the metropolitan area as a whole than in the suburban areas within it, especially for three-bedroom units. This means that if rents in a particular metropolitan building are substantially below the average rents for the MSA, they may be too low, and further analysis is warranted. (Rent analysis is discussed later in this chapter.)

Proportions express the relationship between a demographic subgroup and the entire population—i.e., the subgroup is divided by the entire group. Proportions are helpful in evaluating the strength of one or more elements within an entire population. This would apply to age brackets and income brackets, for example.

Exhibit 1.4 shows the employment in several key industry types as measured against all types of employment in an MSA. Note that three industry types (trade, services, and manufacturing) comprise nearly three-quarters of

EXHIBIT 1.4

Proportions

EMPLOYMENT TYPES BY PRIMARY INDUSTRY DIVISIONS MSA, 1990

Industry	Number Employed	Percent of Total
Trade	3,060,810	25.6
Services	2,981,580	24.9
Manufacturing	2,456,540	20.5
Government	1,451,060	12.1
Finance/Insurance/Real Estate	908,910	7.6
Transportation/Communications/Utilities	620,675	5.2
Construction	500,709	4.2
TOTAL EMPLOYED	**11,980,284**	

all employment within the MSA and that employment in construction industries is the lowest among those cited. This means that employment in the MSA is heavily dependent on the strength of trade, services, and manufacturing companies. While these businesses may be diversified enough to withstand an economic recession, the area's heavy dependence on trade may leave it vulnerable to downswings when there are trade imbalances with foreign countries.

Periodic measures appraise events occurring to all or part of a population during one period of time. These measures can then be compared with the same field at a different time, and the magnitude of any change can be measured. Changes in the size of a whole population and its component subgroups (e.g., distributions by age, race, sex) in decennial censuses are examples. Periodic measures facilitate an analysis of such things as apartment vacancies and can aid in determining the existence of trends.

Exhibit 1.5 shows vacancy rates for the same period in two consecutive years. Increasing vacancy rates might be interpretable as suggesting market softening; however, percentages without actual counts can be misleading. On the other hand, substantial variations among unit sizes, as noted here, could indicate changing popularity of apartment types. Vacancy data of this type should be compared with historical data on pricing and numbers of units in the market to demonstrate whether and to what extent these factors are interrelated. (Vacancy will be discussed later in this chapter in the context of demand and absorption.)

In discussing the hypothetical examples shown in exhibits 1.1–1.5, we have demonstrated how some very basic types of demographic data are relevant to apartment marketing. It is also important to be aware of when the data

EXHIBIT 1.5
Periodic Data

APARTMENT VACANCIES BY UNIT TYPE (Percents)
MSA, SECOND QUARTERS, 1990–1991

	Studio	1-Bedroom	2-Bedroom	3-Bedroom
1990	6.91	10.46	8.27	16.19
1991	10.03	15.29	8.83	17.36
% Change, 1990 to 1991	+45.2	+46.2	+6.8	+7.2

were collected. Specific numbers lose their relevance over time because of changes in the marketplace. Data showing explosive population growth and a fixed number of housing units might be interpretable as indicating a need for additional housing. Yet, those data may have been collected in a time frame that precluded (or excluded) information on new construction—in other words, the need for additional housing may have already been met, but the data suggest otherwise.

For those who have not utilized demographic data extensively or are unsure about where to obtain such information, there are a variety of publications that provide direction in finding demographic information and using it. Three recent books are especially valuable:

- *The Insider's Guide to Demographic Know-How: Everything You Need to Find, Analyze, and Use Information About Your Customers, 2nd Edition,* was written by Diane Crispell and published by the American Demographics Press in Ithaca, New York, in 1990.
- *The Insider's Guide to Demographic Know-How: Everything Marketers Need to Know About How to Find, Analyze and Use Information About Their Customers,* edited by Penelope A. Wickham, is an earlier edition from American Demographics Press, published in 1988.
- *By the Numbers: Using Demographics and Psychographics for Business Growth in the 90's* was written by Judith E. Nichols and published by Bonus Books, Inc., in Chicago, Illinois, in 1990.

The first two contain exhaustive lists of sources of demographic data that are available from federal and state agencies—complete with contact names, addresses, and telephone numbers—and are therefore good starting points for finding information to include in regional analyses. (It is beyond the scope of this book to include all of the state and local sources for such data. Public libraries as well as local governments, chambers of commerce, and newspapers can be useful resources for local data.)

Use of Demographic Data

The U.S. Department of Labor, Bureau of the Census, conducts a decennial census of the population at large and evaluates the information based on race (and Hispanic origin), age, income levels, and education. It also characterizes families (married, with and without children), households (single-person, nonfamily, male- or female-headed), and housing stock (occupied versus vacant, single versus multiple units, age), births, deaths, and mobility (immigration, outmigration, cross-country). Data are compiled by MSA, state, and region.

Data from the decennial census as well as compilations of economic statistics (employment, industries, gross domestic product, price indexes, consumer expenditures, etc.) are selectively updated and published annually in a *Statistical Abstract of the United States*. Comparative statistics on the rate of unemployment, the level of employment, and the rate of new job formation are measures of the economic vitality of an MSA. Information on housing and households is also collected by sampling and issued periodically as an *American Housing Survey for the United States*. Such resources can usually be accessed at public libraries. Renter-occupied housing compared to all occupied housing has remained steady at around 35 percent for most of the period since 1970.

Population projections for the United States reflect current population counts, assumed birth and death rates, and certain levels of migration and immigration. The assumptions underlying such projections have a critical impact on assumed demand for housing. As a result of changes in birth, death, and fertility rates, the age composition of the U.S. population shifts. As the year 2000 approaches, there will be sharp increases in the 45 and over age groups and similar decreases in the under-45 age groups as the "baby-boom" generation—those born between 1950 and 1965—enters middle-age.

The household—the unit of housing occupancy—has undergone a variety of changes over recent decades. In general, households comprising families (persons related by blood or marriage) have been declining as a proportion of all households. Those headed by single persons now represent about one-fifth of the total families, and four out of five of such households are headed by females. Nonfamilies have increased from less than 15 percent in 1960 to nearly 30 percent of households in 1990, and one-person households have almost doubled from 13 percent in 1960 to nearly 25 percent of all households in 1990.

Locally, similar changes in household characteristics suggest niche markets for targeted marketing and leasing. A shift toward nonfamily households may suggest marketing of large units (two and three bedrooms and more than one bathroom) to two or more roommates—in addition to or instead of families with children. Growing numbers of single-person households may create a natural market for studio and one-bedroom units.

Supply, Demand, and Absorption. Demand for apartments in a particular property is a reflection of specific demographic and economic characteristics of the overall population within the market area. Among the specific measures of the strength of a region are comparison of the demand for housing with the supply of available units and evaluation of the market's ability to absorb additional new housing.

Demand for housing is measured in terms of *households*—that is, one or more people who jointly occupy a dwelling unit and constitute a single economic unit in regard to housing expense. This is a different classification than a family, which consists of persons related by blood or marriage. People in a household need not be related. The number of households in the market, their economic and demographic characteristics, their tastes and preferences, and the prices and availability of housing and other goods and services, as well as expectations about future price levels, affect the allocation of housing units among households. This is why it is important to analyze the demographic characteristics of the current local population and compare these statistical data with past compilations and future projections.

Over time, the demographic characteristics of a population change. Age and gender are variables in housing demand, along with population size. Babies are born, and mature adults die. Children grow up and move out of the family home, creating new households. There is movement of households into and out of neighborhoods and regions. These changes all affect demand for housing. Furthermore, preferences for housing types vary with people's ages—young adults tend to choose rental housing while middle-aged adults tend to own their homes. Younger people also tend to move more frequently, and single-person households become multiple-person households via marriage or other social arrangements. Demographers' projections about population shifts, household formation, and other changes are important indicators of future demand for housing (and types of housing). To effectively manage and market apartment communities, real estate managers must keep these types of factors in mind.

Increasing household income is another variable that influences demand for housing. Demographers define income in different ways for different purposes. Most statistical reports show gross income, which is the total wages paid for work done. However, the amount left over after deductions for federal, state, and local income taxes and social security benefits (*disposable income*) is what the household actually has available to spend. This take-home or net income is the basis of a household's ability to purchase goods and services, including housing.

Determination of housing demand requires an analysis of supply. The supply of rental housing in the market area includes both occupied and vacant units. The number of vacant rental units available in the market expressed as a percentage of the total supply of rental units is the *vacancy rate*. The vacancy rate includes vacant units in existing stock plus vacancies in new construction (the unrented inventory of newly built apartments) but excludes vacancies resulting from seasonal occupancy or those unoccupied rental units awaiting demolition, rehabilitation, or conversion—i.e., those vacant units in existing stock that are, for any reason, not available for occupancy. The supply of rental units is only a part of the housing supply. The numbers of single-family houses, condominiums, and other owner-occupied units—and their respective vacancy rates—would have to be analyzed to determine the total supply of housing and the overall vacancy rate in a particular market area.

Vacancies in a particular apartment property are characterized as physical or economic. *Physical vacancies* are units actually available for rent while *economic vacancies* are all vacant units that are not producing income. The latter includes not only physical vacancies, but also units that are not available for lease (e.g., apartments used as models, offices, staff apartments, etc.) as well as leased units that are not yet occupied and occupied units that are not producing rent (i.e., delinquencies). What this means is that the number of unoccupied units may not always be an accurate reflection of the impact of vacancies.

The number of units leased compared to the total number of units available for lease within a certain geographic area over a given period of time is called the *absorption rate*. It relates to both construction of new space and demolition or removal from the market of existing space. When demand exceeds supply, absorption is favorable (vacancy decreases); when supply exceeds demand, absorption is unfavorable (lenders curtail financing and growth slows). A negative absorption rate can also reflect other changes in the marketplace, such as a major industry shutdown (i.e., when there is a lack of jobs, people move away, and new people are discouraged from moving into the area).

Absorption is a concept that is most frequently utilized in commercial markets. Analysts typically consider the square footage occupied at particular rent levels as a way of forecasting the supply (say, of office space) that will be available in the future. Apartment absorption can be measured by examining occupancy levels on the basis of what were earlier described as count data expressed in periodic terms. For example, assume that in Year 1 in a particular MSA there are 200,000 apartments, 95 percent of which are occupied. In Year 2, an additional 50,000 units are built, but occupancy has dropped to 92 percent. The number of units absorbed in the MSA is expressed as follows:

Year 1: 200,000 × 95% = 190,000 occupied units
Year 2: 250,000 × 92% = 230,000 occupied units
Year 2 occupied units − Year 1 occupied units = 40,000 units absorbed

A residential real estate market demonstrates its vitality in part when new product is assimilated—i.e., occupied—and in part when apartment units are re-rented as residents vacate them.

In the field of economics, the *law of supply and demand* explains the pricing of products in terms of their availability. Applied to apartments, this law can be stated: High demand reduces the supply of apartments and thus permits rents to to be raised; conversely, an oversupply of apartment units tends to drive rental rates down.

The principles of "supply and demand" and "absorption" are important in the apartment industry because they provide a useful way of illustrating whether a particular market is "soft." Soft markets are characterized by high vacancy levels and relatively constant (or diminishing) prices. (Strategies for

The Housing Market

The market for real estate is by nature local. Because real property is immobile, it is affected directly by its location and adjacent land improvements. These considerations create a "neighborhood" and give specific value to real estate. Use as housing, tenure as rental occupancy, and physical characteristics of units (number of bedrooms, features and amenities) are used to "disaggregate" the market into submarkets in which the determinants of supply and demand will be relatively uniform.

A submarket consists of a homogeneous supply of housing units occupied by relatively homogeneous households. For example, one submarket might be two-bedroom apartments in a particular neighborhood renting for $600–$750 per month. The homogeneity of apartment residents within that submarket will be determined by such things as household income, age of the household head, stage in the family cycle, the householder's place of employment, and other economic, social, and demographic factors. Household income is usually the measure of housing affordability. This is based on the assumption that a certain percentage of income is spent on housing and a certain level of income is needed to pay the required rent. However, other factors may have to be considered in characterizing the homogeneous subset of households that are the prospects for a particular type of housing unit (e.g., number of people and their ages).

Submarkets of consumers are further separated into distinct groups, and this market segmentation is also based primarily on income. There is a certain income level below which consumers are unable to afford certain types of housing units. In attempting to identify demand for two-bedroom apartments at a certain rental rate, for example, a rent-to-income ratio of 1:4 is often used. This would require prospects to have a monthly gross income of $400 for each $100 of monthly rent. Increasing household income tends to increase the demand for better-quality, higher-priced goods and services of the type already being consumed. Renters move up by paying more rent for larger apartments (extra rooms)—or newer apartments—or for additional features in their apartments (dishwasher, microwave, in-unit laundry equipment) or in the apartment community (swimming pool, exercise facilities, other common area amenities).

Housing markets are often further segmented by demographic characteristics, most commonly age. Individuals in the same age and income group are often distinguished still further based on their attitudes, preferences, and tastes—i.e., psychographic factors. The issues of affordability and desirability may be overcome by a strong preference for a certain location (suburban versus city), a particular type of housing (new versus old), or other "lifestyle" considerations.

---

competing in soft markets are described in chapter 2.) The two concepts can be integrated into a single statement as follows: Absorption rates represent effective apartment demand over a specified period, contrasted and evaluated in terms of competitive supply.

The Neighborhood. While the strength of a region indirectly affects the vitality of apartment buildings situated within it, a property's neighborhood has a direct impact on its economic performance. Apartment buildings generally compete with one another on the basis of such factors as location and rents (prices), as well as their age, quality and type of construction, amenities, and appearance. Their market positions—i.e., their occupancies, in general and at particular rent levels—are determined by their success in competing within particular neighborhoods.

We believe *competition is the key to defining the boundaries of a neighborhood.* Consequently, the extent of the prospective residents' "shopping" area—the physical perimeter within which they are likely to look for an apartment—is the most appropriate way to fix neighborhood boundaries. People customarily choose to live in a particular location because of its proximity to their places of employment, family members, medical facilities, shopping, churches and synagogues, recreational activities, and a variety of other attractions. These assumptions about why people choose to live in particular locales are often reflected in the advertisements for rental apartments—the ads emphasize that a building is close to major freeways or convenient to major employers, schools, buslines, and shopping.

In a suburban community, the city limits may define the neighborhood of an apartment building, but in very large urbanized areas, a neighborhood is likely to be defined as a discrete geographic area within the city. For purposes of consistency, the term neighborhood as used throughout the remainder of this book will refer to the localized area within which an apartment building is considered to compete for prospective residents. The neighborhood for a particular apartment community will depend on such things as the type of building (mid-rise, high-rise, etc.) and its age, the different types and price levels of apartments in it, and the facilities and amenities it offers to residents.

Location is obviously critical. Two other critical competitive factors are, of course, *price* and *quality*. Prospects tend to be price-sensitive and may make their renting decisions based on that criterion alone, especially in tough economic times. For those renters who consider *value* (the constellation of benefits they believe they will enjoy in exchange for their monthly rent—i.e., the quality of the building's construction and the amenities it offers), price considerations are blended into their sense of the quality of their rental lifestyle. Therefore, in establishing the boundaries of the neighborhood, both competitive pricing and competitive value should be considered.

Building types also influence the definition of a neighborhood. Renters frequently prefer to live in a particular type of building—garden-style apartments, high-rises, townhouses—and will often "shop" for such building types. For example, the relative availability of apartments in mid-rise buildings will narrow or expand the boundaries of the neighborhood for the particular mid-rise building that is being marketed.

Property managers and others who market apartments have developed and refined a variety of techniques that can be used for the purpose of analyzing the competitive strength of a property within its neighborhood. Once

> **Understanding the Local Market**
> Major newspapers frequently survey their readership in order to characterize the audience for advertisers as well as focus their editorial content. These types of surveys typically collect demographic data (age, income, sex, marital status, etc.). Often they also include questions regarding lifestyles—preferred reading, recreational and leisure activities, etc. Chambers of commerce may conduct similar surveys when a municipality plans to encourage residential or commercial development. Large shopping centers anchored by department stores sometimes survey their customers, especially when a change in the center's tenant or merchandise mix seems warranted. Real estate managers and apartment marketers should explore these and other types of local information resources.
>
> Apartment marketers need demographic and psychographic information about the local market to target advertising to market niches. Shifts in the dominant age groups suggest both target markets and modifications to existing properties that will increase their appeal to other market segments.
>
> People over age 65 have vastly different interests and needs than people under age 30. Married couples and young families with small children have different needs and desires than people who live alone. Changes in the local population and its income and lifestyle characteristics may suggest accommodation of a more (or less) athletic segment of the population, acceptance (or prohibition) of pets, or any number of different opportunities to achieve the leasing and occupancy goals set for a property. Such changes in the marketplace demand adaptation, not merely to survive, but to succeed.

the composition of the neighborhood has been determined, it is important to analyze the competition. Such analysis will facilitate assessment of rent levels in a particular building so that its net operating income can be optimized. That is the subject of the next section.

Evaluating the Competition

One of the most useful techniques for evaluating the competition is creation of a marketing grid. *Exhibit 1.6* is an example marketing grid form. The grid format permits direct comparison of rental rates and amenities at the subject property—i.e., the manager's building—with the same types of information about the properties that compete with it directly. On the form itself, the features or qualities of the apartments to be compared are listed in the left-hand column. The list should be specific to the comparison being done, including features and amenities present in the subject but not in the competitors and vice versa. (This aspect will be considered in detail later in this chapter.) Columns are also provided for each of the properties to be included in the comparison. The subject property is evaluated in the column adjacent to the features list, and competing properties are evaluated in successive columns to the right. Note that for each competitor there are two columns, one to describe the features and qualities of the buildings and the other to indi-

EXHIBIT 1.6

Example Marketing Grid Form

Type of Unit _____ Date of Analysis _____

Property	Subject	Competitor 1	Competitor 2	Competitor 3
Monthly Rent				
Concessions				
Address				

	Description	Description	Adj	Description	Adj	Description	Adj
Location							
Age							
Curb Appeal (1)							
Square Feet							
Baths (number)							
Patio/Balcony							
View							
Fireplace							
Wallpaper							
Carpet							
Drapes/Blinds							
Washer/Dryer/Microwave							
Dishwasher							
Disposal							
Air Conditioning (2)							
Cable TV							
Elevator							
Pool							
Sauna/Exercise Room							
Tennis							
Party Room							
Security							
Garage (3)							
Parking Fee							
Tenant Pays Heat							
Rental Rate							
Less Monthly Discount							
Effective Rent							
Adjustments (Total Net)							
Adjusted Comp Rent							
Adjusted Rent/Sq Ft							

(1) 3 = poor; 4 = fair; 5 = good; 6 = excellent curb appeal
(2) W = wall unit; C = central AC
(3) R = aboveground, open ramp; U = underground parking

NOTE: This example was adapted from a grid used by the authors. For any specific evaluation, the comparison items for the subject property and its competition might include such things as specific utilities, other parking options, and vacancy rates.

cate adjustments to the rent amount (ADJ)—addition or subtraction of a particular dollar amount for each feature. (Entries in these columns will be discussed later.)

A marketing grid is intended to be a data-driven assessment of the current competitive position of an apartment community within its neighborhood and, therefore, *objective*. However, the results are by nature *subjective* because the choice of features to be compared in a marketing grid and the assignment of values to them are usually arbitrary. Managers should keep this limitation in mind, especially when a marketing grid is used in setting rents.

The best marketing grids compare a subject with at least three other properties. When more than three competing properties can be identified, the results will be even more useful. A separate grid should be prepared for each unit type that will be studied (studio, two-bedroom/den, etc.), and each grid should be dated to provide a ready reference as to when the analysis was done. A major use of the marketing grid is for comparison of rents.

Comparing Rents. A comparison of the rents at competing properties provides an overall understanding of the pricing structure in the neighborhood under study. The first row at the top of the grid (see exhibit 1.6) is for listing the rent for the particular type of apartment at each property (at the time the analysis is done). This should be the amount of monthly rent that a prospective resident is quoted for a particular apartment type by a leasing agent at a particular property.

The person constructing the grid should think through the best means for arriving at a definition of the rent to be used in the grid. Property managers use a number of different terms in discussing rents. The quoted rent is also sometimes called *face rent, street rent,* or *contract rent.* By definition, the latter is the rent stated in a specific lease. The term *market rent* is often used interchangeably with contract or street rent, but true market rent is the amount a comparable unit would command in a competitive market. The actual rent being paid for a particular one-bedroom apartment may or may not be equal to the market rate for one-bedroom apartments generally. For comparison purposes, some analysts recommend using rent amounts that are believed to be "typical" for that unit type in the subject property and among the competition. Alternatively, the *lowest* rent for available units among the competing properties in the market may be listed—we prefer the latter approach.

The purpose of the marketing grid is to capture the current state of the market, and pricing comparisons are essential to this task. If a figure other than the lowest rent amount is used, the picture thus created can be deceptive. Presenting rent ranges, for example, will require calculation of an average rent for comparison purposes, and there may be no one apartment priced at that amount. Similarly, trying to arrive at a typical figure requires a judgment about which particular apartment in the subject building and each competitor is representative of the others in their respective properties.

As a further complication, the sources of information—typically on-site leasing personnel in other properties—may have only a very general impression of rent ranges for occupied versus vacant apartments. However, they are likely to know the lowest-priced available apartment of each unit type with reasonable accuracy. While using the lowest rent does not permit comparison of all rents for all unit types in the market, it does facilitate evaluation of the rents for available apartments. These numbers are not perfect, but they will provide valuable information. The key is to be consistent.

Once the lowest rents for a type of unit in the neighborhood are known, a variety of relationships can be calculated. The *mean* (arithmetic mean or average) is calculated by adding together the rental amounts for all of the competing properties and dividing the sum by the number of competitors in the study. The *range* would be a listing of the lowest and highest rents in the market. It may also be desirable to calculate a *median* rent—i.e., the middle value among a series such that there are an equal number of items above and below it (for example, in the series $345, $346, and $350, the median is $346; in the series $345, $346, $347, and $348, the median is $346.50). A comprehensive statistical analysis might also include the *mode* (the most frequently occurring value or amount) as well as the *standard deviation* (the square root of the average of the squares of the deviations from the mean). Whatever the method of analysis, it should be apparent where the rents for different apartments in a particular building fall within their market.

Head-to-Head Comparison. A simple comparison of rent amounts might be called *head-to-head price correlation*. This information is useful because many renters in particular markets make their housing decisions predominantly on the basis of price considerations, with all other factors being decidedly secondary. Knowing where a property is priced relative to its competition—along with such other component factors as vacancies (in and of themselves and according to unit type), seasonal variations in price and vacancy levels, and other influences—can facilitate a decision whether to modify a rent structure.

In creating marketing grids for properties we manage, additional rows are included at the top of the grid for recording rents from past evaluations (see exhibit 2.1 in the next chapter). This allows us to analyze historical pricing in a market. If pricing data are rigorously compiled on a monthly, quarterly, or (minimally) semiannual basis, the price history of the neighborhood can be charted. This information is helpful not only in evaluating the long-term strength of the market, but also in adjusting rents if it is apparent that there are seasonal pricing or other variations across the neighborhood.

The row labeled "concessions" permits listing of specific rent concessions being offered in the neighborhood (e.g., one month free rent on a one-year lease). The rent per month reduced by the monthly value of the concessions is the *effective rent* per month for that unit. (From the property owner's viewpoint, effective rent is a better measure of the actual income derived from the lease for an apartment than the monthly rent stated in the lease.) It may be desirable to monitor effective rents over time as a way to study the prevalence of concessions in the market and to note their presumed impact on vacancy rates and net operating income. (Usually effective rent is recorded near the bottom of the grid, as in exhibit 1.6.)

The marketing grid discussion thus far has been based on the assumption that price (especially the effective rent)—coupled with quality—is the primary determinant of the success of an apartment community. Such straightforward calculations (using either quoted or effective rents) underscore the limitations of a comparison based solely on price. It does not factor into the selection criteria such significant considerations as unit size, property age and appearance, unit and property amenities, etc.—i.e., the other items listed on the grid. These are the desirability or "buy" factors that may be expected to influence prospective renters to (1) choose a particular apartment community and (2) be willing to pay a particular rental differential to obtain them. The next section will address these concerns.

Comparing Buy Factors. The features and qualities listed on a marketing grid will vary according to the manager's assessment of the buy factors he or she believes local prospects consider important. The list may be shorter or longer than the one in the example (exhibit 1.6), depending on the type of building being evaluated.

Whatever the buy factors in a particular list, it is important to be aware of the consequences of including some features while omitting others. Because the use of a marketing grid is an attempt to provide an objective assessment of the market, every significant amenity that exists in the neighborhood—whether related to the apartment or the common area of the property—is a potential item to be included on the grid for comparison purposes. This may lead to a decision to list features in the market that are not present in the subject property. For a property in an upscale market, for example, such things as fireplaces, fitness centers with the latest equipment, and in-unit washers and dryers may be common features among the competition. Some properties in the neighborhood may also provide unique staff services such as laundry and dry cleaning pick-up and delivery, valet parking, on-site restaurants, and transportation to downtown work locations or to recreational facilities. Each of these characteristics represents a potential buy factor that could influence a prospect's renting decision. This means that a dollar value can be assigned to the characteristic (in the adjustments column), thereby adding to or detracting from the property's desirability in the market—and thus changing its monthly rent.

By assigning specific values to the buy factors, the manager is attempting to decide how much these factors are worth to the renters in the market. This is admittedly a subjective exercise. What is a tennis court worth per month to prospects? Five dollars? Ten dollars? More? How about a patio or balcony, or an underground parking garage? The best way to assess the value of such features is to ask the residents in the building what they think or to question prospects about their preferences. Undoubtedly this would be beneficial in terms of accuracy and objectivity, but it is unlikely that a manager will have the time to undertake a comprehensive study of this type just to prepare a marketing grid. (If the manager lives in an apartment community in the area, he or she should already be attuned to the popularity of various amenities among residents there.) As a safeguard, however, it is worthwhile to ask a few people what dollar amounts they would assign to certain features.

On the other hand, some buy factors can be valued fairly precisely. For example, if the subject property does not charge for parking but one of its competitors charges $40 per month, the differential for the comparison is $40. Regardless of the absolute values of particular features, the adjustment exercise is worthwhile—as long as the manager keeps in mind that the adjustments are fairly subjective and that such subjectivity will affect the validity of the results.

Because the subject property is being measured against its competition in economic terms, the dollar amounts assigned to various features and amenities will be indicated in the adjustments column as either positive or negative values. Thus, if the competitor is superior to the subject property with respect to a particular feature or quality, the adjustment for the competitor will be a negative amount; if the subject property is superior, the adjustment for the competitor will be positive. The various adjustments for each competitor are added together to calculate the net (positive or negative) adjustment to the competitor's rent. In short, the rent of each competing unit will be adjusted up or down relative to the subject property in an attempt to make it—and the rent it commands—more nearly comparable to the subject property.

Making Specific Adjustments. Although making rent adjustments on a marketing grid is inherently subjective, the ultimate goal is to estimate the values that prospects would assign to particular features. One mistake often made in constructing a marketing grid is to overvalue the features of competitive properties. When the value of a particular item is uncertain, the wisest practice is to make adjustments in smaller, rather than larger, amounts.

In making specific adjustments, the manager must consider the potential renters of the apartments being compared. For example, some prospects may state a preference to live in an older building (rather than a brand-new one) because they believe that newer apartments lack "charm." However, such a stated preference does not always translate into a specific action and, consequently, negative adjustments to the competitors simply because they are older than the subject would be erroneous, at least for these prospects.

On the other hand, compilation of data for the marketing grid may indicate that competitive apartment communities have a vast array of amenities that are not available at the subject property—e.g., jogging trails, solariums, concierge services. Theoretically, such would be a basis for downgrading the competitor. However, if a large number of prospects are corporate transferees—i.e., people moving in from other states who are looking merely for quality housing at low prices until they can buy or build their own residences—it would be inaccurate to record large positive figures in the "adjustments" columns for the competitors, at least for these prospects. All that can be done in these circumstances is to make the best estimate of the value of a feature or quality to *average* prospects.

The admonition to use smaller amounts is especially relevant if you are adjusting for vacancy rates in the market. (Vacancy adjustments would be made on a separate line; the example grid in exhibit 1.6 does not include such an item.) If a manager concludes that a competitor's vacancy rate is elevated because its rents are too high, the "adjustments" column might show a negative amount equal to the rent "reduction" that, ideally, would lower vacancy in the competitor to a level that will maximize its net operating income. On the other hand, an extremely low vacancy rate in a competitor might lead to the conclusion that its rents are less aggressive than they should be. In which case the "adjustments" column might show a positive amount equivalent to the rent "increase" that would achieve a suitable vacancy rate.

However, it is difficult to know with any certainty the vacancy situation in competing properties or the rental rates that will maximize their net operating incomes. We have found that site staffs at competing properties are extremely reluctant to share accurate information, and any figures gleaned from them are likely to be understated. Except during initial lease-up, high vacancy rates are considered indicative of failure, and leasing and management personnel are inclined to believe that excessive vacancies are symptomatic of their own inadequacies. These considerations reinforce the need to make extremely conservative estimates when preparing a marketing grid. While competing properties may have a higher or lower vacancy rate than the manager believes is appropriate for the subject property, the goal of the grid exercise is to set rents for the subject property at the level that will maximize its net operating income.

Once all the buy factors have been compared, adjusted rents and base units of value can be calculated.

Calculating Adjusted Rent and Base Unit of Value. The "adjusted" rent for each competitor is computed by adding together the positive and negative amounts in the "adjustments" column and increasing or decreasing the effective rent by the total. (Remember: Effective rent equals contract rent minus concessions amortized over the lease term. Effective rent plus-or-minus total adjustments yields the *adjusted rent* for each competing property.) Once the adjusted rent for each competitor is known, the *adjusted rent per square foot* can be calculated by dividing the adjusted rent by the area (square footage) of the representative apartment.

Having arrived at these figures, the *base unit of value* for the subject property can be determined. There are two ways of doing this. One is to calculate the average adjusted rent for the competition by adding together the adjusted rents for a particular unit type and dividing the sum by the number of competing properties involved. The other is to add together the adjusted rent per square foot for each of the competing properties and divide the sum by the number of competitors—the result is the average adjusted rent per square foot for the competition. These two values should be entered in the appropriate spaces for the subject property.

The base unit of value should be calculated for each of the apartment types being studied and expressed in terms of both the average adjusted rent and the average adjusted rent per square foot for the competition. The reason for calculating two values is that the average adjusted rent does not include apartment size as a factor that may influence prospects' renting decisions. When the average adjusted rent per square foot is multiplied by the area of the unit in the subject property, the result may be substantially different than the average adjusted rent amount. If renters in the area are known to consider apartment size as a buy factor, or if units in the subject property are substantially larger or smaller than those in the competition, the rents for the subject property should reflect this. The average adjusted rent per square foot provides a means of computing rent based on unit size. On the other hand, if other features in the apartments or common area are known to be more important to prospects, or if floor plans are more influential than apartment sizes, the average adjusted rent is the more appropriate base unit of value to use.

The base unit of value is an accepted means of comparing the effective rent of the subject property with rents of competing properties in the market. Whether the rent structure for the subject should be modified in light of the calculated average adjusted rents or average adjusted rents per square foot may be open to question. However, these two values provide a rational basis for evaluating whether the rents set for each apartment type in the subject property are appropriate. The results of these calculations are substantially more than a simple head-to-head comparison of rents. Rather, they reflect the assortment of buy factors that are considered important to renters. In essence, use of a marketing grid indicates that prospects are faced with a variety of alternatives for housing and that their deliberations extend beyond price to include features and amenities that are available to them.

[NOTE: In setting rents for a brand-new or newly rehabilitated property, it is desirable to identify and select only nearby properties that are truly comparable in location, amenities, and other characteristics. In such a marketing grid exercise, the average of the adjusted comparable rents or the final rent for the comparable property with the fewest adjustments is likely to be the ideal market rent to be set for the unit in the subject property. For an established property, however, a marketing grid may be used to show how the rent in the subject compares with the adjusted rents for similar units in competing properties. This will help the manager quantify differences between the subject property and its competition. The differences may indicate whether and how much more rent can be obtained for units in the subject property because of their superiority to the competition or, conversely, whether expected rents are too high because the subject is inferior compared to the competition. In practice, rent reductions are rarely endorsed by ownership because they go directly to the bottom line—they reduce both net operating income and property value. However, a marketing grid may identify types of concessions that could be introduced or features that might be added to or upgraded in the subject property so that it can compete more effectively.]

Other Uses of Grid Data. As a marketing exercise, a grid creates an awareness of the features of a particular managed property that constitute its competitive advantages. It will provide clear indications of buy factors that can be used to sell the property to prospects—information that can and should be utilized in developing advertisements and other promotional materials.

Marketing grids for all the available unit types can be posted on a wall in the leasing office. They should be sufficiently prominent so that staff will be aware of and refer to them, but out of the view of prospects. Leasing agents should be encouraged to review the grids each time they prepare to interview a prospect. Furthermore, as they talk with prospects who are residents at competing properties, they should gain additional insights. Knowing a prospect comes from a particular property should ultimately facilitate identification of specific features about the subject property that can be promoted to that individual. In addition, comments made by the prospect may provide details about the competition that can be used to fine-tune and update information on the grid. In other words, knowing a property's advantages—and disadvantages—will give the manager and the leasing staff a competitive edge.

Focusing on the Property

As already described, numerous external factors (demographics, competition, supply and demand) affect the success of an apartment property even though property owners and managers cannot control them and can influence them only indirectly. In addition, a building's internal performance has a potential impact on its economic success, and such factors as appearance and maintenance are entirely within the control of the site staff and the property manager.

In truth, prospective residents base their renting decisions primarily on two factors: The quality of the apartment presentation made by the leasing agent and the quality of the apartment product they see. Prospects evaluate the quality of the product in part by deciding whether the physical features of the apartment building (common area amenities, apartment size and design) will meet their needs and in part by judging whether those features are clean and in good repair. Because maintenance and housekeeping are decisive factors in prospects' renting decisions, they are crucial elements in the overall success of an apartment community.

Curb Appeal. The impression a building makes when a prospect first sees it is the result of its *curb appeal*. When we train our marketing and leasing personnel, we explain to them that curb appeal goes beyond the appearance of the exterior of the apartment building and its grounds to include the hallways, interior amenities, and other common areas—virtually everything prospects see as they approach the property and tour the building *before* they are shown an apartment.

Prospects make judgments about quality when they drive into the parking lot, as they walk along a sidewalk next to the building, or when they overhear residents talking about their experiences living there. Consequently, it is imperative that the product they are evaluating is made attractive and kept that way as a matter of habit.

Successful apartment owners and managers are very much aware of the significance of curb appeal. They know the truth of the saying: You never get a second chance to make a first impression. These first impressions either (1) motivate prospective residents to enter a particular apartment building and find out more about what it has to offer or (2) convince them that the quality they are seeking in apartment living is more likely to be found somewhere else.

To be sure the property is looking its best, apartment managers often hire consultants to "shop" their buildings, using a checklist to record and comment on their observations. *Shoppers* are asked to evaluate the appearance of signage, common areas, exterior maintenance and upkeep, snow removal, and a host of other factors. They are also asked their opinions about what they see and how they are treated by the site staff, including and especially the leasing personnel.

With respect to building and common area maintenance and housekeeping, a shopper might be directed to answer yes or no to the following questions on a printed checklist.

1. Was your first impression of the property favorable?
2. Were the grounds, parking, and trash collection areas clean?
3. Were lawns, shrubs, and landscape foliage neatly trimmed and healthy-looking?
4. Were the directions easy to follow?
5. Was the signage attractive and easy to see?
6. Did signs lead you directly to the office?
7. Was the intercom (if any) easy to understand?
8. Was the lobby neat, clean, and painted?

9. Were the halls neat, clean, and painted?
10. Were there any noticeable odors?

In addition, space would be provided at the end of the checklist for the shopper to note personal comments about the appearance and condition of the exterior and common areas of the property.

Shoppers assume the roles of actual apartment prospects, and owners and managers often decide to take corrective action based on shoppers' evaluations of the physical appearance and maintenance of the property and the professionalism and leasing skills exhibited by the site staff. (Consultation with an attorney may be advisable since some states require such shoppers to be licensed as "private investigators.")

The same kinds of questions can be used by the manager, who should walk the property at least once a day using a checklist to note those areas that need improvement. Any deficiencies should be corrected as soon as possible, either by the manager personally or with the assistance of the staff. Because objectivity is vital, someone else whose opinion the manager respects should be asked to walk the property every week or so and evaluate its condition using the same checklist.

Unit Readiness. Just as the quality of an apartment community is illustrated by its curb appeal, its desirability as a place to live is embodied in the condition of the apartments that prospects are shown. Apartments must be "rent-ready" at the time they are marketed to prospects and when new residents move into them. Apartment preparation is important for four reasons:

1. It affects the "salability" of the apartment.
2. It reflects the image of the property and contributes to its reputation.
3. It represents the professional caliber of the manager and the staff.
4. It establishes a relationship among the manager, the property, and the prospects and residents.

Determining whether an apartment is truly rent-ready requires it to be checked thoroughly by a person sensitive to details to make certain it is in perfect condition.

Here, again, a daily walk-through by the site manager or another designated staff member, using a specially prepared apartment inspection checklist, will assure that any furnishings are in place, fixtures are always sparkling clean, carpeting has been vacuumed, and all litter has been removed. This person should ask himself or herself: "Would *I* want to live in the apartment in its present condition?" If the answer is, "No," the apartment should not be shown to prospects, nor should new residents be allowed to move into it. The manager should also maintain an accurate inventory of vacant units, showing apartment size, location (unit number), carpet color, and other specific features, updating the list as units are leased and others are vacated. These inspection records and inventory lists will ultimately facilitate the leasing program.

Apartment Marketing and Economics

Because an investment property derives its income—and therefore its bill-paying capacity—almost exclusively from rent collections, setting rents is one of the most important functions that an apartment owner or manager performs. Consequently, estimations of the property's "gross potential income" and "effective gross income"—the latter takes into account vacancy and collection losses—merit close attention. The rent structure for a property should be designed using a marketing grid and taking into account the economics of the building itself. This means that rent-setting is linked to budgeting, whether the property is new to the market or already well-established. A budget is an estimate of income and expenses, projected for a future period. Current income and expenditures coupled with known changes in costs (e.g., utility rates, taxes) and receipts (rent increases in place) form the basis for these projections. Funds for marketing and advertising to lease apartments are a component of an annual operating budget. (Budget preparation, in general, is beyond the scope of this book; budgeting for marketing is addressed in chapter 2, and specific advertising considerations are covered in chapter 4.)

While marketing grids facilitate setting rents according to apartment types, they are less useful in deciding what rent levels are achievable within each type. This is because particular apartments have "desirability factors" that others of the same type may not have. A manager may find, for example, that all the one- and two-bedroom apartments on an entire floor in a building have spectacular views while other units in the building do not. The spectacular view is a desirability factor that should be taken into account when setting rents for those particular units. Other apartments may be located close to elevators, trash chutes, or exercise rooms—what might be considered "*un*desirability factors." For those units, it may be appropriate to set rents somewhat lower as a way to compensate residents in them for unpleasant noises they may experience.

Because of such considerations, the optimum rent for a given unit may be higher or lower than the projected rent for the unit type. Rents that are set too high will increase vacancies; rents that are too low may create high occupancy levels but generate less-than-optimal net operating income (NOI). However, if the only way to lease the unit is to decrease rent, more can be lost from NOI if the rent is not adjusted and the unit remains vacant.

Every time a downward adjustment is made in the rent for a particular apartment, the NOI of the property is affected negatively. Just as important, the value of the building is correspondingly diminished. This is based on the *income capitalization approach to value,* which derives the value of a property by dividing its NOI by what is known in the industry as a *capitalization or "cap" rate.* This economic reality explains why established apartment rents should not be reduced as a leasing concession.

Also, determining which apartments in a building's inventory have particularly desirable (or undesirable) features requires more than common sense. For example, if a manager believes the views from some apartments may be especially pleasing, that impression should be tested. Views should be evaluated at a time when residents would be expected to be physically present in the apartments to enjoy them because daytime views differ from those seen at night, and that difference affects value. If residents are expected to be at work during the day, then evening views should be observed as the basis for any rent adjustments. The opposite is also true. An especially important consideration is *what* the occupants will see. Mountain or garden views that are spectacular in the daytime may become nothing to look at after nightfall. Conversely, cityscapes may seem unimpressive in daylight but become spectacular after dusk.

Arriving at the appropriate rent level for one apartment, a group of apartments, or an entire building cannot be done in a vacuum. Apartment rent-setting is essentially a matter of finding the proper "price point" for a particular apartment based on its acceptance by prospective renters in the competitive market. This means that apartment product will at some point find its own price level. The maximum amount a prospect will pay for an apartment is the rent that should be set for it.

The concept of price points should be kept in mind for two reasons: (1) They will eventually be established by the market, and (2) they tend to be higher than at least some apartment managers believe them to be. The market will determine price points regardless of the rent levels projected in a *pro forma budget* prior to development of a new property. Thus, they will operate as a reality check if owners or financial institutions are more aggressive in their income projections than the market will justify.

Our experience has indicated that site staffs prefer rent levels to be low. They lobby apartment managers to lower rents or to approve rent (or other financial) concessions because lower prices make their jobs easier. Furthermore, leasing personnel typically fail to "close" their sales because they are often uncomfortable with the rents they are expected to charge, and they tend to favor low prices because they expect prospects will be less likely to object to them. In other words, they anticipate that pricing objections will be difficult to handle. (Chapter 6 addresses this issue in more detail.)

There is a natural—and desirable—tension between an owner's aggressive, optimistic projections about achievable rents and an on-site marketer's pessimistic assessments of them. It is a rare occasion when these estimates will be in agreement. The professional property manager recognizes the relative validity of these divergent perspectives, reaffirms the concept that business considerations require rents to be set in the maximum amount the market will accept, and justifies rent-setting decisions to these different factions on the basis of marketing grids, historical experience with price points, and personal knowledge of the market.

A Practical Example—
Competing Against Concessions

In our market area, management of large properties has traditionally remained in the hands of the original development companies, which have large budgets; opportunities for fee management typically come as major challenges—i.e., when a property is experiencing problems. Sometimes competition for residents becomes very fierce, and it can be extremely difficult and discomforting not to follow along. These are the conditions under which we undertook the marketing and management of Steeplechase.

Steeplechase is an upscale apartment property in a major downtown market. Its neighborhood is a discrete physical area in which there are some 750 apartment units of types similar to those at Steeplechase. Pro forma rents for this property had been established by bankers in another city nearly eighteen months before it opened. During its first year, Steeplechase leased up rapidly (to the 80-percent level), and the effective income projected by the development pro forma was achieved.

Directly across a city park from Steeplechase is a multiple-use property, which we will call Maxima. Maxima contains approximately 250,000 square feet of retail and office space as well as 100 high-priced condominiums and 250 rental apartments. It opened some four years before Steeplechase and, unfortunately, was a spectacular failure in the market. The retail component was opened first, with perhaps only 50–65 percent of its space leased; subsequent leasing of store space for nonretail commercial uses made the retail space less desirable. In addition, the rental apartment component was managed by people whose prior experience had been exclusively with commercial properties. These management choices were coupled with less-than-top-quality construction. Maxima proceeded through a variety of refinancings and foreclosures and was eventually taken back by one of its successor financial institutions (an entity willing to absorb huge losses). At that point, Maxima began to offer substantial leasing concessions—as much as five months' free rent on a one-year lease—as well as drastically reduced rents. Other properties followed Maxima's example, and a devaluation stampede was under way.

We soon found that the property we managed (Steeplechase) was competing in a market that seemed to have collapsed virtually overnight. In succeeding weeks, its competitors (led by Maxima) continued to modify their rent structures, vying with one another to offer—and advertise, often in half-page Sunday display ads—more startling discounts, move-in allowances, and cash incentives. Security deposits were no longer required; health club memberships, sumptuous dinners, and river cruises abounded.

While others chose to reduce their rents we did not. Through it all, Steeplechase floated serenely above the fray. As its managers, we had panicked very briefly, reassured our jittery out-of-state owner, and steadfastly maintained our rent structure—by now, our contract rents (monthly rates stated in leases) were averaging $150 per month more than our competitors'. We had capitalized on the heightened interest in the neighborhood that had been spawned by the competition's screaming advertisements and actually improved the leasing velocity at Steeplechase.

Price wars of the type we encountered are not uncommon in overheated apartment markets where there is an abundance of product. This phenomenon is also characteristic of markets similar to that of Steeplechase, where repeated take-backs and failures impel managers to focus on a dizzying variety of giveaways and thereby further devalue their properties. Some owners and managers anxiously react by competing solely on the basis of price considerations; however, we took the opposite position with Steeplechase. We believed a variety of benefits offered at the property—e.g., top-notch construction and a newer building, recreational and fitness facilities, concierge services, and a guaranteed 20-minute response to service requests—constituted value to the current residents and would enable Steeplechase to continue to compete on the basis of quality. We saw no need to be stampeded into the wholesale use of concessions that characterized the market. Instead, we proceeded to promote the building to the niche market of prospective residents who (1) were suspicious of giveaways, (2) recognized that price cuts inevitably downgrade housekeeping, maintenance, and service generally, and (3) were willing to pay extra for superior rental housing.

Techniques for selling *value* will be addressed again in a later chapter. Here we simply reiterate that the interplay between financiers' and site marketers' projections of achievable rents often requires judicious assessment of the environment in which an apartment property functions (its breadth and depth), adherence to the principles that seasoned managers of multifamily apartment properties have developed and tested, and optimism about the capacity of a quality product to succeed—despite temporary market conditions. The approach we advocate begins with a marketing plan—the subject of the next chapter.

CHAPTER 2

Strategize Marketing

In preparing to write this chapter, we called a friend to ask if he had some really good marketing plans he would be willing to share with us. His response? "I'm embarrassed to tell you that the closest we have ever come to a marketing plan is to ask, 'Where's the leasing brochure?' and 'Who's going to place the ad in the Sunday paper?' " Furthermore, a survey of property managers in our area revealed that more than 80 percent did not routinely prepare written plans for their intended marketing activity during a given period. When a particular approach did not work, they would simply modify their marketing effort—with little or no understanding of what had failed, or why. (We call this approach "Alaskan-winter marketing" because it is done totally in the dark.)

One of the major themes of this book is that marketing and its components should be considered in terms of their ability to influence the behavior of prospective renters. We believe there is a direct causal relationship between marketing planning and marketing achievements and that marketing achievements are vital to the financial well-being of apartment communities. If apartment marketing could be likened to waging a war, then a marketing plan would be like a battle plan. While planning will not assure victory, it will lessen the likelihood of defeat. Success should be more than the result of a series of lucky guesses. For the manager who approaches apartment marketing with knowledge and forethought, it is. Planning forces the apartment manager to analyze, question, and focus, all of which stimulate creativity. Planning permits the manager to control the outcome of apartment marketing efforts and influence their success.

A *marketing plan* presents the entire marketing program for an apartment community over a particular period of time. It details how the program will be coordinated and specifies how the marketing tasks will be allocated among the site or central office personnel. Usually such a plan is based on a budgeted allocation of funds for marketing expenditures. However, it is also appropriate to develop a marketing plan that suggests various strategies, projects their estimated costs as a basis for comparison, and makes specific recommendations as to which alternatives would be most efficient or cost-effective or both. Such a marketing plan might well include an estimated budget for all proposed expenditures related to the full spectrum of the marketing effort. Such a presentation will facilitate choices and decisions by ownership or others in positions of authority.

The foundations for the marketing plan are the owners' goals for the property (discussed later in this chapter) and an objective in-depth analysis of the competitive position of the apartment community in its region and neighborhood (see chapter 1). The plan should include objectives to be achieved—numbers of apartments to be leased, at what rates, and during what time frame. It should outline the thrust of the specific promotional campaign on the basis of the positioning statement or theme that is proposed for the property and develop a specific program for accomplishing the listed objectives using that theme. This means it should include the advertising media that will be employed and the contents of the advertising that will be placed (issues addressed in detail in chapter 4).

A comprehensive marketing plan will spell out the roles and responsibilities of the leasing staff who will implement the plan. It should suggest approaches to be utilized in interviewing prospective residents, screening devices for qualifying applicants, and techniques for acquiring signed leases. If concessions are to be offered, the plan should describe the limits that will be placed on acceptable concessions and the market conditions that will allow their use. Finally, the marketing plan should specify how the plan will be monitored and the criteria that will be used to measure its success. It may also be appropriate to indicate acceptable alternatives (mid-course corrections) for achieving the required results.

Because knowledgeable apartment marketers are becoming increasingly aware of the importance of reducing resident turnover, the best marketing plans include the specific contents of the resident retention program that will be in place at the site. (A formal document incorporating the elements listed here—i.e., including the specific leasing activities that will be conducted—might also be called a *leasing plan.*)

Before you can begin to develop a meaningful plan, you must know the size of the marketing budget.

Budgeting for Marketing

Customarily, a budget for apartment marketing has been approached as some arbitrary percentage of gross income devoted to advertising or as a specific dollar amount based on anticipated apartment turnover. Some owners and managers may simply ask, "What can we afford?" However, the process of arriving at an appropriate marketing budget for an apartment community is more complicated than a merely subjective determination of what might be necessary. It requires knowledge of both the costs that are likely to be incurred and the potential availability of funds to pay for them. Ultimately, the money made available and spent on marketing will depend on the owner's goals for the apartment community in terms of expected occupancy and rental income levels. It does not make sense to create a marketing plan that will cost thousands of dollars if ownership will approve spending only a few hundred dollars. Nor is it particularly sensible to skimp on marketing expenditures (use only occasional classified ads in newspapers, for example) if there are numerous vacancies to be filled quickly, and ownership is willing to spend whatever it takes to get the job done. What this all means is that you have to know up front what kinds of costs might be incurred for different marketing activities you want to propose, how successful you expect them to be, how effectively they will fulfill ownership's goals, and whether they are "affordable." (Ownership goals are discussed later in this chapter in the context of marketing strategies.)

A helpful starting point is to identify the activities that will (or are likely to) generate the expenses that will be charged against the marketing budget. In the broadest sense, marketing may encompass showing apartments, obtaining signed leases, moving in new residents, renewing leases with current residents, and monitoring the results of specific advertising campaigns in addition to attracting prospects—in short, all the costs related directly or indirectly to the marketing of your apartments. The line item in the annual budget may be labeled "marketing" or "advertising"—or something else altogether. Regardless of the label, it is important to have one place for recording all of these types of expenses.

Generally, the costs associated with production and placement of individual advertisements (the actual dollar amounts) are the most obvious candidates for this category. Because they are likely to be the biggest expenditures as well, we will discuss them in detail in chapter 4. Charges for design and printing of brochures, guest cards, stationery, and business cards, plus postage and any "welcome home" gifts for new residents or other items directly related to the leasing effort are also obvious marketing expenses. In addition, there are numerous other, less-obvious, costs that should be considered in this budget category. A model apartment is one. Signage is another. Supplies of preprinted applications, leases, and traffic report forms might also be included, along with any required staff uniforms. Strictly speaking, salaries and benefits (and bonuses) for the leasing staff are "marketing" costs as well.

Some costs related to resident retention may also be considered marketing expenses. Apart from lease renewals, these might include such things as newsletters and social activities for residents. Resident newsletters involve costs for personnel and production in addition to those for printing. Summer or holiday parties for residents are other items for which considerable amounts of money may be committed, and such expenses are often charged to the marketing budget (although some managers budget for these types of expenses in the "administration" budget category). We recommend a more expansive view because analyzing these related expenses in a marketing context is the best way to get a handle on all of the costs of acquiring leases and retaining residents.

The size of the marketing budget and the activities it is likely to support mean that careful thought must be given to exactly what the budgeted dollars are expected to buy. In the apartment industry, there is a tendency to spend both money and energy turning over one resident after another in apartments. We believe it is shortsighted to devote the entire marketing budget solely to attracting new residents. It is much wiser to concentrate some of the effort and dedicate some of the dollars to the comfort, happiness, and consequent retention of the residents who have already been acquired.

Put a different way, the expense that is the consequence of resident turnover ought to sensitize apartment managers to the wisdom of continuing to do business with current residents. Resident turnover can be illustrated with a simple analogy that likens an apartment community to a bathtub: Water from the spigot flows in to fill the tub; the advertising campaign and on-site marketing comprise the spigot that fills the apartment building with residents. However, unless the tub is plugged, the water will flow out the drain at the bottom at nearly the same rate as it flows in. Similarly, dissatisfied residents move out of their apartments, and no amount of advertising and on-site marketing will be able to keep the building filled. However, efforts invested in resident retention (i.e., service) can be a useful plug for the resident turnover drain. If it were not for the fact that residents move out of apartment buildings—often for reasons directly related to their dissatisfaction with the quality of the service and attention they received—most of the expense of advertising established properties could be avoided. (Resident retention is addressed in chapter 8.)

Remember, too, that current residents are not immune to the ads for vacancies where they live. What is being offered to entice new prospects could add to the dissatisfaction of current residents who did not or will not receive the same (or comparable) inducements to rent or renew leases. It is risky to promote concessions or other giveaways that are not also available to your current residents. That is yet another reason not to grant rent concessions.

Developing a Marketing Plan

Creation of a marketing plan is merely one of the later activities in something much larger—the marketing process. The marketing process encompasses analyzing marketing opportunities, researching and selecting target markets, designing marketing strategies, planning marketing programs, and organizing, conducting, and monitoring the marketing effort. In major retail operations, these duties are parceled out among various company divisions because they involve research, strategic planning, marketing, sales, and financial tasks. Retail marketing is a collective enterprise involving large numbers of people schooled in a variety of disciplines who work single-mindedly at their crafts. Because of the numbers of specialists who have contributed to it, the resulting marketing plan is likely to be more painstaking and more comprehensive than a similar effort in the apartment industry. In truth, retail marketing is substantially more sophisticated than apartment marketing because retailers have long recognized the value of meticulous planning as a prerequisite for spending marketing dollars. Consequently, they have organized and refined their planning processes, and this is reflected in their staffing structures.

By contrast, the apartment marketing process is often handled by one person or, at most, a handful of people whose marketing responsibilities may have been assumed by default. Because of staffing limitations, they may find themselves scrambling to design a leasing brochure and place classified ads in the local newspaper. In these circumstances, preparing a marketing plan seems a luxury that neither time nor available skills will permit. As a result, these marketers will be engaging in "Alaskan-winter marketing."

Although marketing planning is more highly developed and better funded in retailing than in the multifamily housing industry, it is just as crucial to apartment marketing success. Whether an apartment property is in the design and development stage or already on the market, the need for effective marketing planning is obvious. However, marketing an established property should be somewhat easier because its history can suggest new approaches, both to build on previous successes and to avoid past mistakes. The fact that planning for marketing is a long-accepted practice in retailing provides a model for property managers—retailing methods can be modified and applied to apartment marketing.

To reiterate, the essential elements of the marketing process are:

1. Analyzing marketing opportunities.
2. Researching and selecting target markets.
3. Designing marketing strategies.
4. Planning marketing programs.
5. Organizing, conducting, and monitoring the marketing effort.

The next sections of this chapter will cover these elements, addressing strategies and monitoring in detail. The next chapter on market research will expand on targeted marketing, and the following chapter on advertising will develop the components of a marketing program in depth and introduce additional methods for evaluating what has been accomplished.

Marketing Opportunities. The essence of marketing is distinguishing your product from the competition, which means finding and capitalizing on your product's strengths. "Know your enemy" is a well-known tenet of war, and marketing can be likened to a battleground. More linear feet of closet shelving, for example, or more cubic feet of refrigerator space, a greater R-value (insulation factor), or a 10-ounce greater weight in carpeting may be the ammunition a leasing agent needs to convince prospects that his or her apartment community is the best value available to them.

The previous chapter described preparation of a marketing grid. Much of that discussion focused on the uniqueness of the subject property—the factors that make it special in its market—highlighting techniques for translating those unique features into a rent schedule. Beyond structuring rents, the marketing grid exercise should identify what differentiates the subject property from its competition—the "buy" factors that will form the basis for your marketing strategies. *Exhibit 2.1* is a marketing grid we prepared for one of the properties we manage showing several properties that are its effective competitors.

In a well-prepared marketing grid, the property's strengths—its marketing opportunities—will be obvious. The strengths of a property are the foundation of much of its overall marketing thrust. Identifying marketing opportunities is the first step in creating a marketing plan.

Target Markets. The next step is to research and select target markets by matching the list of marketing opportunities with certain demographic characteristics of prospects in the immediate market—people in particular age groups and income categories, whose households are of a particular size and composition. (Demographers call these clusters of prospects cohorts.) Target markets are comprised of the people who can afford to rent the apartments available and will be interested in doing so and for whom the property is appropriately located—in other words, segments of the overall market for whom the specific apartment product is likely to be appealing. The focus on specific target markets enters the realm of *psychographics* because it relates to lifestyle characteristics.

Marketing products to particular segments of an overall population is economically sensible because it means that advertising resources will be concentrated on certain likely customers, rather than scattered among an entire universe where many will be indifferent. However, for target marketing to be successful, certain assumptions must be made about both the product and the cohorts who will respond positively to it. For example, a marketing grid may reveal that two unique attributes of a property are its lovely wooded jogging trail and its well-equipped playground. The first feature may entice

EXHIBIT 2.1

Marketing Grid Evaluating Competition for Haverhill

ONE BEDROOM APARTMENTS

PROPERTY	(Subject) Haverhill	Steeplechase		Calumet	
Monthly Rent as of November 1989	$782	$635		$660	
Monthly Rent as of March 1991	$775	$592		$580	
Monthly Rent as of July 1991	$762	$510		$555	
Concessions*	none	½ month		½ month	
Address	Haverhill Drive	1310 Conant		Calumet & Hwy 9	
	Description	Desc	Adj	Desc	Adj
Age of Building	1 year	4 yr	5	4 yr	5
Curb Appeal (1)	6	4	5	4	5
Square Footage	584–1,338	580–855	20	700–960	13
Number of Baths	1	1		1	
Patio/Balcony	No	No		No	
Fireplace	Yes	No	5	No	5
Wallpaper	Yes	No	5	No	5
Carpet	New	Yes		Yes	
Drapes/Blinds	Miniblinds	No	10	No	10
Washer-Dryer/Microwave	Yes/Yes	No/Yes	5	No/Yes	5
Dishwasher	Yes	Yes		Yes	
Disposal	Yes	Yes		Yes	
Air Conditioning (2)	C	C		C	
Cable TV	Yes	Yes		Yes	
Elevator	Yes	Yes		Yes	
Pool	No	No		No	
Sauna/Exercise Room	Yes/Yes	No/Yes	2	No/Yes	2
Tennis	No	No		No	
Party Room	Yes	No	5	No	5
Security	Yes	Door	5	Door	5
Garage (3)	U	R		R	
Parking Fee	$0	$30	30	$30	30
Tenant Pays Heat	No	Yes	15	Yes	15
Monthly Rent	$762	$510		$555	
Less Monthly Discount*		21		23	
Effective Rent	$762	$489		$532	
Adjustments (Net)			+112		+105
Adjusted Rent	$762	$601		$637	

*Rent concessions on 1 year lease; amount based on monthly rate.
(1) R = aboveground open-air ramp; U = underground parking
(2) 3 = poor; 4 = fair; 5 = good; 6 = great curb appeal
(3) W = wall unit; C = central air conditioning

Strategize Marketing 37

1 Greenlee		Plantation		The Warrens		Oaks on Six	
$670		$650		$665		$540	
$620		$670		$650		$545	
$575		$645		$495		$535	
1 month		1 month		2 months		none	
Greenlee Plaza		Highways 13 & 9		Warren at 26th		4420 Highway 6	
Desc	**Adj**	**Desc**	**Adj**	**Desc**	**Adj**	**Desc**	**Adj**
4 yr	5	5–6 yr	5	18 yr	20	15 yr	20
5	5	5	5	3	10	3	10
688–763	20	569–849	25	700	26	680–725	25
1		1		1		1	
Yes	−5	Some	−2	Some	−2	No	
No	5	No	5	No	5	No	5
No	5	No	5	Some	2	No	5
Yes		Yes		Yes		Yes	
Blinds		Some	5	No	10	No	10
No/No	10	No/No	10	No/No	10	No/No	10
Yes		Yes		Yes		Yes	
Yes		Yes		Yes		Yes	
C		C		W	10	W	10
Yes		Yes		Yes		Yes	
Yes		Yes		Yes		Yes	
Yes	−5	YMCA	−5	Yes	−5	Yes	−5
Yes		YMCA	−5	Yes/Yes		Yes/Yes	
Yes	−5	YMCA	−5	Yes	−5	No	
No	5	No	5	No	5	No	5
Door	5	Yes		Yes		Yes	
R		R		U		U	
$0		$0		$0		$45	45
Yes	15	Yes	15	Yes	15	Yes	15
$575		$645		$495		$535	
48		54		83			
$527		$591		$412		$535	
	+60		+63		+101		+155
$587		$654		$513		$690	

NOTES: Steeplechase was described in chapter 1. It is located in the same geographic area as Haverhill although it does not compete with it. (We manage both properties.)

EXHIBIT 2.1 *(continued)*

The marketing grid on the preceding pages was prepared to identify the range of marketing opportunities for Haverhill. The property and unit characteristics listed in the left-hand column—the "buy" factors—are the ingredients we evaluated. As it turned out, the grid provided a "snapshot" of the situation in our marketplace after a period of fierce competition, which was characterized by slashing rental rates and offering concessions in the form of free rent and merchandise.

This particular grid compilation resulted from our efforts to understand the apparent disintegration of our market. Typically, markets show a gradual increase in rents; this example demonstrates that that is not always true. Major disparities can arise in any market where competing properties are substantially different, as was the case with Haverhill and its competition. As data on the grid indicate, apartment sizes in our market were markedly different; features in individual apartments and amenities at the properties were also varied. At Haverhill, heat was included in the rent; at the competition, the resident paid for this expense. Only by compiling this marketing grid were we able to see all of these differences and better understand the situation we were facing.

In particular, the rent history shown in the grid is *atypical* for this neighborhood because rents were *reduced* substantially at all of the properties during the approximately 16 months over which we captured pricing data; rents continued to plummet in the months between March and July 1991, even though rent concessions were escalating.

Monthly discounts are the amounts of the rent concessions divided by twelve months, which is the typical lease term in this market. In some instances, we have not listed a dollar amount for an adjustment factor; this means that we could not fix a "measurable" value difference among the properties in the amenity or condition we were evaluating.

As noted on the grid, rent concessions ranged between one-half month and two months' worth of rent on a one-year lease. For purposes of our analysis, we chose to compute the amount of the concession and divide it by twelve to reflect out-of-pocket costs to residents over the one-year term. These concessions may have taken the form of a period of "free rent" for a particular month during the lease term, in which case a one-month concession would mean eleven months' rent paid on a twelve-month lease. (In chapter 1, we described the negative impact of rent concessions on the net operating income and the value of the property.) While we try to avoid rent concessions of any kind, a period of free rent is preferable to an outright reduction in the rental rate, and its impact on property value can be tempered somewhat by extending the term of the lease (to thirteen months, for example). Such an approach means the landlord will receive twelve months' rent at the market rate.

Note that "location" is *not* one of the factors we evaluated in this market—we believed all of the properties were situated in equally desirable locations. However, location is a particularly important consideration in comparing multifamily properties but, being intangible, is difficult to measure in terms of dollar values. Proximity to public transportation, highway access ramps, schools, shopping, and an array of other attractions and facilities within the community should be considered in rating the desirability of a property's location. What you are estimating is the amount of additional rent people are likely to pay for convenient access to such amenities.

In some markets, there are other, equally important, intangibles to consider in evaluating a property's competitive position. These include the quality of construction of the building, its reputation, and the caliber of the personnel who are responsible for marketing and managing it. Although it is especially difficult to assign dollar values to such characteristics, they can be very important in motivating prospects' renting decisions. Regardless of whether such intangibles are assigned separate values in the preparation of a marketing grid, they deserve special consideration in the assessment of the competitive position of your property and in the determination of the characteristics (marketing opportunities) that you will promote in your advertising.

fitness enthusiasts while the second may be attractive to families with young children. These, then, are two potential target markets for whom that apartment community may be appealing and to whom some marketing attention may be appropriately directed.

Research and analysis of potential target markets should include the demographic profile of *current* residents. It may seem obvious that considerable marketing effort should be devoted to attracting more residents who are demographically similar to the current ones. Yet, we have found that few apartment marketers are aware of the particulars related to their own residents. (One repository of demographic information about your residents is the property's collection of rental applications.) The marketing plan should focus on attracting prospects who are similar to many of the established residents in income, occupation, recreational interests, or other characteristics. Because household size is a determinant of space requirements, it should also be a marketing consideration in apartment leasing. The target markets chosen will shape particular marketing strategies.

Marketing Strategies. A marketing plan should express the ways in which the available marketing weapons can be deployed, driven by budgetary considerations and the owner's goals for the property. Property managers generally assume that an owner's goal for a real estate investment is to maximize cash flow, and that assumption is usually correct. However, owners sometimes have other objectives for their properties. They may prefer to have a building appreciate in value over time so their investment will produce an attractive return for their heirs. If so, they may want the cash return to be invested in upgrading the property. Other owners take particular pride in the fact of ownership and want their residents to be free of any worries about rent increases. Still others may have been interested initially in the tax advantages that flowed from apartment ownership, although such advantages have virtually disappeared during the last few years, being supplanted by the objective of simply covering the mortgage. In formulating a marketing plan, it is important to recognize that the owners' objectives must be reflected in the marketing projections. It is always wisest to ask the owners to indicate their expectations at the outset. Achieving them is the measure of the effectiveness of the marketing plan.

Specific marketing strategies will be related to attributes of the property, its market, and the people who will do the work. A good way to start is by taking three separate sheets of paper and heading them as follows:

Strengths
Weaknesses/Solutions
Resources

Strengths will be a catalog of positive features of the property (from a marketing grid, as in exhibits 2.1 and 1.6). On this sheet, every significant marketing opportunity that can be exploited in an advertising campaign and on-site marketing efforts should be listed. Each entry should be accompanied by notes that suggest how to take advantage of these opportunities. The following are some examples of annotated entries.

- *Excellent curb appeal*—new building, great signage, terrific landscaping. (Good for photographs in leasing brochure and apartment locator magazine. Leasing agents should make positive comments during presentations.)
- *Large apartments, unique design*—largest one-bedroom units in neighborhood; only two-bedroom split layout in market—good for roommates. (In positioning statement, emphasize as an appropriate option for nearby college students. Carry through in all advertising and in site presentations by leasing staff.)
- *Strong amenities*—only indoor pool and tanning beds in market; washers and dryers in units. (Use in advertising and apartment showing opportunities.)

In summary, the list of strengths should contain a recitation of each major competitive weapon that can be utilized in marketing the property, along with references to strategies that can be used effectively to exploit them.

Weaknesses/solutions should detail the impediments, in both the market and the property, that can hamper the marketing effort (weaknesses). These should be accompanied by short statements of possible means for overcoming these marketing deficiencies (solutions), as suggested in the following examples.

- *Inadequate number of three-bedroom units*—most popular unit in the market; just three apartments of this type available in the building. (Could combine some two-bedroom units with small one-bedroom apartments facing freeway.)
- *Diminishing number of prospects in target age category*—prospects in age 25–35 target market vacating largest two-bedroom units at end of lease to purchase single-family housing. (Possible economic recovery in short term may drive interest rates upward, limiting prospects of home ownership. Alternative: Market apartments to corporations for short-term rentals to transferees.)

The list of weaknesses and solutions should be a working document that is revised and updated frequently by management and marketing personnel (we recommend biweekly intervals). This list will grow as additional, unexpected marketing problems are uncovered and will diminish only after appropriate solutions are found. The leasing staff should discuss the problems on the list and brainstorm remedies that can be tested and implemented, bearing in mind that some specific problems may require capital expenditures which can only be funded over time. (Actual funding may depend on the owner's financial position and goals.)

The weaknesses/solutions list is one of the most important documents that will be compiled during the life of an apartment community. Properly utilized, it can be an effective marketing research tool. Leasing, maintenance, and other site personnel should be encouraged to add to the list even though particular items may seem to be incidental. The objective should be to identify concerns that require action—before they become major problems. The following is an example from our personal experience.

> We assumed management and marketing responsibilities for a major upscale apartment property which was situated two blocks north of a major highway and almost totally hidden from view by a stand of trees. We were dismayed to learn in the first few weeks that drive-by prospects—which the owner had expected would be the major source of traffic to the community—were almost nonexistent. To compound the problem, the county re-routed the highway during an extended period of road construction, reducing our traffic to a trickle. The notation "no traffic" headed the sheet of property weaknesses that the staff listed in the initial weekly meetings, and the inventory of solutions was disappointingly short. We began to experiment with solutions, first by placing maps in the Sunday newspaper display advertisements and in the monthly apartment locator magazines. We had some success, but traffic was still inadequate. Then, in a flash of inspiration, one of the staff decided to research the local city ordinances. He discovered that the local municipality had no signage restrictions. This meant we could place directional signs (with the property's logo and a large arrow) at nearby intersections and along city streets. We repeated this theme on a billboard adjacent to the entrance, where it remained for several months, and we even erected a huge sign on the top of one of the buildings, making its location easily visible to all passersby. This highly visible signage resulted in leasing velocity that exceeded the most optimistic projections.

From this example, it should be obvious that the goal of creating a list of weaknesses and solutions is to identify the marketing predicaments facing the property and to involve as many problem-solvers as possible in fixing them. This exercise should challenge the manager and the site staff to become proactive in confronting the difficulties that are inherent in marketing multifamily properties, transforming obstacles into marketing opportunities.

Resources will be defined to a large extent by the marketing budget. (Specific budget considerations regarding advertising are detailed in chapter 4.) Although financial resources are of paramount importance, there are also human and physical resources in any apartment marketing arsenal. The former are the site staff and the latter are the physical characteristics and quality of the apartment property itself. (The personnel component of marketing strategies is covered separately in chapter 4. Hiring, training, and motivation of staff is the subject of chapter 5.) The available resources will determine how the apartment community will be presented to prospects and residents and how they, in turn, will perceive it. In this discussion of resources, we will address the property's physical attributes as they relate to product presentation.

The first and most important element of product presentation is *curb appeal*—the external appearance presented by an apartment community. Its caliber will be the initial impression that the property makes on prospective residents. Ideally, the appearance of the property will convey the message: Here is an apartment community that is well cared for by a devoted staff and occupied by people you would love to have as neighbors.

Curb appeal includes cleanliness, of course, but it also encompasses all aspects of a property's appearance. Fresh paint, manicured lawns, flourishing flower beds, neatly swept or plowed parking lots, and attractive, coordinated window treatments all have an impact on prospects' perceptions of the quality of a property. The manager who doubts that curb appeal is an essential facet of an apartment marketing campaign need only recall his or her feelings or reactions when visiting an apartment building that was shabby or in disrepair. No amount of advertising, salesmanship, or lowered rent would induce a quality prospect to rent an apartment in such a place.

Signage is another physical characteristic of an apartment property and is therefore part of its curb appeal. Signage is often regulated by municipal codes, and managers must know what those codes are. However, within the limitations that city ordinances impose, every effort should be made to maximize the advantages that derive from color and good design. The print (type) for a monument sign must be easily read from the street. A sign that will be viewed and read from a freeway 200 feet away, where vehicles are passing by at speeds of 55 or more miles an hour, will have to show larger print and a more succinct message than would a sign that is less than 30 feet away from drivers who are about to enter the school zone down the block from the community's entrance. It should be easy for prospects to read the message. Thin or elaborate (e.g., flowery) type may be elegant, but it is not likely to be readable. Similarly, safety orange and fluorescent pink are striking colors but rarely appropriate for marketing an apartment property. A sketch of the sign—as close to full size as possible and in the colors that will be used—should be prepared so the manager can visualize whether and how well it will enhance the community. Consultation with an architect or a graphic designer will help assure appropriate choices of type and colors as well as accurate preparation of any scaled-down drawings. If the concept and presentation are wrong, it is better to discover this before hundreds or thousands of dollars have been spent on the final product.

Signage is one of the marketing tools—along with stationery, business cards, brochures, and print advertisements—that are often professionally designed to establish and perpetuate a visual *theme*. There may be a symbol or logo that appears on every item, and the same typeface is used throughout to present a consistent package. A unified graphic theme provides a visual identity for a property, something that is characteristic and will be recognized because of its repetition. Such a thematic approach requires a thoughtful evaluation of the property and the type of image to be projected. The theme should be chosen with long-term continuous use in mind.

Model apartments are often included as a marketing strategy, but it can be enormously expensive to outfit models properly. Because models can consume a large part of a marketing budget, we are often asked whether their cost is justified. We believe that models are *not absolutely necessary* to a successful marketing effort. Models can provide some advantages, and many apartment managers would not be without them; but when they fail, they do so for several reasons. In the first place, developers of new apartment communities may think they know who they wish their market to be, but they rarely conduct the necessary research to validate their assumptions. Consequently, they often provide inadequate direction to decorators who, in turn, create models in motifs that are appealing to themselves rather than the target market (in a traditional market that favors solid wood furnishings, the model might be decorated in chrome and glass).

Another problem with model apartments is that the most popular floor plan is inevitably used. When all of these units are rented, the model may be relocated to another apartment, but the resultant presentation is never the same (the furniture may not be arranged as artfully; the pictures may not be hung in the most appropriate rooms, and there may be more or fewer furnishings than the new space will accommodate). In other words, whatever magic there was in the original model is lost forever.

More significantly, however, model apartments are often used to demonstrate that a certain array of furnishings (X pieces of furniture and Y decorations) can be accommodated in a particular living space. A prospect must imagine whether his or her own furniture and decorative items will fit into a particular space, and the decorated model intrudes into that visualization.

Nonetheless, models are a staple of apartment marketing. Because of that, we make the following recommendations.

1. Decorate your model apartments tastefully. Hire a professional decorator and use the likely preferences of the target market when selecting furniture and other items.
2. Choose a unit for the model that is representative of the *least desirable* apartment layout in the property rather than the best. The decorator should be able to enhance any difficult design features of the apartment so that prospects can see ways they, too, can address the problems they will encounter.

3. Resist the temptation to upgrade items such as cabinetry, carpeting, and light fixtures in the model. Mirrored and wallpapered walls are not appropriate if residents' apartments have only painted walls. It is not fair to raise prospects' expectations to a level that cannot be achieved or is not in keeping with the delivered product. (It may be stretching the point here, but "truth in advertising" is a legal—and ethical—requirement in apartment leasing.)
4. If the model must be moved within the property, have the decorator come back and direct the arrangement of the furniture and the incidental decorating in the new location. The cost is likely to be nominal, and the results will be well worth it.

The leasing office is central to the success of the marketing effort. The goal in designing it should be to provide ease of access to the sales activity for both prospects and staff. While the leasing center is a part of the property's overall "curb appeal," it also transcends that concept. What is at issue might better be called apartment-marketing ergonomics. *Ergonomics* is an applied science related to the design (and arrangement) of such things as tools, equipment, and office furnishings so the people who use them can interact with them most effectively. Ergonomics has its roots in computer and automobile design, and its purpose is to make the activity user-friendly (any directions should be easy to figure out and the object should be fun to use).

In apartment marketing, ergonomics translates into a need to remove any barriers to successful leasing. In other words, it should be easy for prospects to find the leasing expert they are seeking. Customer parking should be clearly marked and convenient to the leasing center, and there should be appropriate directional signage with clear instructions for finding the center. Apartment marketing ergonomics can be evaluated by asking the question: Is there any risk that a prospect could be made to feel at all uncomfortable in making a rental decision and signing a lease? (We are talking here about a very low level of discomfort or inconvenience, such as one might feel when faced with a locked room and given no directions for accessing it.)

The following should be kept in mind when the leasing center is being established.

- When a choice is available, put the leasing center as close to the point of prospect entry as possible.
- Provide designated parking stalls for "future residents."
- Make sure that prospects can be readily seen and immediately acknowledged by the staff when they enter the leasing center.
- Make the leasing center a special place, comfortably furnished for transacting business with prospects.
- If music is played in the background, be sure it does not dominate the atmosphere.

- Provide an adequate number of telephones—and phone lines—to accommodate the business being transacted.
- If both apartment marketing and resident business are conducted in the same space, do everything possible to physically separate these two very different activities.
- Avoid cluttering the leasing center with packages or supplies.

These points may seem simplistic. However, many leasing offices have been designed so that no staff member could see the entry (prospects had to stand and wait for attention, and waiting makes prospects uncomfortable). Furnishings and decor of the leasing center should foster the marketing activity, not hinder it. A circular table with upholstered chairs is preferable to the typical office configuration in which an authority figure presides over and directs the discussion (a round table creates a feeling of equality and provides an opportunity for relaxed conversation).

The general atmosphere should be conducive to leasing discussions. Any background music should be consistent with the image and demographics of the property rather than the tastes of the staff (for example, heavy metal music is likely to be unattractive to senior citizen prospects); noise should generally be kept to a minimum; intrusions of any kind should be avoided.

An adequate and appropriate phone system is imperative. Prospects who encounter busy signals when they call for rental information are unlikely to call again. Also, a poor-quality or feature-loaded telephone system can itself be a marketing deterrent. "Call waiting" may be a terrific innovation for personal use, but it is irritating to customers. It is better to have additional phone lines installed. It is also a good idea to include in the leasing center a phone that prospects can use for outgoing local calls.

Leasing activities should be conducted away from the area where management staff handle rent collections, service requests, and other resident contacts for good reasons. Sometimes interactions between residents and the management staff become unpleasant. If resident business and leasing are conducted in the same area, disagreeable situations can intrude on the marketing activity, and that can impede sales. Also, much of the information provided by prospective residents is extremely personal, and many people are uncomfortable discussing sensitive issues in public.

The best arrangement is to set up a private area where the manager and staff can converse with residents or leasing business can be transacted. A separate room is ideal but not always possible. However, privacy can be maintained by rearranging the desks in a large open space, perhaps using file cabinets or bookshelves to create a dividing barrier. Advising other staff members when leasing appointments are scheduled and asking their cooperation in sustaining privacy during that time will also help.

Other uses of available office space can also pose problems. Packages delivered and held for residents, as well as accumulations of maintenance items, can give the leasing area a cluttered look. This, too, can hinder sales.

If at all possible, packages and supplies should be delivered to a designated area such as the separate management office.

Having considered the physical resources of the property and their potential to enhance the marketing effort, the next step is to formulate a specific advertising campaign.

Marketing Programs. Each discrete marketing program is an *advertising campaign*. It begins with a one-sentence positioning statement for the property. This should be a clear, believable expression of the distinguishing attributes of the apartment community to be conveyed to the target markets. An advertising agency gave us this analogy for a positioning statement: If you're going fishing, you've got to have a single, sharp hook. The following are three examples of positioning statements we have used.

1. Feels like home (for a townhouse property with tuck-under garages and separate entries).
2. Rent the heart of the city (for a high-rise apartment building in an attractive downtown location).
3. The charm of the 1920's, the lifestyle of the 1990's (for a fully renovated property).

The positioning statement is the cornerstone of the entire advertising effort, and it will determine to some extent where specific advertisements will be placed. The content of the advertising should develop the idea embodied in the chosen theme. For a positioning statement such as "feels like home," the ad copy should evoke impressions of comfort and coziness—pictures of fireplaces, fresh-baked cookies, and family dinners might be shown. The salient features that have been isolated as marketing opportunities will also appear, either as images or in writing. Equally important, focusing on the positioning statement means refraining from advertising other qualities that are inconsistent with this theme because they dilute the primary message and thereby confuse prospects about what the property has to offer (e.g., great location, terrific shopping, and nearby buslines would detract from the "feels like home" theme in the example).

The next step is to decide which media will be employed to convey the positioning statement as well as the overall advertising message. One probable choice is some type of print medium, perhaps one or more of the following: community or metropolitan newspapers, apartment locator magazines, direct mail, specialty publications such as church directories. Electronic media, such as radio and television, may be used as an adjunct to the primary advertising campaign. (If electronic media will be used, the marketing plan should include the reasons for choosing this expensive technique.) There are, of course, other delivery systems that can be productive. For example, billboards can be very useful as directional signs, especially if the location of the property is a hindrance to the marketing effort. In locales where billboards are restricted or prohibited, ad benches or other devices may be available. (Media selection and other aspects of advertising campaigns will be detailed in chapter 4.)

Once an advertising campaign is launched, it is crucial to have established procedures for tracking its productivity.

Monitoring Results. We have found that few companies evaluate the success of their marketing campaigns in detail, and those that do so rarely make changes in their programs based on the observed results. Prospect traffic may be recorded conscientiously, and sources of the traffic may be noted, but these exercises tend to be conducted in a vacuum.

Results of your marketing efforts should be monitored scrupulously. At a minimum, the number of telephone calls and visits to the property should be recorded, noting the source of the traffic and the result of each such contact. If no lease results from the visit, the leasing agent should be required to note the reasons why. For example, a phone call may not produce an appointment for a showing because the caller believed the quoted rent was too high; that reason should be noted on a traffic log. A visit may not result in a lease because the prospect intended to visit two other competitors; that reason should also be logged. Tracking these types of information can be useful in evaluating such things as the competence of individual members of the leasing staff in generating appointments and leases from telephone inquiries as well as the overall effectiveness of the advertising campaign. In particular, it is important to know the numbers of appointments and leases (i.e., volume of business) resulting from various types of advertising.

There are numerous ways to collect information about leasing traffic and the results of specific prospect contacts. The next group of exhibits shows a series of traffic report forms used to monitor marketing results for properties we manage. *Exhibit 2.2* is a daily record of apartment showings. Note that there are indications of specific media and a checklist of results across the top and a column to record the time of day. We use the comments column to track individual prospects; if they do not rent one of our apartments, we try to find out where they ultimately sign a lease and why they did not choose our property. *Exhibit 2.3* is a weekly record of the total number of contacts. Here, again, we link marketing vehicles and other sources of prospects to specific rental results (phone calls, showings, leases signed). This is a seven-day log covering Sunday through Saturday, and the daily logs are to accompany this report to the main office. *Exhibit 2.4* is a log for recording telephone calls received, linking individual contacts to sources and results—in this case appointments. Individual prospects may be identified here and on a later daily showing report. The week's results are compiled along with those of the specific showings on the weekly report form in exhibit 2.3. All three of these forms are used by staff at the site.

Exhibit 2.5 is our monthly compilation of marketing results for an individual apartment community. This allows us to assess the total numbers of

EXHIBIT 2.2
Example Daily Traffic Report—Showings

Apartment Community _____ Date _____
Leasing Agent _____ Weather _____

Time	Name	Phone Number	Apartment Size Desired	Newspaper — M/SP (Sunday)	Newspaper — M/SP (Daily)	Newspaper — Local	For Rent Book	Living Guide Book	Other Magazine	Signage/Drive-by	Referral Agencies (Identify)*	Resident Referral	Other (Identify)*	To Return	Not Qualified	Rent Too High	No Amenities	Size	Looking for Future	Pets	Other	Rented/Apt #	Comments*

(Columns grouped under: **Source** — Newspaper through Other (Identify); **Results / No Lease** — To Return through Other; **Rented/Apt #**; **Comments***)

*Use comments column to provide supplementary information.

This type of form permits identification of the source for each prospect contact and specific results of a showing.

Adapted with permission from Mid Continent Management Corporation in St. Paul, Minnesota.

EXHIBIT 2.3

Example Weekly Traffic Report

Apartment Community _____
Week of _____ through _____ (Sunday through Saturday)

Total Number of Phone Calls _____
Total Number of Appointments Made _____
Total Number of Showings _____
Total Number of Rentals _____

TRAFFIC ANALYSIS:	Phone Calls	Showings	Rentals
Newspaper—M/SP (Sunday)			
Newspaper—M/SP (Daily)			
Newspaper—Local			
For Rent Book			
Living Guide Book			
Other Magazine			
Signage/Drive-by			
Referral Agencies (Identify)*			
Resident Referral			
Other (Identify)*			

RENTALS:	Name	Apt. No.	Move-In Date

EVALUATION*
_____
_____
_____

*Was the week productive from a rental standpoint? Any comments or suggestions for advertising?

THIS REPORT MUST BE MAILED (OR FAXED) TO THE CENTRAL OFFICE, IMMEDIATELY ON MONDAY MORNING. **DAILY** TRAFFIC REPORTS MUST ACCOMPANY THIS WEEKLY REPORT.

This type of form is used to record the accumulated counts of prospect phone calls, showings, and resultant leases. Indicating the counts in relation to the advertising source permits analysis of the promotional vehicle's effectiveness.

Adapted with permission from Mid Continent Management Corporation in St. Paul, Minnesota.

EXHIBIT 2.4
Example Daily Traffic Report—Phone Calls

Apartment Community _____ Date _____
Leasing Agent _____

Time	Name	Phone Number	Apartment Size Desired	Newspaper — M/SP (Sunday)	Newspaper — M/SP (Daily)	Newspaper — Local	For Rent Book	Living Guide Book	Other Magazine	Signage/Drive-by	Referral Agencies (Identify)*	Resident Referral	Other	Appointment Made (Show Date/Time)	Comments*

*Use comments column to provide supplementary information.

This type of form permits identification of the source for each prospect phone call and whether it results in an appointment for a showing.

Adapted with permission from Mid Continent Management Corporation in St. Paul, Minnesota.

EXHIBIT 2.5

Example Monthly Traffic Analysis Report

Apartment Community _____ Month of _____
Total Number of Phone Calls _____
Total Number of Showings _____ (_____ % of Calls)
Total Number of Rentals _____ (_____ % of Showings)

Identification of Sources

	Phone Calls	Showings	Rentals	Conversion Ratio
Newspaper—M/SP				
Newspaper—Local				
For Rent Book				
Living Guide Book				
Other Magazine				
Signage/Drive-by				
Referral Agencies (Identify)*				
Resident Referral				
Other (Identify)*				

Advertising Used During Month

	Number of Rentals	Total Cost	Cost Per Rental
Newspaper—M/SP			
Newspaper—Local			
For Rent Book			
Living Guide Book			
Other Magazine			
Referral Agencies (Identify)*			
Other (Identify)*			

Analysis of Advertising Program: _____
_____

Effectiveness of Leasing Agents' Efforts: _____
_____

This form is used to record the accumulated counts of prospect phone calls, showings, and resultant leases for a one-month period. It is used to analyze the promotional vehicles used in terms of *conversion ratios* (number of rentals compared to number of showings, expressed as a percent) and *cost per rental* (ad cost divided by number of resulting rentals).

Adapted with permission from Mid Continent Management Corporation in St. Paul, Minnesota.

contacts derived from specific advertising media and measure the success of particular sources (numbers of rentals accomplished) and the effectiveness of our leasing personnel. Further, we can easily calculate prospect-to-resident conversion ratios and estimate the cost-effectiveness of particular ads and individual media. These results are used to guide future marketing efforts for each property and evaluate overall leasing performance of the program and the people implementing it.

It is often desirable to have leasing agents record certain other information, which can be noted on the daily traffic logs or reported as comments on the weekly traffic report. Walk-in and drive-by prospects—passersby attracted by the property's curb appeal rather than any specific advertising—fall into this category. Also, weather conditions can affect traffic on a particular day. Heavy rain or deep snow may or may not keep prospects at home. However, a clear, sunny day may bring out an abundance of people who are only "shopping"—they may be unhappy with their current housing, but their leases do not expire for some months. These contacts can be important, even though they do not yield immediate results. Savvy leasing agents will try to learn when such prospects' leases are due for renewal and plan to contact them in the future—provided there are vacancies that would meet the prospects' expressed needs at that later date. There is also the possibility that these shoppers will be impressed and tell their friends who are in the market for an apartment now or will be later. Word of mouth is still the Cadillac of advertising vehicles.

The example forms included here are very straightforward; more sophisticated methods can be used, of course. The data can be entered into a computer or word-processing file where it can be stored and added to, reorganized and resorted based on specific elements, and retrieved as traffic reports or as compilations of particular facts—e.g., numbers of contacts generated by each advertising vehicle, highest and lowest counts based on time of day or day of the week, etc. These data may suggest changes in the advertising schedule.

It is also possible to track prospects by their zip codes, logging this information according to where they work and live. Such data can be helpful in suggesting geographic areas to target with advertisements. It may also indicate whether the traffic generated by particular advertising vehicles is qualified to lease the advertised apartments (i.e., whether prospects can afford to pay the rent).

Conditions in the local market can be very important considerations. Apartment managers sometimes find that their traffic increases when other apartment communities in the neighborhood are advertising heavily, simply because people were there already. Knowing what the competition is offering and how often they advertise can help a leasing agent focus his or her contacts with prospects. Also, such things as observed holidays can increase traffic, while street or highway repairs or a nearby construction site can reduce it.

It is important to establish a policy that sets the hours and days of the week when the leasing center will be open (and staff will be scheduled to work). In major metropolitan areas, Sundays are often the busiest days for apartment leasing and shopping. Retail stores routinely open on Sundays but are usually closed for observance of traditional family and religious holidays such as Easter, Thanksgiving, Christmas, and New Year's Day. Such lack of commercial activity hinders leasing on these days. On the other hand, President's Day and other designated Monday holidays are widely observed, with schools, local government offices, and some businesses being closed for the day. Having a day off from work allows consumers to shop and pursue other activities—including searching for housing. Prevailing practices in your market area can guide you in establishing a policy about leasing on Sundays and holidays, and advance advertising can help you take advantage of these leasing opportunities.

Evaluation of marketing results from data collected on traffic reports may be done by the leasing staff or by the apartment manager. Performance of the leasing team as a whole may be addressed in group meetings; that of individual leasing personnel is best handled in one-on-one discussions.

A marketing plan may only apply for a limited period, and the time frame is likely to be the current fiscal year for which specific funds have been budgeted. Unless low leasing results indicate a change is necessary, a specific advertising campaign is likely to be in place for the entire plan period. Lease-up of a brand-new apartment community may require greater advertising expenditures in a shorter time period while handling of low levels of vacancies and turnovers may call for annual renewal of a minimal budget. Measuring the success of any plan in terms of prospect traffic and signed leases permits the real estate manager to make sound, justifiable decisions regarding repetitions of ads in certain media as well as specific changes to ad contents or placement schedules. However, this decision-making process will take into account more than the measured success of a current advertising campaign. It will also consider changing market conditions.

The Impact of Market Conditions

When we set out to write this book, our intention was to equip the reader with all of the ammunition necessary to wage apartment marketing wars under all conditions. Thus far, we have discussed the marketing plan from the perspective of the property only, and we have assumed normal or at least stable market conditions. However, changing market conditions play a very important role in apartment marketing success.

Shifts among population segments (age and income groups) result from births, deaths, and migration into and out of the market area. Development of shopping centers and construction of public facilities such as roads and schools create additional attractions to bring people into a neighborhood and encourage them to stay. Population growth, changing employment opportunities, and variant levels of governmental regulation all contribute to changes in the market at the regional or MSA level (see chapter 1). Successes and failures of nearby rental properties, as well as their marketing activities, will contribute to market changes in the neighborhood of competitors. All of these types of changes pose challenges for real estate managers of apartment communities, but the most demanding conditions are those encountered in so-called soft markets.

Real estate activity is cyclic in nature and tends to lag behind and exceed the peaks and troughs of the business cycles that characterize the general economy. The real estate cycle reflects shifts in supply and demand and is lead by single-family construction activity. As the business cycle recovers from a recessionary period, the general economy is expanding. Population and family size increase, wages are raised, and employment levels are high. Demand for housing increases and vacancies decrease as housing units are sold or rented. This leads into a period of general prosperity when rental occupancy is high, rents are rising, and absorption rates are high. Real estate sales are strong, and large amounts of money are available to lend at acceptable interest rates, thus favoring new construction to meet accelerating demand. However, planning and construction of large-scale multifamily rental housing properties take more time than do single-family homes for sale. Then, construction peaks and an excess of new space becomes available all at once. Pent-up demand is satisfied and begins to decline, absorption slows, and rents weaken. The result is an overbuilt market in which vacancies increase to unacceptable levels—the market for rental apartments becomes "soft" because the supply far exceeds the demand. Until demand makes inroads into the oversupply and approaches equilibrium, construction levels will remain low. As vacancies decline, demand cannot be met by the available supply, and the cycle repeats.

A soft market in which there are many more apartments than there are potential residents for them is feared by owners and managers but eagerly welcomed by prospective renters. The following phenomena contribute to oversupply.

- Easily obtained financing for apartment properties despite reduced market demand (market changes between date of loan commitment and completion of construction).
- Demographic changes resulting from population shifts.
- Major employers leaving the region (and not being replaced).

- A lack of consumer confidence in the economy of the region or the neighborhood (this often foreshadows recession or worse).
- Unemployment being high.
- Interest rates for home mortgages being low.
- Several new apartment communities opening in the same locale at the same time.

Sometimes the softening of a market is so gradual it is difficult to detect a trend developing. However, there are usually numerous signs that point to this phenomenon. The first might be lower conversion ratios—fewer prospects are becoming residents. Prospect traffic may dwindle, or the quality of prospects may diminish—fewer prospects may be qualified to become residents. Numbers of residents who "skip" (abandon their apartments and their leases) and evictions for nonpayment of rent may soar. Often the best barometer of an apartment market's strength is the newspaper classified advertising section. If there is a profusion of ever-larger display ads competing for attention on the basis of ad size and concessions (e.g., low rent, free rent, other giveaways), the market is probably soft.

Increased unemployment translates into greater difficulty paying rent and lowered rent collections. Some residents may still be employed but in other, lower-paying jobs (they may work fewer hours or, having lost the jobs they held when they applied for residency, taken a cut in pay). Finding it increasingly difficult to stretch their paychecks to accommodate a standard of living they can no longer afford, these residents are consistently late in paying their rent until they cannot pay it at all. Many of them will simply skip out rather than face the embarrassment of eviction. Others may try to lengthen their tenancies by faulting the landlord—either claiming breaches of promises supposedly made or probing their leases to find hypertechnical violations. Still others delay the inevitable by progressing through the tortuous process of eviction.

Some of these developments may appear gradually. A manager may discover one skip and three eviction actions filed in one month compared to no skips and a single eviction in the same month of the previous year. Some of the most reliable residents may suddenly petition to pay part of their rent on the first of the month and the remainder two weeks later. Perhaps a handful of residents, all employed at a major local firm, ask to meet with the manager to discuss the possibility of paying their current rent when their annual bonuses are received. Part of the problem in recognizing a softening market is that few management firms monitor and quantify market information, and fewer still use it to forecast trends.

A number of cities in the United States are heavily dependent on the economic vitality of a particular company or industry. As the company or industry goes, so goes the local economy in general and the apartment business in particular. Petroleum, lumber, railroads, and heavy equipment manufacturing are a few such industries. The automobile industry, which in addition to assembly of the vehicles themselves includes manufacture and distribution of components and replacement parts (aftermarket) as well as supplies used in manufacturing (e.g., masking tape used in painting and finishing), is a particularly strong example. The success (or failure) of such industries dictates the size of the local population and the number of people who can afford to pay rents in particular amounts. Layoffs and plant closings can destroy the vigor of an apartment market almost overnight.

We have several friends who owned apartment buildings in flourishing municipalities that became ghost towns. Most survived, although barely. However, some prospered, primarily because they were forced to work leaner and smarter than they ever had or thought they could. The key to their success was that they made friends with the soft markets they encountered. One way of making friends with this problem is recognizing that if markets never softened, there would be very little need for site managers, property managers, or asset managers. A rental property in a strong market can be run like a military barracks. Similarly, residents can be treated like cattle, housed in whatever apartments might be available at whatever prices landlords choose to charge, with no concern for their satisfaction. In a soft market, however, there is more product available and fewer residents to occupy it. This accelerates the level of competition and intensifies the need to sharpen marketing skills.

Typical Reactions to Market Softening. One characteristic of a soft market is that owners rarely view the challenge in appropriate perspective. Their first reaction is to try to make the difficulty disappear by throwing money at it. They compete on the basis of ever more expensive giveaways, either as free rent or other concessions. Furthermore, they advertise these "giveaways" in increasingly expensive ways (experimenting with display advertising and four-color magazine ads; buying radio and television time; coupon promotions; advertising on billboards and at bus stops). Promotion of giveaways is not a marketing strategy we recommend. This reaction to a soft market can be characterized as: Let's do something, even if it's wrong. Meanwhile, the property's net operating income (NOI) continues to plummet, and the neighborhood acquires a reputation among prospects as a place where deals can be made.

Another characteristic reaction to diminishing occupancies and faltering NOI is to fire the staff, or at least pare it down. When a property owner is faced with impending disaster, the tendency is to assess blame and, in this type of situation, site personnel often bear the brunt of it. The staff may or may not be part of the problem. Clearly they are not responsible for a recession or even a slight downturn in the market. So holding them responsible for failure in a soft market only compounds the problem and delays finding a solution to it. Wholesale staff dismissals are often coupled with reductions in the quality of maintenance and grounds keeping and postponement of capital expenditures. This leads to additional problems in replacing such personnel because of the time involved in hiring and training them. After all, owners may argue, if there is not enough money to pay for normal operations, what alternative do they have except to slash expenses?

The most compelling challenges facing those who market apartments in these circumstances are two in number. First, those who own and manage the apartment properties must be persuaded to resist the temptation to panic, especially when the pressures to do so are almost overwhelming. Nearly as daunting—and a consequence of the first challenge—is finding a way out of the soft market. There is only one way out, and that is to apply the skills the professional apartment marketer has learned from working in robust markets, as well as the techniques outlined in this book, to the obstacles presented by the soft market. There is no substitute for hard work; that is one key to survival. There is also no substitute for experience, and that is another key.

Recommended Approaches to a Soft Market. It is true that managers cannot avoid or even influence the economic forces that affect the business of renting apartments, but the impact of those forces can be reduced by managers who apply their knowledge, analytical skills, planning, and creativity—and hard work—to the challenge of the soft market. Whether you are currently operating in a soft market or not, you need to be prepared to do so.

- If you do not currently monitor prospect traffic, begin to do so.
- Find out why prospects do not rent your apartments.
- Find out why some current residents stay and others move out.
- Monitor market conditions.
- Periodically evaluate operations at the property.
- Analyze and compare these different types of information over time.
- Modify your marketing and advertising strategies based on the results.

These activities take on new meaning in the context of a soft market.

Your information and the system used to collect it should be user-friendly—easily read and readily understood. Computers make it easy to compile and update different types of information, especially once the process has been initiated. They also facilitate manipulation of the data for different types of analyses. However, you should not become so enthralled with the process of collecting and reporting information that you forget why you are doing it. The reason is to enable you to evaluate your property's leasing performance and, from that, to determine whether there is a downturn that needs your immediate attention.

Focus on the Property. Begin by compiling certain information into a data base, then routinely maintain and update it. You need to know the numbers of telephone calls your property attracts from prospects on a weekly basis as well as the numbers of apartment showings and leases that result from them. These figures should be expressed as *conversion ratios*—numbers of telephone calls converted to apartment showings and numbers of apartment showings that resulted in leases, expressed as percentages. If ten phone calls resulted in six showings, and three of those showings led to signed leases, six out of ten calls is a 60-percent conversion to showings; three out of six showings is a 50-percent conversion to leases. (Conversion of showings to leases is sometimes also called a *closing ratio.*)

Apart from success (or the lack of it) in acquiring new residents from marketing efforts, it is also important to determine *why prospects do not rent* at your property. The reasons may or may not be directly related to economic conditions. A reaction to the property or the way it was presented—or even personal considerations—may have influenced a prospect's rental decision. (Follow-up of prospects who do not rent at our properties is described in chapter 3.)

Each month you should track lease renewals—the number of leases renewed compared to the number of leases up for renewal, expressed as a percentage—as well as rents received late (as dollar amounts), and numbers of skips or evictions. You should also track general demographic information about your resident population—at a minimum, age, gender, type of employment, and salary. Marital status and household size are also useful to know. (The rental application form is where much of this information will be gathered. In some markets, state or local laws may not permit some types of information—e.g., age, marital status—to be requested from applicants.)

When established residents move out, it is important to find out *why they chose to leave.* This can be difficult to do, and a conversation with the resident who is leaving may not yield accurate information. Sometimes people are relocated by their employers, and that is a valid reason for moving although a mid-term move may be complicated by an established lease. Others move out to live in single-family homes they have bought. Such economic factors increase vacancy rates but only in the short term. On the other hand, your occupancy problems may not be due to a soft market but, rather, to a lack of responsiveness to residents' needs. Dissatisfaction with the property or the personnel managing it is not likely to be stated in an exit interview, and move-outs for such noneconomic reasons can have long-term impact on vacancies.

If you do not find out why your residents are leaving, you will be missing important information that can be used to improve your apartment product and your resident services. The market as a whole may recover from high levels of vacancies caused by market softening or other factors. However, resident dissatisfaction increases turnover, also resulting in extended vacancies. In the absence of information about the reasons for your residents' having moved out, your apartment community will not be able to recover—and you will not know why.

To find out for sure why a resident moved out, ask former residents to tell you anonymously. Exiting residents should be required to leave a forwarding address; use that information to send a follow-up questionnaire that asks about their satisfaction during their period of residency and their reason for leaving. To assure more candid responses, do not require them to identify themselves. The information you obtain can be used to help forestall other move-outs. (Use of questionnaires to measure resident satisfaction is discussed in chapter 8.)

Focus on the Market. It is also important to know what is happening in the market where your apartment community competes. Information on rental rates (quoted or market rents) for each apartment type in your neighborhood, the types of concessions being given, and the circumstances under which particular concessions were made should be compiled routinely, at least once a month. You should also try to find accurate information on occupancy levels.

Compiling data is not enough. You need to review that information frequently and compare it month to month and year to year. What happened in March of this year compared to March a year ago? Two years ago? Ten years ago? What changes have you been seeing over the past two or three months compared to the same time period a year or two or longer ago? Compared to the preceding two- to three-month period? If your firm manages more than one apartment community within a neighborhood or region, you will be able to compare and contrast their performances.

These comparisons will allow you to distinguish between short-term, perhaps anomalous, situations and those that are more serious. A number of factors can cause a sudden (but fleeting) downturn in the performance of a property, and these should not be confused with negative economic conditions or a softening market. For example, weather conditions can discourage prospects from venturing out to look for a new residence. The loss of a valued employee who was effective in retaining residents may lead to a lower occupancy level. A change of ownership or management can suspend resident confidence. All of these consequences may resemble market softening, yet they are generally only temporary effects that can be reversed rather easily.

Remember, too, that apartment properties are affected by economic conditions both locally (neighborhood and region) and at the national level. If economic indicators suggest that your region and neighborhood are in a boom period, yet figures for your property indicate otherwise, your internal operations should be scrutinized. Find out what your property's problems are—be they staff, building maintenance, service delivery, or something else—and look for ways to improve its internal performance. Boom times are characterized as a seller's market because demand exceeds supply, and if you are not converting prospects to residents, you may have to improve your product so that prospects will become renters. On the other hand, if economic indicators and your figures both forecast a bust, your management and marketing efforts have to be adjusted to meet that situation. Oversupply creates a buyer's market, and you will be faced with strong competition for a diminishing pool of potential renters. Your objective should be to promote your property as the most desirable choice among the many properties competing for the same prospects.

In good times or bad, *value* is the key to the success of an apartment community. Real estate managers and apartment marketers must focus on value in advertising a property, promote value in the apartment leasing process, and deliver value to residents. These are the means of achieving and maintaining optimum occupancy at optimum rental rates, and that optimization is indispensable to a property's economic performance.

The key to survival in a soft market is not only to apply these principles, but to be smarter and leaner in doing so. The only difference between succeeding in soft versus healthy markets is that the challenges are greater when times are tough. If your property averages 96-percent occupancy and enjoys a steady flow of prospect traffic—no matter how much or how little you advertise—its performance is likely to be consistently good but not outstanding (it does not have to be). On the other hand, necessity truly can be the mother of invention. When it becomes apparent that traffic is down from a comparable period, take another look at your marketing plan and analyze your situation.

- Check demographic trends
- Assess lease renewal rates
- Review (and revise) marketing grids

The demographic profile in your neighborhood or region may have changed. There may simply be fewer prospects in the market. In which case, your advertising campaign may need sharpening to convey the right message to a different segment of the market than has been pursued previously. If your lease renewal rate is down from last year, a personal survey of departing residents can tell you why. Learn from that exercise and apply the lessons to your current prospects and residents. Your marketing grids should be reviewed periodically regardless. In tough times, they may suggest additional competitive advantages that you should be selling to prospects. Post the grids where leasing staff can see and use them. Highlight the features that should be promoted. Train your staff to capitalize on those qualities during their sales presentations and monitor their performance.

Focus on Professionalism. Striving to be the best in their market should be every apartment manager's and leasing agent's professional goal, no matter what that market is. This can be accomplished by maintaining an awareness of and being knowledgeable about current market conditions and accepted practices for meeting the challenges posed by the market. Market information sources include publications that feature reports and assessments of economic trends. These can be obtained as personal subscriptions or accessed at local libraries. Having the information available is one thing; understanding and using it is quite another. Joining and participating in professional organizations is another way to access such information. The Institute of Real Estate Management (IREM) is an organization whose local chapter meetings, publications (journals, newsletters, books), and educational programs offer immediately usable information.

The stresses of soft markets either inspire productivity or foster inactivity. The techniques we have outlined here are designed to improve residential marketing and leasing productivity. The soft market environment offers apartment marketing professionals an opportunity to discover and develop their own talents and those of their co-workers.

CHAPTER 3

Understand Your Customers

One of the most important marketing developments in recent years was the discovery that end-users of a product can be asked about the qualities the product should have before it is offered to them for sale. This breakthrough in consumer marketing is called *market research*. Sellers are able to pose questions directly to actual or potential consumers, and respondents' answers are used in making decisions about the products. Such consumer responses are likely to be crucial to a product's success. They may even determine whether the product will be brought to the market at all. An example is provided by a product that is known worldwide.

> In the mid-1980s, Coca-Cola Company replaced the 100-year-old formula for Coke with a new blend that tasted very much like its nearest competitor, Pepsi. There was a tremendous negative response from consumers, and within a few short weeks, the original product was returned to the market. Classic Coke, as the original formula was now called, was to be sold side-by-side with the new-formula Coke. When asked whether this had been done on purpose, Coca-Cola executives denied having any objective other than to change an old formula, claiming, "We're not that dumb and we're not that smart." Regardless of the truth in their comments, the Coca-Cola executives should have done their homework. The consumer rejection of the new-formula Coke amounted to very expensive market research.

The Concept of Market Research

Marketing is the business of moving goods from producers to consumers. It starts with finding out what consumers want or need and then determining whether a product that meets those needs can be made or sold at a profit. *Marketing research* is done to determine the general characteristics of the marketplace (population size, age, income distribution, etc.) and assess the competition. *Market research,* on the other hand, is more specific. Manufacturers and sellers talk directly with consumers to find answers to questions they have about their products. Optimum pricing levels are sometimes determined in this way. However, market research is also used to explore product design, packaging, size (quantity), and other marketing-related issues.

Market research provides the means of collecting information about consumers' wants, needs, and preferences. More broadly, it is the process of defining a marketing problem and then systematically collecting and analyzing information from consumers in order to recommend actions to improve a product's success in the market.

Yogi Berra, former catcher and manager for the New York Yankees and all-purpose philosopher, put it best when he observed, "It's amazing what you can see if you look." Market research is simply a means of formulating questions to be directed to a list of interviewees, then evaluating what their responses suggest as a course of action. This chapter will help those who market apartments decide what to look for and how to utilize what they see.

Types of Data. In earlier discussions, we touched on two types of market data, demographics and psychographics. *Demographics* is the statistical analysis of populations. It utilizes information derived primarily from census records—the age, gender, occupation, and income characteristics of the people who live in a geographically defined area—and is used in characterizing discrete markets. Such concurrent data as household size, numbers of children and their ages, and levels of homeownership are of particular interest to apartment developers and marketers because they relate to requirements for living space in the form of rental apartments. *Demographics is a tool of marketing research.*

Psychographics, on the other hand, is more qualitative because it describes people's lifestyles. It is a way to determine what might be called "hot buttons" or buy factors (i.e., specific perceptions that individual consumers have) in a particular market. Thus, psychographics goes beyond demographics to uncover personal preferences and attitudes that the numbers alone do not reveal. *Psychographics is one of the specific tools of market research.*

The distinction between demographics and psychographics can be illustrated as follows: Suppose two men are next-door neighbors. They are both wage earners, employed in white-collar professions and earning gross incomes of $60,000 a year. Each is between 35 and 45 years old and owns his single-family home. These data are *demographic factors*.

Further exploration may reveal that one of these men spends most of his leisure time at a fitness club. He subscribes to *Architectural Digest* and has considered remodeling his home to add bay windows and wallpaper in the living room and an oak-paneled study. However, he much prefers apartment living, likes stall showers, stores his Suzuki motorcycle in the garage, and would be willing to spend 50 percent of his gross income for the right kind of housing. The sale of his home is scheduled to close within 90 days, and he has not yet begun looking for an apartment. His neighbor, by contrast, spends his leisure time skeet shooting and playing billiards. He has been a copyright lawyer for 17 years, gets his news mainly from *USA Today,* and believes that $545 is the right monthly rent for a two-bedroom walkup apartment. He recently decided to let his sister move into his house, and he is currently looking for a nearby condominium to rent. These additional characteristics of the two neighbors are all *psychographic factors* that reveal critical features of their individual personalities and lifestyles. Notice how specific they are—and how helpful they would be to a developer or apartment marketer. We will return to these concepts later in this chapter.

Applications in Retailing. Market research has been employed by consumer products manufacturers for many years. It has been used for such diverse purposes as designing automobiles, naming spaghetti products, and pricing refrigerators. Any doubts about the extensive application of this technique are easily dispelled by a trip to a supermarket. The diversity of product types and brand names, package sizes and pricing, containers and colors are all the results of specific market research. For example, why does a certain brand of chewing gum have a light green package showing a darker green arrow and the trademark "Doublemint?" For that matter, why does Doublemint gum taste the way it does? Why do some packages contain only five sticks while others contain seven or nineteen sticks? Other examples abound, and many seem to be at cross purposes. Why are hot dog buns packed in eights while hot dogs are packed in tens and twelves? Toothpaste in tubes sold very well; why package it in pumps, too? Why name candy bars Milky Way, Kit Kat, Butterfinger, etc.? Why use a picture of a smiling little girl on the packaging for a popular margarine? For that matter, why call it Blue Bonnet margarine? The answers to these questions may be closely guarded secrets, but the decisions behind them were not made accidentally. They were arrived at only after painstaking research conducted by trained professionals who talked in great detail to large numbers of consumers. Like us, you have probably had your dinner interrupted more than once by someone calling to ask if you would be willing to take a few minutes to participate in a survey. Obviously, market research is all around us. In fact, its large-scale use is not limited to consumer products; the marketability of such diverse things as professional publications and political candidates is also evaluated using these same techniques.

The results of market research are ubiquitous. Every time a person goes to a showroom or shopping mall, every time someone views a billboard or magazine advertisement—literally every time consumers are invited to buy goods—someone somewhere probably conducted some kind of market research about the product or its advertising before it was made available to the public.

Like all things worth having, there are costs involved, and market research can be quite costly. The research described so far probably involved face-to-face in-depth interviews of large numbers of potential consumers, a process that is very expensive. However, market research techniques can be applied in ways that are much less expensive. In truth, the cost of bringing to market a product that has no customer appeal is invariably greater than the expense associated with market research. To put it another way, if such research helps to keep out of the market a product that will not be successful, or suggests refinements to a product that will increase the likelihood of its being successful in the market, the cost of that research is insignificant.

The point has already been made, but it is important enough to justify repetition: Market research allows producers to know the market receptivity to every aspect of a product *before* it is marketed. Thus, thorough market research can predetermine the success of a product. Consumer product manufacturers also conduct market research on an ongoing basis after a product is launched, looking for ways to improve the product and increase its market penetration.

Why Do Market Research on Apartments?

Despite the potential benefit of research as a marketing tool, such techniques have generally escaped the attention of developers and owners of multifamily housing. Apartments, condominiums, and townhouses have generally been designed according to the tastes of developers, who relied on the "feel" of the project rather than the preferences of potential renters. Most likely this was unintentional. It may not have occurred to developers to design housing projects any other way, but this oversight has become increasingly problematic. When there was a surplus of residents for the existing multifamily housing stock, mistakes in design were of small consequence. Consumers who preferred apartment living—or could not afford to buy single-family homes—simply chose from whatever apartments were available. However, when there are more apartments available than people to live in them, prospective residents can be much more selective about their housing. Because there is more vacant product in the marketplace, renters are free to choose housing that offers features and amenities they find attractive. In all likelihood, they can afford what they prefer because, in this type of environment, rents are likely to be lower. (Indeed, as this book was being written, many multifamily housing markets in the United States were soft. When supply exceeds demand, prices can be increased only nominally, if at all. Some apartment product will remain vacant, generating no income; and because rent increases may encourage residents to move out, those apartments that are occupied are likely to generate only a static amount of income until market conditions improve. These are typical outworkings of the law of supply and demand.)

Many owners and management companies react to overbuilding by conducting price wars. They compete with one another by offering concessions in the form of free (or reduced) rent or by giving away consumer goods (microwave ovens, color television sets) or vacation trips. (We presented a specific example of this in chapter 1.) This method of marketing apartments diminishes their value; it cheapens the product and tarnishes its reputation. It can also alienate residents who signed leases without such incentives. Renters are sophisticated enough to know that if landlords have to give their product away, it may not be worth what they are charging. In the short run, competing to give away more (and more valuable) prizes as rental inducements may be just a less-than-desirable marketing ploy; for the long run, however, the consequences of such giveaways must be weighed carefully and their impact understood. In particular, rent concessions subtract dollars from the bottom line—the property's net operating income (NOI)—and thus reduce the value of the property. Their impact is doubly damaging because expenses related to the upkeep of leased units are the same regardless of the rent they generate. The reduction in income resulting from rent concessions means that operating expenses consume an even larger proportion of a property's income than they would if rents were at market rates.

Another way of looking at this phenomenon, and one that involves a certain irony, is that concessions—especially in the form of consumer goods—often reflect what consumers want in their apartments in the first place. Viewed in this way, concessions are a kind of belated market research—if a renter receives a free microwave in exchange for signing a lease, chances are the prospect wanted a microwave all along. If the apartment had been outfitted with a built-in microwave oven initially, the landlord would have invested in something that would remain in the unit rather than leave with that resident when his or her lease expires.

In an environment in which there is both an oversupply of housing and housing that is not matched to the tastes of consumers, real estate managers must necessarily be extremely skilled in the marketing of their portfolios. One of the primary responsibilities of property management—and, sometimes, the biggest challenge—is to maintain high occupancy levels at optimum rents. It is the manager's job to improve net operating income, irrespective of prevailing market conditions. Thus, real estate managers tend to find themselves in an uncomfortable position: They must discover markets for properties that either never had any markets before or whose previously established markets have more or less evaporated.

Paradoxically, one of the results of the lack of market research in the apartment industry is that talented marketers of multifamily housing will find their skills in increasing demand. These skills can be vastly improved by the judicious use of market research techniques. The importance of market research is exemplified by our own experience with a property called The Laurels.

> The Laurels is a 255-unit high-rise apartment building overlooking the Mississippi River. It is owned by a national financial institution, and apartments there are priced above the upper end of the market. Historically, the property's occupancy level has been in the 80–85-percent range. Demographically, The Laurels' residents have been primarily senior citizens. At the time we did our research, the average age of the residents was 68; many were much older, and all were financially secure.
>
> In an effort to increase occupancy, we decided to conduct an intensive advertising campaign. We contracted with an advertising agency to design a print advertisement that could be used in many different ways—e.g., in the local apartment locator magazine, as a direct mail piece, and as a newspaper advertisement. The goal was to develop a single ad that could be used to market The Laurels by employing a variety of print media throughout the year. We intended to use the entire advertising budget for the year to make this particular ad as widely seen as possible, using every print medium available to us. What we were planning was an all-or-nothing media blitz driven by a single advertisement.
>
> Our first task was to select a positioning statement for the property—a one-sentence description designed to appeal to a particular group of prospective residents (the target market for the property). In the case of The Laurels, the target market was elderly, affluent prospects, and we identified a doorman, the serene and secluded location, and an on-site cafe as features that were likely to appeal to them.

When formulating positioning statements, the characteristics of both the apartment property and the market have to be considered. The link between the positioning statement and the target market for an apartment property deserves consideration here. In essence, the positioning statement is a definition of the property—a succinct description of its capacity to meet the special needs or preferences of consumers in the market. It dictates an analysis of what makes the building exceptional or unique and why it is an especially appropriate choice for certain types of people. For example, amenities such as a well-equipped exercise facility, tanning beds, indoor and/or outdoor swimming pools are likely to be attractive to a market segment comprising young, athletic men and women.

In an ideal world, an apartment building would have been developed, designed, and constructed with specific users in mind so there would be a ready-made market for the property when construction was completed. However, this is rarely the case. In the typical scenario, the market for a structure is only dimly defined before it is built, and those responsible for leasing it have to determine the primary market of renters in retrospect. Although target markets may be more or less unknown at the time a property comes on the market, that does not mean they are unimportant. Without a good idea of the types of people who will find the building attractive, the marketing campaign will be unnecessarily extensive, all-encompassing, and very costly. The marketer will probably cast a very broad net, hoping to catch as many prospects as possible, and when a prospect is caught, it will be pretty much by accident.

By contrast, when a target market is known beforehand, the entire marketing effort can be crafted to appeal specifically to it. Take the example of an apartment building designed for the athletically inclined. Its advertising will spotlight the particular features of the building that will appeal to those prospects. The headlines and language of the ad (the ad copy) will be written narrowly, and an athletically oriented advertising medium might be used (e.g., a sports-related magazine, a radio spot following sports news). This marketing approach can be likened to fishing at a particular level in a small pond, using special bait, and catching fish that are known to be swimming there.

> In the case of The Laurels, we decided to try to attract the same kinds of people as those who were currently living there—we wanted to reach prospects who were older and wealthier than the community population in general. The Laurels' very favorable location in an upscale neighborhood, coupled with its state-of-the-art controlled-entry system, became our focus for positioning it as a residence that is tranquil and comfortable.
>
> Our actual positioning statement was: *The Laurels is a refuge from the concerns of contemporary society; our staff will take care of your every need.*
>
> The ad that was developed from that premise is shown in *Exhibit 3.1*. The idea of sanctuary was conveyed by the ad headline and the art: "Some people confront the problems of city life only once a day"— and then only by reading about them in the newspaper. The premise was that if the prospect prefers this approach to city life and its problems, he or she will choose to live at The Laurels.

EXHIBIT 3.1

Example Display Ad

Some People Confront The Problems Of City Life Only Once A Day . . .

Living in any city is an increasing challenge. At The Laurels, we go to every effort to make sure you are comfortable in your apartment home.

Order a meal delivered from our restaurant if you don't feel like cooking. Have the maid help you get ready for a party or, if you're traveling, have us water your plants and pay special attention to mail and deliveries.

When you come home to The Laurels, you're entitled to more than just a spacious apartment. You're entitled to a wide range of services . . . and the luxury of confronting city life only once a day.

Call Jayne at 555-5555 for more information.

Apartment Living at The Laurels.

Image courtesy of Cowles Media Company, Minneapolis.

As experienced property managers know, security issues can create liabilities for both owner and manager. The word security is rarely featured in ads for just that reason. However, The Laurels has state-of-the-art controlled-entry equipment and a trained safety-conscious staff, all supported by a substantial budget. For these reasons, we were comfortable with mentioning security as a marketing feature for this particular property.

As was the case with every ad we developed, we showed the ad for The Laurels (see exhibit 3.1) to our staff and our friends and refined it somewhat. Soon, however, we arranged to have the ad placed temporarily in the various print media for which it had been designed. We waited anxiously for a positive reaction—measurable as increased traffic to the property on the part of the neighborhood's wealthy, elderly population. Ten days passed, then two weeks, and still there was no reaction. Finally, one of the residents dropped by the management office. She was furious!

"How dare you imply that I and my friends are helpless old fogies living in a rest home?" she exploded. She considered herself an active, middle-aged woman who was totally able to care for herself (even though she was actually over 70 years old, partially blind, and wheelchair-bound). "When I'm ready to live in a rest home," she fumed, "I will move out. But not a minute sooner!"

We thanked her for her input and dismissed her complaints (though not without some concern). We thought her reaction must be atypical, but we were not absolutely certain. So we asked our manager to chat about the ad with several other residents. What we learned was that our carefully planned advertising campaign was on a collision course with disaster. Many of our residents were merely annoyed. Others were outraged. A few were somewhat amused about the furor.

We also found out that the masthead of the newspaper we had featured in the ad was from a neighboring city—*not the local paper*. We had not even noticed that, but our residents had. It made them very angry. They thought we surely should know better than to support a rival city's newspaper in our advertisements. Well, yes, we should have, but it had never occurred to us that that particular detail would matter.

We had relied on our own instincts in creating a positioning statement, and we paid a high price for it. The issue of the newspaper masthead merely compounded the error.

We learned several important lessons from that experience. First, and most important, we learned not to base an advertising campaign solely on our own instincts. Our gut reactions are not perfect, particularly when we are using them to anticipate the reactions of others whose age and income level—for that matter, any demographic classification—are very different from our own. To assume that we can somehow hypothesize the psychographics of people who are fundamentally different from ourselves is to believe that our intuitions are infallible. Common sense should tell us otherwise.

Second, we learned that factors we may consider unimportant—even overlook entirely—can wreck our best efforts. They can even create animosity. When we checked with our advertising agency, they claimed the ad looked better with the other newspaper masthead. Later, they admitted that they had not thought about it either. There had been an old newspaper lying around in the designer's office, and she simply picked it up and copied it.

How could we have foreseen that positioning The Laurels as a place guaranteeing "security" to prospective residents who probably did not feel a need for such assurances would destroy the effectiveness of an ad? That, of course, is the point. We could have known it. We should have known it. It was easy and inexpensive to know it. We might have tested the ad with a group of our residents before we placed it, which would have alerted us to the obvious errors we had made. We also could have conducted a more scientific inquiry, by sampling larger numbers of people who were similar in age and economic status to the people in our target market. Either alternative would have constituted market research. The question is, what methodologies are appropriate for conducting market research on multifamily housing?

Market Research Methods

There are a multitude of techniques for conducting market research. One of these is the focus group; another is the questionnaire. Both are helpful in conducting market research for apartment communities, focus groups particularly so.

Focus Groups. The focus group is a major tool of market research that can be employed in the multifamily housing industry. It allows owners and managers of apartment communities to explore subjects of interest with people who are similar in perceptions and preferences to their current resident population.

A *focus group* consists of a number of people brought together in a group interview setting to focus on a specific product, organization, or service. Because the intent is to obtain personal viewpoints, the group is usually small—as many as twelve people but rarely larger. They are asked to answer questions posed by a moderator about their personal buy factors. The members of the panel are carefully chosen so that the group's composition will have the same general demographic characteristics as the target market (age, economic status, occupations, etc.) and therefore be representative of their attitudes or opinions. In short, a focus group consists of people with similar demographic characteristics gathered together for the purpose of exploring psychographic factors.

The session is typically held in comfortable surroundings, with seating arranged in a semicircle or horseshoe shape. Participants are paid a minimal fee for attending, and refreshments are served. The proceedings are often tape recorded or videotaped, and the meeting may last as long as two hours. Panel members are encouraged to participate actively, but the moderator may have to intervene to ensure that no single member of the group dominates the discussion.

The moderator is trained in group dynamics and consumer behavior. In addition, he or she will have some knowledge about the subject matter and the overall purpose of the discussion. However, *the moderator must be absolutely disinterested in the outcome of the discussion.* This distancing is crucial to the success of the focus group effort. Otherwise, the moderator might become an active member of the group and influence the discussion by intruding into the proceedings (via tone of voice, body language, etc.). In general, the moderator for an apartment marketing focus group should not be a property manager or anyone who is associated with the marketing or management of the particular apartment community that is the subject of the session.

Consistent with that principle, participants in a focus group are told very little about the subject matter they will be discussing. The selection of panel members for an apartment marketing focus group is dependent on two things: They must have demographic characteristics similar to those of the target market, *and* they must have moved to an apartment building in the neighborhood of the subject property recently or otherwise indicated their intention to do so within a fairly short period of time. These qualifications of the panel members are designed to create a group that is as similar as possible to the market of prospective residents. The people recruited will be told that they will be involved in a panel discussion about their housing preferences; they will not know that the discussion will concern a particular apartment building.

There are any number of applications of focus groups in apartment marketing and management. We used a focus group session to evaluate the advertising campaign for The Laurels. (A partial transcript of that session concludes this chapter; the use of focus groups in evaluating resident satisfaction is discussed in chapter 8.)

Questionnaires. Questionnaires are a particularly productive means of finding out information. Two specific applications in apartment marketing are to learn what influenced renters' choices of residence and to find out why prospects did not become residents. Factors that strongly influenced residents' choices should be considered for incorporation into (and emphasis in) future advertising campaigns and on-site marketing efforts. Question-

EXHIBIT 3.2

Example Resident Questionnaire

**THE LAURELS APARTMENTS
RESIDENT QUESTIONNAIRE**

Your opinion is important to us! We are trying to improve the quality of your apartment. Please complete this questionnaire and return it in the envelope we have provided. WE WILL APPRECIATE IT IF YOU EXPLAIN YOUR ANSWERS ON THE BACK OF THIS SHEET. Thanks for your help!

1. Why did you choose to live at The Laurels Apartments? (Please check all reasons that apply.)

 _____ Convenient location
       _____ Close to business
       _____ Close to shopping
       _____ Close to other things (Which ones?)
       (1) _____ (2) _____
 _____ Apartment design/appearance of the building
 _____ Building amenities (party room, exercise room, lobby, etc.)
       Which ones?
       (1) _____ (2) _____
 _____ Price
 _____ Reputation of the building
 _____ Management/Maintenance staff (please list names, if known):
       (1) _____ (2) _____
 _____ Other reasons:
       (1) _____ (2) _____

2. Please CIRCLE the reason above that was MOST IMPORTANT in influencing your decision to live at The Laurels.

3. What do you like BEST about apartment living at The Laurels?

4. What could we do to IMPROVE your enjoyment of your apartment?

_____
Signature/Apartment Number (Optional)

---

naires are also useful in measuring resident satisfaction and finding out why residents leave (see chapter 8).

In evaluating our apartment marketing success, we send new residents a questionnaire shortly after they move in. *Exhibit 3.2* is a form we use at The Laurels. It combines questions regarding residents' satisfaction with their new apartments and questions pertaining to factors that influenced their choice of

EXHIBIT 3.3

Example Telephone Questionnaire for Nonrenters

THE LAURELS APARTMENTS "NO RENT" SURVEY

Name: _____ Phone Number: _____
Date: _____   Interviewer: _____
                                Time Start: _____
                                Time End: _____
                                Length: _____

Ask to speak with _____
                         (Name)
(Greeting)

My name is _____. My company is conducting a survey about people's attitudes about rental housing in the Tarnhill Park area.

This will take only a few minutes of your time.

We are **not selling** anything.

Your name will **not be used** in my report.

Your answers will be used for **statistical purposes** only.

1. Where are you currently living?

2. Are you living in:
    _____ An apartment (Name) _____
    _____ A condominium
    _____ A single-family home
    _____ Other (Specify) _____

3. What was the **single most important reason** you chose to live there?
   (First mention:)

   (Additional mentions:)

4. If respondent is a **renter only** (if respondent is not a renter, skip to question #7):
   Did you receive a **concession in the form of free rent** (or other premium) when you signed your lease?
   _____ Yes   _____ No
   (If Yes) What was the concession? (Record response exactly.)

5. On a scale of 1 to 5, 1 being "extremely important," 3 being "neither important nor unimportant," and 5 being "not important at all," **how important was the concession** in making your decision to rent?
    _____ Very important
    _____ Somewhat important
    _____ Neither important nor unimportant
    _____ Somewhat unimportant
    _____ Not important at all

6. What size apartment do you currently rent? _____
   (Number of bedrooms) _____

7. Is your (monthly rent) (house payment):
    _____ $500 or less
    _____ Between $501 and $600
    _____ Between $601 and $650
    _____ More than $650

8. Before you made your recent housing decision, did you visit any of the following apartment communities? (Read list)
   _____ Mary Hill
   _____ The Tarnhill
   _____ 11 On the Plaza
   _____ The Laurels
   _____ Other (Which ones?) _____

9. Of the apartment communities listed above, which one do you believe would be the **best choice for you**? (Read list)
   _____ 11 On the Plaza
   _____ The Tarnhill
   _____ The Laurels
   _____ Mary Hill
   _____ Other (Specify) _____
   Why do you say that? (Record responses exactly.)

10. Which apartment community do you believe would be the **least desirable** for you? (First mention)
    Why do you say that? (Record responses exactly.)

These last few questions refer to **The Laurels Apartments** in Tarnhill Park.

11. Please complete this sentence: "The thing **I liked best** about The Laurels was (record response exactly):

12. On a scale of 1 to 3, 1 being "much too expensive," 2 being "too expensive," and 3 being "about right," please describe the monthly rent charged at The Laurels for the apartment you liked best.
    _____ Much too expensive
    _____ Too expensive
    _____ About right

13. On a scale of 1 to 5, 1 being "very important," 3 being "neither important nor unimportant," and 5 being "not important at all," how important is it to you that the landlord pays all utilities (except telephone) at an apartment you rent?
    _____ Very important
    _____ Somewhat important
    _____ Neither important nor unimportant
    _____ Somewhat unimportant
    _____ Not important at all

14. Assume that you intend to rent an apartment in Tarnhill Park, and that the cost of underground parking is not included in the rent payment. How much per month additional would you be willing to pay for an underground heated parking space?
    _____ $0
    _____ Between $1 and $10
    _____ Between $10 and $20
    _____ Between $20 and $30
    _____ More than $30

15. This is the last question. If you had considered The Laurels to be a good place for you to rent, what would have been necessary for you to sign a lease? (Record response exactly.)

(Thank you)

residence. The combination design is effective because it allows residents to suggest ways in which management can improve their apartment living, and it allows the manager to discover and quantify residents' most important reasons for choosing their apartments.

Sometimes, though, no matter what apartment marketers do, they are not as successful in filling their multifamily buildings as they think they should be. They wonder whether there is something fundamentally wrong with the apartments, the amenities packages, or the rent structure. Maybe the living rooms are too small, or perhaps the amenities are outdated; maybe the rents are overpriced. The manager can choose to worry about these possibilities and attempt to address them, say, by painting the living room walls blue or tinkering with the rent schedule. However, one is more likely to find out if something is actually wrong by going out into the marketplace and asking.

Exhibit 3.3 is a questionnaire we use for telephone follow-up of nonrenters at The Laurels. (Such a questionnaire can be administered by a member of the site staff.) The example in exhibit 3.3 was drafted primarily to explore renting or buying motivators for prospects. Note, however, that it also includes detailed questions pertaining to the presence of concessions in the market, price-sensitivity, and responsibility for paying utilities charges. This particular vehicle was designed to help us find answers to the following questions.

1. What factors led the prospect to choose his or her current living situation?
2. How much money is he or she spending for rent now?
3. How familiar was the prospect with our competition?
4. What is his or her opinion of the competition?
5. What good and bad things can he or she tell us about our building?
6. Are we too expensive?
7. How important were concessions in his or her rental decision?
8. How much does it matter to the prospect that utilities were not included in the rent at our property?
9. Would that have been outweighed by the fact that underground parking is included in the rent at our property?
10. What (if anything) would have led that individual to sign a lease with us?

This type of follow-up of nonrenters enables the manager to determine buy factors throughout a particular market. An apartment manager or marketer may think he or she knows what those buy factors are, but there is always a possibility that the results will be something of a surprise. Even if the research only validates what had already been assumed, the results can be used to rank the property's features based on preferences expressed by the individual respondents. This process facilitates targeting of advertising and on-site marketing because it gives the marketer a better idea of what actual prospects are likely to consider important.

Note that the questionnaire in exhibit 3.3 includes The Laurels as an optional choice among several others, but it focuses on The Laurels only as the telephone interview is being concluded. This allows us to learn about the prospect and the competition without prejudicing the respondents' answers. Prospects may be very familiar with the competition for a particular property, and we have learned that they often have negative impressions about those buildings. They might think that the competitors are poorly maintained or that their apartments are too small—or even that the leasing office is inadequately staffed. On the other hand, they might think that the amenities in our building are superior, that our location is particularly appealing, or that our maintenance is outstanding. Even though these prospects actually rented someplace else, their comments have helped us restructure our advertising campaign to emphasize those features that are perceived favorably by the market.

Choosing a Methodology. The difference between focus groups and questionnaires is primarily one of format. In deciding whether to proceed in person (by using a focus group session) or on paper (with a questionnaire), the apartment marketer must recognize that each method has its advantages and disadvantages.

The focus group format is intrinsically more personal and more intense. It is conducted by a person whose position indicates to the participants that their landlord is interested in their reactions. Because of the length of time involved, a focus group can explore a relatively large number of subjects and do so at length. Its limitation, however, is the small number of participants; the results cannot be subjected to statistical analysis. On the other hand, a well-chosen panel of prospects can yield information in the form of personal opinions that no amount of generalized gathering of statistical data can provide.

The questionnaire format, while less personal and less intensive than a focus group, provides a vehicle for participation by every person who chooses to respond. If space is included on the questionnaire for additional comments (e.g., by inviting residents to write on the back of the page, as in the example in exhibit 3.2), it enables the respondents to explain their answers in more detail or to raise additional issues that are not covered by the questionnaire.

The choice of methodology raises a collateral issue, that of sampling. For purposes of choosing between a focus group and a questionnaire as the means of finding out what residents believe, the issue of sampling is very important. *Sampling* is the process market researchers and pollsters use to determine whether the results of their studies are valid—a large number of respondents permits generalizations to be made from partial results. The per-

Focus Groups versus Questionnaires

The purpose of a focus session must be clearly defined, and it is the moderator's responsibility to keep the participants focused on the subject. In general, there should be a single objective—discussions of apartment features, resident services, and advertising campaigns would be conducted separately—but the scope of a single session may be expanded to discover a variety of insights beyond the initial objective. The moderator should have no vested interest in the outcome of the focus group session he or she conducts.

The purpose of a questionnaire, on the other hand, is to obtain specific types of information. Use of precise language and rating scales will yield quantifiable results; open-ended questions that call for descriptions or opinions gather information that is not easily quantified but is almost always interesting and worthy of consideration. Consultation with a market research professional will assure the effectiveness of a focus group or questionnaire.

While it is beyond the scope of this book to address specific costs of market research, factors that contribute to the costs of focus groups and questionnaires can be identified. In general, a focus group session is more complex and has a wider range of potential costs to be considered. Questionnaires, on the other hand, are not particularly expensive.

The moderator of a focus group is often a professional market researcher whose responsibilities may include recruiting focus group participants and developing the program content. This person is usually compensated with a consulting fee. Consulting fees and participant compensation vary widely and depend on the nature of the "product" being analyzed and the qualifications of the participants. Participants typically receive token compensation which may be money but can be merchandise. (Professionals asked their opinions about a technical product related to their work are usually compensated differently than consumers who participate in a product evaluation.) In addition, refreshments may be served as a means of making everyone comfortable, and the type and amount of food and drink will affect the costs. Use of a "neutral" location may incur some expense as well.

Usually a focus session on apartment marketing or management issues would not be conducted at the subject apartment community. However, a focus group session related to resident services would be appropriately conducted on site, with current residents as the only participants.

Development of a specific questionnaire may be a one-time activity for a marketing consultant or the responsibility of the manager of the property. Use of a marketing consultant will incur a fee, of course, depending on the complexity of the project and the amount of work done by the consultant. Unless a mass mailing is being made to the marketplace (as opposed to a captive market of community residents), postage costs for mailing each questionnaire—plus postpaid return—would be nominal, and personnel costs (staff preparation of the "mailing") should be negligible. Mailing costs may be avoided altogether by hand delivering questionnaires to residents on site and having them returned to the management office.

A telephone survey will take staff time (probably at least 15 minutes for each contact) plus the cost of the telephone call. Local calls may accrue time charges; long-distance charges are based on time and distance.

Ultimately, the decision to use a focus group or a questionnaire depends on the type of information to be obtained and whether varied points of view are more important than being able to quantify results.

son who will use the resultant information must decide whether a clear majority opinion is required and how many people must be surveyed to obtain such a majority view.

A focus group is usually composed of a dozen or fewer people whose opinions are applicable only to them and not to the entire population. If a property has only twelve residents, a properly conducted focus group would include all twelve of them as participants and yield everything the manager needed to know about resident opinions. It would then be possible to make generalizations about all those residents from what the group said. On the other hand, if the resident population is substantially greater in number than the focus group, it would be inappropriate to draw specific conclusions from the opinions expressed by this small group and assume that all of the residents share them. It is important to keep in mind the fact that focus groups are simply what they appear to be—several people who represent different (and, hopefully, relevant) points of view that exist in a particular population group.

By contrast, use of a questionnaire does permit results to be quantified. People can be asked to respond to particular questions using a numerical scale to indicate differing levels of intensity. (See exhibit 3.3, the telephone interview questionnaire.) Thus, at least theoretically, questionnaires permit the researcher to obtain a response from every person from whom one is desired and to gauge how strongly the respondent holds his or her opinions. The number of responses of any one type can be added together and divided by the total number of respondents to arrive at an average gradient of opinion.

You can use the techniques discussed in this chapter to survey your markets. They are easy to use—and relatively inexpensive—and your findings can sharpen your overall marketing efforts and improve the efficiency of your advertising campaigns.

A Practical Example—A Focus Group Session

Picture a conference room with several rectangular tables arranged in a U-shape, with upholstered chairs around the outer edge. Ten well-dressed people (seven women and three men) are seated around the U, eating sandwiches and drinking coffee and soft drinks. They are chatting amiably, getting to know one another after initial introductions. Two of the women, who appear to be in their mid-sixties, are discussing opportunities for volunteer work; news about grandchildren and social security developments are shared. One elderly gentleman is trying to enlist support for a rent-control effort that he is apparently spearheading. Midway down one leg of the U is a younger, professionally dressed woman who is distributing name tags, yellow pads, and pens. Her name is Maggie; she's the moderator of this focus group session.

Maggie introduces herself and states the name of her company. She tells the group that she does market research, that her job is to travel around the country and talk to people about different products and services. Maggie says that the focus session will last approximately one and one-half hours and that she'll be showing the participants some things and asking for their opinions and reactions. She emphasizes that she wants the group to be "very candid and honest" in their responses. They should understand that she does not work for any of the companies involved and that none of the materials she will be showing them are her ideas. She notes that both favorable and unfavorable responses are welcome, that nothing said in the session will hurt her feelings. Finally, she assures the panel that she does not expect them to agree about everything and mentions that she will be tape-recording the session to help her write her report.

Then Maggie gets down to business. She proceeds around the table, asking each of the panel members to tell her something about their backgrounds. She asks them to start with where they live, how long they have lived there, and what they enjoy doing in their spare time.

She learns that they all live in a particular geographic area known as Tarnhill Park (where The Laurels is located); some live in single-family homes, others in duplexes, and several in apartment buildings. All would be considered prospective residents for The Laurels, and their responses illustrate a variety of reasons for preferring the neighborhood and the particular living situations they have chosen.

Karen, a resident of the Tarnhill area for 35 years, says: "After being widowed 19 years ago, I moved into an apartment building in a neighboring suburb. I hated it, because the residents were all old and sick—and I'm not that old." Several members of the group chuckle, and Karen continues: "I don't know why everybody thinks that after you get to be a certain age—sixty or so, . . . I'm 67—you have to be taken care of. I don't want that. Sure, I like to have the snow shoveled off my walk, and it's harder for me to do repairs. But I'm living in a 17-unit apartment building where I know everybody. I don't like those high-rises where the elevators are always going out and, if there's a fire, you have to walk down all those stairs."

Margaret interrupts: "Well, . . . I don't agree. I live in a high-rise, and I really like it. Everybody—the manager, the maintenance crew, all of them—they're so nice to me. I know all my neighbors, and we get along fine. There's a security system at the front entrance that lets me see my visitors before I buzz them in. The only thing I don't like is that every year when I renew my lease, my rent goes up."

Maggie, beginning to direct the discussion, asks Margaret how she arrived at her choice of an apartment: "Tell me a little bit about the process you went through when you were selecting your apartment. What apartments did you

APARTMENT FEATURES

Room size [big!] (5)
Price/low rent [most important/#1] (ALL)
Layout, floor plan [big bedroom] (3)
No long hallways (2)
Security [#3] (9)
Friends live there (3)
No expensive amenities (2)
Quiet/soundproof/good construction (8)
No dark hallways (6)
Neighborhood/location [#4] (9)
In-unit laundry (2)

Big closets (4)
Near shopping (4)
Screen tenants [#2] (10)
Close to busline (3)
Upkeep (clean) (7)
Heated garages (2)
Secure garages (5)
Looks good from outside (1)
Entertainment room/party room (1)
Central air (1)
Pest control (2)

HOW TO FIND

Friends/relatives (3)
Newspaper (6)
Apartment locator magazines (5)
Signs near building (10)

---

look at? How did you evaluate them? How did you find out what was available?"

Margaret responds: "I wanted to find a place to live that was near my church. Other parishioners helped me locate the apartment I eventually chose, and I had seen an apartment ad on the church bulletin board."

An extended discussion ensues. Maggie moves to a blackboard, and begins to list the most important reasons—the buy factors—that group members have offered for choosing their current housing. After approximately half an hour, the blackboard is scrawled with two lists, with parentheses indicating the number of responses in a particular category (see box).

> We shall return to the focus group discussion shortly, but it is worthwhile to interrupt at this point to consider what the panel had communicated to us in the list, which was incorporated into Maggie's report.
>   We recognized that what we were seeing was important information, and some of it was unexpected. We were surprised to learn, for example, that *tenant screening* by the management company was one of the most important buy factors the panel had isolated. We had not thought about that as a marketing tool at all; credit checks were just a routine administrative task that we normally conducted at all of our properties. While screening could be considered an adjunct to the security component [we had anticipated security as being a key element], it clearly deserved separate attention. The members of

the focus group, who were themselves prospective residents at the property, believed it was important for management to carefully screen residents before they moved into the building.

Further, in considering the list of items as buy factors, it was possible to rank them and then think about constructing our advertising in response to what the focus group had told us. In other words, the things we should emphasize were price (although we were reluctant to do so, given the rental structure at The Laurels), tenant screening, security, and location. These items were ranked 1 through 4 in the list.

However, we also found out that the quality of construction at the building and its soundproofing were factors that prospects actually knew about and considered in arriving at their decisions to rent. Both were excellent at the building. Also, while we knew that the maintenance and housekeeping of any apartment property are important, we decided to feature them more prominently in our marketing of The Laurels, along with its location.

The panel also verified some of our beliefs that had not been proven before. For example, appropriate signage is a key to attracting prospects, including those who are elderly. We also found out—contrary to what had been reported on our guest cards—that word of mouth was the primary source of traffic at The Laurels [we had thought, instead, that newspapers and apartment locator magazines were relied on by prospective residents]. All in all, we had gained a wealth of information that could be useful in the future.

Now let's return to the focus group.

The final part of the discussion was devoted to an in-depth consideration of four proposals for print advertisements, including the one we mentioned earlier in this chapter. Focus group participants were shown preliminary sketches with headlines.

Maggie begins: "I want to show you some ideas for advertisements. They are not finished ads; they're not meant to be. As you'll see, there's no printing on them, and the pictures are rough drawings rather than photographs. As I show these to you, I want you to write down what you consider the main idea to be—what is it they are trying to communicate to you?" She begins by showing Ad #1 (it contains sketches of three faces below a headline, "Live Among Good Friends, Quiet Times"). She allows approximately 90 seconds for writing, then asks Edith to begin.

Edith responds: "Sociability. Comfort. I think it means that people watch out for one another."

Marie: "Feel secure and happy in your surroundings. I don't mean security; just that when you're around friends, you feel secure and comfortable. You're at ease."

Jo: "This means community living; friendship."

Karen: "The first thing I wrote down was retired people; but when I look at the picture, I don't think they're retired. I think they're younger."

Rosemary: "I wrote 'living around friends and no noise.' "

Maggie interjects a reminder: "Focus on your reaction to the idea contained in the headline."

Edith: "A lot of people like to be around children; I don't know. I haven't lived with children for a long time. I like the idea of being with older people. I only see my grandchildren once a year, and I don't even know how to act when I'm around them. It makes me uncomfortable. *Maybe the drawing should be of retired folks.*"

Martha speaks up for the first time: "I can visualize lovely grounds, woods where you could walk. This is what this ad makes me feel." Others murmur approval.

Rosemary: "It's very important to live around good friends, especially if you live alone—as I do. You feel secure when you have friends around you that you can depend on."

Mary interrupts: "I think (the ad says) 'contentment,' and we're all looking for that. And it's important to have neighbors whom you can call on, and they'll call on you, in need. The ad also suggests 'care in selecting occupants with similar values.' "

Jo: "I disagree. The ad reminds me of a nursing home. Sometimes there's too much closeness. You don't want to have the feeling that you have to do everything with somebody else. That's what a nursing home is for, and I'm not ready for that."

Maggie senses that others agree with Jo's criticism. She asks Karen to respond to this point.

Karen: "It has a somewhat negative connotation. It just feels as though recreation has to be a group thing—and planned for you—whether you want it or not."

Margaret: "This is the kind of advertising that they used for Lake Villa. I lived there awhile, and everybody was old and sick. I don't want any part of that. . . . My friends are people I've known for years. I think the ad should use the word neighbors, not friends."

The others nod agreement. Several participants make positive comments about this refinement. Maggie moves on, displaying Ad #2 (a sketch of an older woman reading to a young child below the headline, "Have More Time for the Little Pleasures of Life"). Comments begin immediately.

"That sounds like retirement."

Maggie asks the panel to write down the main idea of the ad.

Martha: "This means time to enjoy your grandchildren, without spending a lot of time doing housework and yard work, that sort of thing."

Rosemary: "I think that the wording means that you can enjoy your leisure time if you live in an apartment, without having to do a lot of maintenance—like there is with a house. But I think the picture has a somewhat negative connotation, because it suggests that it's only a place for retired people. I like the headline, but they should change the picture. I abhor the idea of living in a retirement village."

Jo interrupts to offer a pointed comment [showing an unexpected weakness in this ad that we hadn't considered]: "Most of us don't want our grandchildren around all the time. It would be okay if they had a place where residents could go, say, to have a birthday party for a younger person. But I don't think that they ought to have an ad that promises that you can have grandchildren with you in your apartment. I wouldn't rent a place because of that."

Karen expands on that idea: "I lived in two apartments that advertised like this. And I hated both of them. I thought my neighbors were going to be active people, and they weren't. I'm an active 73-year-old, and I'm not ready for the scrap heap."

Maggie asks Karen: "Does the ad itself convey this idea? Or is it just that your experience in the two places you mentioned was negative?"

Karen responds: "It's from my experience. And the way they advertise. All those seniors' magazines have ads like this. They aren't like you think they are, and you don't find out until you get in there and live it."

Maggie moves on to Ad #3 (from the original ad shown in exhibit 3.1, the rolled-up newspaper and the headline, "Some People Confront the Problems of City Life Only Once a Day"). She allows time for writing.

Jo begins: "Well, I like living in a big city. I like all the activity. To me, this ad suggests that skimming over a newspaper for a few minutes is all you need to do to keep in touch with the city. This ad doesn't have anything to do with renting an apartment. What it really means to me is either that living in a big city is a mistake—which I don't agree with—or that you can enjoy everything a big city has to offer by reading a newspaper—which is stupid." [This was a criticism that had not dawned on us, and it sparked other unexpected comments.]

Marie: "I think it's just the opposite. It means that if you live out in the country, you don't have to worry about city life. But I agree with Jo—I don't understand what this ad has to do with apartments at all."

Rosemary: "I feel that the ad conveys the idea that life should be boring. 'Confront the problems of city life only once a day' means getting out of bed, I suppose. I want things to be more exciting than that. This ad is sort of insulting."

Maggie displays Ad #4 (the sketch of a young man in dinner clothing occupies the left of the ad; the right is dominated by the headline, "There are Two Places You'll Find a Concierge and a Good Restaurant: A Fine Hotel and The Laurels"). The panel is quick to criticize this one.

"The Laurels is a status symbol."

"Meant for the upper class."

"Only certain types of people—not me."

"Advertising for the elite—where the elite meet to eat."

"I couldn't afford it—and I'm not sure I'd want to, even if I could."

"The man with the tuxedo would turn some people away. I'm not sure I have the right clothes to live there."

"You'd better be in an exclusive financial bracket, or don't bother living here."

Maggie then conducts an exercise. She asks the panel to rank the advertisements on a scale of one through four, as effectively indicating places where they would want to live based on the ideas contained in the ads. As might be expected, there is no consensus—except that the participants generally agree that none of the ads appeals to them.

> In listening to the tape afterward, we were startled to hear Karen summarize her reaction to that last exercise. "I have always wanted to live at The Laurels," she remarked, "but none of these advertisements would make me even want to go there for a visit. I think you ought to go back to the drawing board."
>
> As it turned out, we *did* go back to the drawing board. The focus group experience taught us that our expensive print advertising program was very likely destined to fail. It was obvious that the proposed illustrations and headlines conveyed vastly different images and impressions to these prospects. On the other hand, we already knew that established residents liked their apartments and the amenities at The Laurels—we had overheard their favorable comments to others. So, we chose instead to rely on this high level of resident satisfaction (i.e., word of mouth) as the vehicle for "advertising" The Laurels. We created and publicized a program that rewarded resident referrals. When a resident's recommendation resulted in a signed

lease, the new resident and his or her mentor (and their spouses) received a certificate for a specially catered dinner at the on-site cafe. These special "thank you" gifts became desirable in themselves, and the program worked well. As a result of this change of focus, we were able to fund additional activities and services within our established resident-retention program.

CHAPTER

4

Advertise

Professional managers of apartment communities are required to have working knowledge of a variety of complicated disciplines that may be foreign to them. Most apartment managers would probably never dream of writing an insurance policy for a building they manage or overhauling its heating system. Yet, they often create their own advertising campaigns, budget the money to pay for them, and then proceed to write and place their ads in various media.

What most apartment managers know about advertising is a result of what they have learned over time as consumers. Because of this, their approach to apartment advertising may be based more on their experiences and feelings—their personal preferences—than on principles learned from textbooks. People are apt to believe they have developed some special competence in the field simply because of having been passive consumers of advertising all their lives. American consumers are bombarded by thousands of advertising messages in the form of television and radio commercials, newspaper and magazine ads, billboards, signs, bushels of so-called junk mail, and a host of other items from the time they are barely old enough to understand language. (Experts say we see as many as 500 advertising messages every day of our lives.) Americans live in a commercial culture.

One may be impressed by the power of a particular piece of advertising, but often the thought comes to mind, "I'll bet I could do as well as that" or, "If I had a huge ad budget, I could produce a better commercial than that one." These opinions are rooted in the notion that advertising is essentially a matter of taste. The presumption is that any literate person with a sense of style can design and produce a professional advertisement. On the contrary, we believe that good advertising, while perhaps more an art than a science, results from the application of skills that, once learned, are developed and enhanced by repeated experience.

In this chapter, we will discuss advertising from the perspectives of determining advertising objectives, formulating specific strategies, developing an advertising budget, deciding who will do the work (staff or an outside agency), and choosing specific media to use—in other words, creating a specific advertising campaign as part of the overall marketing effort to lease apartments. (Development of a marketing plan, evaluation of marketing results, and monitoring what the competition is doing are discussed in chapter 2.)

Advertising Objectives

Much of real estate management is reactive. It is easy to forget that apartment buildings deteriorate with time and use. (Things like roofs, heating systems, and sidewalks are only fixed *after* they break. Preventive maintenance is a fairly recent concept.) Similarly, advertising of apartments is often done in an environment best characterized as crisis management—dictating newspaper ad copy over the telephone to an account representative minutes before the deadline or frantically trying to create a last-minute ad campaign for placement in an unfamiliar medium because an owner insists on it.

Apartment advertising is an area in which waste is endemic. Advertising mistakes are often the result of inexperience. An ad in a newspaper or rental magazine may be run unchanged for several months (or years). Often it is doubtful that the ad is there because it has been productive. More likely it is being run out of habit or because the building owner or manager does not know how to compose a better one. Managers often fail to plan for advertising, and such plans as are made are rarely guided by research. A target that is uncertain cannot be expected to be reached with any accuracy; when a target is hit, the achievement is probably accidental.

The best way to avoid operating with a crisis mentality, counteract inexperience, or overcome an apparently mindless expenditure of money is to plan your advertising program. Advertising is one of many components of the overall business strategy for an apartment building. The decisions involved are just as important as the decision to renovate a lobby, refurbish a community room, or provide a new amenity. The decision to advertise is not automatic. It should be the result of setting specific marketing goals within an overall management plan coupled with an objective assessment of the value that advertising will add to the attainment of those goals. One advantage of a thoughtful approach is that advertising becomes a strategic tool. It increases the confidence of the property's owners (and the others involved in the process) that the manager is spending a particular amount of money in order to achieve predetermined—and desirable—goals.

As a prelude to the development of a specific advertising campaign, it is important to identify the expectations of the owners and everyone else who has a stake in the performance of the property (the manager and the leasing team in particular). Their expectations may be identified from the answers to one or more of the following questions.

- Do they anticipate that advertising will generate a certain volume of traffic—i.e., large numbers of qualified prospects? Is such traffic likely to be seasonal or steady throughout the year?
- Do they expect particular conversion ratios—i.e., that a particular percentage of signed leases will result from a specific volume of traffic? What ratios are achievable?
- Do they want to project a specific image for the building (positioning) in the marketplace? What is that image? Is it likely to be believed by prospects?
- Are there certain media that they expect will produce the greatest numbers of qualified prospects (e.g., newspapers, magazines, billboards, radio, television)? Is this expectation based on prior experience?

The expectations listed here may seem to be somewhat amorphous. When specific numbers are added to them, they may seem constricting. The point is, it is important to begin the planning process by writing down what you believe are the underlying assumptions of the people involved in the success of the advertising campaign at the property you manage. This should not be an exploration of personal preferences and conjecture but, rather, the starting point for developing a specific advertising campaign. Once the expectations have been identified and stated, the next step is to set specific objectives and create a strategy for achieving them through advertising. Because the goals and strategies will vary from property to property, as will the demographic and psychographic characteristics of their target markets, it is wise to avoid a cookie-cutter approach to advertising—i.e., something that will be applied to every apartment property in your portfolio.

In marketing apartments, the goal is to generate signed leases. Thus, the objective for an advertising plan might be stated: *To achieve 97-percent occupancy within six months after the campaign is launched.* Note that the percentage in this example could be higher or lower, and the time frame could be shorter or longer. In stating a specific objective for your advertising campaign, you should consider what can be achieved realistically for your property in your market. The parameters for lease-up of a new apartment community might be stated progressively (e.g., 50 percent in three months; 75 percent in six months, and 95 percent in one year), while closing a small vacancy gap at a very desirable, well-established property might be stated very narrowly (e.g., 98 percent in eight weeks). The size of the property, the condition of the market area, the number of vacancies to be filled, and the rate of turnover are some of the factors that will affect your advertising objectives for a particular campaign.

Sometimes what an owner believes will happen is markedly different than what reality dictates—an owner may expect to achieve occupancy goals that are infeasible in a depressed market. On the other hand, it does not pay to be too cautious; goals should not be set so low that reaching them is extremely easy—it is human nature to stop running when the race is finished. In establishing a marketing goal, it is important that the occupancy level selected is desirable, achievable, and optimistic.

Goal-setting in the apartment industry inevitably involves occupancy figures. The financial success of an apartment property depends in large part on achieving high occupancy rates—that is what generates income. However, the achievement of high occupancy rates should not be at the expense of net operating income (NOI). Concessions are usually very effective in improving occupancy, but they are also very seductive. Many months of rental income may be sacrificed to achieve an occupancy rate that is ultimately deceptive. In fact, rent concessions actually diminish net operating income and reduce the value of the building as an asset. Thus, a property can have a high occupancy level and, because of concessions, generate less income than would have been collected with a substantially lower occupancy rate at market rents with no concessions. Free rent goes straight to the bottom line. Every one-month rental given away reduces the value of a one-year lease by one-twelfth—a loss of more than eight percent of the annual rent amount for that apartment. If concessions are part of a marketing strategy, it is important to calculate the costs involved and be sure that everyone knows the impact they will have on the property's net operating income (and its value).

From personal experience, we recommend that an advertising goal statement include a description of the owner's (and manager's) philosophy regarding concessions. In that vein, we would amend the previous goal statement to read as follows: *To achieve 97-percent occupancy within six months after the campaign is launched, at market rents with no concessions.*

Advertising Strategies

Regardless of how the goals for a property are stated, the means of achieving those goals must be formulated. The result should be one or more strategy statements that delineate a methodology. Inherent in such a strategy is the assumption that the results will be measurable. The goal statement presented earlier can be carried to this next step, thus: To achieve the stated occupancy goals—*by promoting the property's most prominent benefits in biweekly newspaper advertisements to attract maximum traffic of qualified potential residents.*

The portion of this statement that deserves particular attention is the phrase "prominent benefits." A list of what the apartment manager believes are the prominent benefits of the property should be prepared. The more obvious items might be such things as an elegant lobby, a remarkable exercise facility, or unique apartment amenities—or, perhaps, the competitively low rents that are being charged. The buy factors identified in a marketing grid would be likely candidates for the list as well (see chapters 1 and 2). However, determination of the prominent benefits of the property—as perceived in the marketplace—is facilitated by conducting market research (as discussed in chapter 3). After the results of the market research have been tallied, the two lists should be compared. There will probably be some duplicate items, but the manager may be surprised to find out what the market considers attractive about the property—often the market singles out aspects that would never have occurred to the manager. The prominent benefits on the combined lists will be the basis for part of the specific ad copy to be developed.

A close look at the revised strategy statement reveals a limiting factor—qualified traffic. Unqualified prospects waste the valuable time and energy of the leasing staff and result in unnecessary wear and tear on the property. If an ad attracts large numbers of people who are unwilling or unable to rent the available units, that ad is misguided.

In choosing apartments, prospects target particular neighborhoods based on location. They may prefer to be close to work or to shopping or recreational activities. They may want to live near to relatives or far away from them. Proximity to schools, a hospital, or other facilities may also be a consideration. Having targeted a neighborhood, they will identify what types of apartments are available in each building. Then, based on such factors as price, amenities, and floor plans, they will visit the most promising apartment properties in person. At that point, the on-site leasing team will take over.

It should be readily apparent that the reasons for choosing a specific apartment building and a particular apartment in that building are personal (idiosyncratic is a better word). *The challenge is to design an advertising campaign that will appeal to the ideal prospects for the property.* The best way, as we noted earlier, is to find out from current residents what they like best about the apartment community. Those are the features to advertise. This approach might be called copycatting—it assumes that there are prospective residents who have the same preferences for location, price, and features as the current residents do. This tactic is an attempt to expand a particular target market using specific demographics and psychographics.

Market research repeatedly indicates that location and price are important to prospects. Because of that fact, we believe that this information should be included in apartment advertising. Doing so enables prospects to sort through the available apartments merely by scanning the ads—looking first

EXHIBIT 4.1

Example Display and Liner Ads

WILLOWGATE AT NORTHTOWN
Spacious 1, 1+Den, 2 Bedroom Apartments from $410
At I-18 and Boulder Road
Across from Southgate
Washer/Dryer, Private Entry, A/C,
Fitness Center, Garage w/Opener
Call Lisa, 555-5555

WILLOWGATE AT NORTHTOWN.
Spacious 1 BR, 1BR+Den, 2BR apts. From $410. I-18/Boulder Rd., near Southgate. W/D, Priv. ent., A/C, Fitness, Garage. Lisa, 555-5555.

All apartment advertising should include the words "equal housing opportunity"; in a display ad, the fair housing logo may be substituted.

---

for particular locations, then carefully reading the ads that initially caught their attention, and finally deciding for themselves which ones are geographically convenient and affordable and have features that are appealing to them. Thus, if the building is close to certain landmarks—e.g., a major business, a shopping center, or a freeway—those attractions should be advertised prominently. If the medium being used has a short life and is easily changed (e.g., all type copy in the Sunday newspaper), pricing should be included. *Exhibit 4.1* shows two different approaches to the same basic ad, one a boxed display ad and the other a standard want ad (classified ad).

An important consideration regarding strategies is the element of time. Although specific details are beyond the scope of this book, the apartment marketer should keep in mind that time is required for design and execution of advertising art. The review and approval process requires time for appropriate people to see and comment on ad copy, graphic components, art, etc. Changes or corrections to an ad take time as well. A particular limiting factor will be the deadlines imposed by selected media. Advertising agency personnel and media representatives can provide guidance on allocation of adequate time for different stages. A schedule showing when each step must be completed, the order in which they must be done, and who will be responsible for each one will help the apartment manager stay on top of the advertising campaign's development and implementation. (Time must also be al-

Creating Effective Advertisements
- Describe the apartment for lease—e.g., number of rooms, number of bedrooms and bathrooms; availability of eating space in the kitchen, a dining room, or a dining area extension of the living room (may include square footage).
- Name and/or describe special features of the apartment, amenities of the property, or characteristics of the neighborhood or community—e.g., built-in microwave oven, wood-burning fireplace, spectacular view; availability of parking, laundry facilities on site, indoor swimming pool; proximity to public transportation, schools, shopping.
- Identify the location—name the general area (e.g., north side), town, or neighborhood; give names or numbers of nearby cross streets or a major intersection.
- State the price—a specific rent for a single unit, a starting or minimum rate for several apartments of the same type (e.g., one-bedroom units), a range of rents (lowest to highest) in an ad for the entire array at a property.
- Provide a contact—the name of the management firm or the person to call, with a telephone number (unless the market area includes more than one area code, the seven-digit number is sufficient).

Classified advertisements usually show standardized abbreviations used by the newspaper unless the advertiser asks to have everything spelled out. Apartment size, property location, rental amount, and whom to contact are minimal information to show. It may be appropriate to indicate a date when the apartment will be available, especially if it is being advertised more than 60 days in advance. Stated time periods for acceptance of calls may also be appropriate, particularly when "business hours only" (9:00 to 5:00) or "evenings" (after 5:00 P.M.) are preferred. Fair housing requirements are usually satisfied by inclusion of the words "equal housing opportunity" in ads.

Display advertisements can accommodate much more information, and apartment marketers often choose to present features and amenities as bulleted lists. When illustrations are used, ad copy usually is presented in narrative form and accompanied by a headline reflective of the "positioning statement" for the ad campaign. Regardless of format, no abbreviations should be used. Illustrations should be chosen carefully for two reasons. One is to achieve a good fit with the image being created for the property; the other is to avoid legal problems regarding discrimination. The apartment community's name and logo graphics are usually included in display advertisements, and the equal housing opportunity logo should be used.

Other considerations regarding advertising content relate primarily to legal issues (see chapter 7). Federal fair housing laws include specific requirements regarding choices of words and illustrations to avoid discrimination. State and local fair housing laws may extend protections beyond those mandated under federal law. It is a good idea to seek competent legal advice if there is any question or concern about the content of advertisements.

located for printing of forms, stationery, and other advertising and marketing adjuncts because they have to be available when prospects respond to specific advertisements.)

Budget Considerations

The amount of advertising that is done will be driven by the marketing budget (see chapter 2). Budgeting for an apartment advertising campaign is especially challenging. It requires the manager to forecast the number of ads (and their variations in size and content) that will be created for the year and the media that will be utilized to deliver them. Undoubtedly, the single greatest expense in an advertising budget is the media that are used to convey the message to the public. Assuming that the printed word will predominate, the size, shape, and color of each ad and its frequency of placement in various publications (number of insertions) will determine the costs involved. It will be necessary to identify not only which ads will be run and when, but also the publications in which they will appear.

Often apartment managers find themselves trying to market their properties in an environment in which the competition is offering unprecedented concessions in the form of free rent or other inducements. A sudden drop in mortgage interest rates may make home ownership especially desirable to long-term apartment residents, resulting in unexpected move-outs. As a result, a manager may have to employ different ads or different media than had been predicted during the budgeting exercise. Whether such a response is termed reactive, strategic, or crisis advertising, the fact remains that market factors inevitably put extraordinary pressures on scarce advertising dollars.

If use of other media is contemplated, the budgeting process becomes even more complicated. Billboards are rented to advertisers for a fixed period of time. Because they are usually positioned for viewing by people in moving vehicles, the ad message must be short and specific. The location of billboard ads is critical—by far the largest number of people who see such ads from major highways are *not* likely apartment rental prospects because they are usually intent on their specific destinations (going to work or home from work, etc.). Radio or television advertising requires buying discrete amounts of time (ad spots) in a certain number of time slots (frequency and time of day). Charges for broadcast advertising are based on ad length (in seconds), number of repetitions, and programming context (rates for morning drive time may be substantially higher than those for late night in a particular market, or vice versa). Production costs also vary radically. A radio spot can be read by a live announcer or prerecorded (the latter guarantees uniform quality of delivery). However, television ads are generally prerecorded, and they may be presented very simply—a voiceover with still photographs or reading copy that appears on the screen. To take fullest advantage of this visual medium—presentation of high-quality video images showing people and action—can be very costly because of the people (acting talent), the time (repetition to get it right on film), and the technology involved in producing it. The audiences (target markets) for whom the broadcast ads are intended will dictate when and where they will be placed, but the number of times they will be repeated also has a great impact on the cost.

Media rates are generally based on the ad size (print area, length of broadcast time) and positioning (front, back, or middle of a publication; broadcast programming context). They are also weighted to reflect the amount of exposure the advertising will receive in the marketplace of prospects. The size of the captive audience is one of the factors in determining advertising rates, whether the vehicle is printed (newspaper or magazine) or broadcast (radio or television). Broadcast media, by definition, reach very large, very diverse audiences. For targeted marketing via television, a local cable channel may be a better value than regular or network-affiliated channels. Any advertising medium should be able to provide a "media kit" containing demographic data on the size and composition of its audience to help the advertiser optimize the effort to target a specific market. (Media selection is discussed later in this chapter.)

John Wanamaker, a pioneer in retailing, is credited with saying, "I know half the money I'm spending on advertising is wasted. Now, if I only knew which half!" That comment generates a word of caution about the advertising budget: A review of last year's expenditures may reveal that $10,000 was spent on advertising. The manager may simply decide to allow for inflation by projecting $10,500 for the coming year and stopping at that point. However, such thinking does not go far enough. It is just as important to examine what was accomplished with the amount spent. If last year's $10,000 attracted only 42 qualified prospects, the manager should be thinking about doing something different to improve the results. (In this example, it cost more than $235 to attract each of those 42 prospects; if only 10 of them signed leases, the cost of acquiring each lease was actually $1,000. Last year's advertising was not cost-effective.)

The point is, the performance of your advertising campaign—and the feasibility of reaching the goals you expect it to achieve—should be reviewed periodically, preferably at very short intervals. It is very likely that a careful review of the advertising campaign for the coming year (and the thinking behind it) will suggest ways you can improve its effectiveness. Such scrutiny may even reveal where your advertising dollars are being wasted. You should also be prepared to learn two equally disquieting truths—first, that you are actually *underspending* for the results you want to achieve and, second, that you cannot fully achieve your occupancy goals, no matter how much advertising money you spend. You may find yourself in the uncomfortable position of having your advertising agency pleading for more money on the one hand while the owner you work for is demanding a reduction in spending because

Costs of Advertising

Many factors contribute to the cost of an advertisement. These include:

1. **Ad size**—classified advertisements may be priced by the word, by the line, or by column inches; display rates may be based on columns (width) and inches (depth) but are more often defined as whole pages or fractions of pages. In broadcast media (radio and television), ad size is measured as time, usually minutes, fractions of minutes, or numbers of seconds.
2. **Timing**—when the ad appears—is critical. Classified newspaper advertisements often have higher costs for Sundays than for weekdays. Display rates may vary with the time of year; broadcast ad rates vary with the time of day and surrounding programming. Ads accepted after a deadline may carry additional penalty charges.
3. **Frequency**—the number of repetitions—is a major consideration. Each repetition adds to the overall cost, but multiple print insertions and broadcast spots usually carry lower "per ad" costs. A one-time insertion might cost $500.00, and four insertions of the same ad within a specified time period might be billed at $450.00 each.
4. **Audience**—how many copies of a print vehicle are circulated, how large a population is reached by a broadcast. The size and characteristics of the audience (demographics, psychographics) reached by the medium will determine rates. It may cost more per targeted prospect to reach a narrowly defined market because a particular medium may reach a small segment of an area's population, all of whom are likely rental prospects.
5. **Creative elements**—development of print ads usually proceeds through several stages—sketches of ideas (images and headlines), developed components of the chosen ad (written copy, art, photography), completion of camera-ready art (keyline and paste-up)—before they can be printed in the magazine or other vehicle. Broadcast ad costs include scripts, sound recordings for radio, audio and video recordings for television, and voice (and acting) talent. Broadcast production often requires repeated "takes" and editing (out-takes) to create the final, timed advertisement. Agency charges for creative elements may include a factor to cover "overhead"; charges for work contracted out by the agency (e.g., special typography, illustration art, photography, broadcast production) are passed on to the advertiser.
6. **Variables**—factors such as geographic location and time of year. Advertising rates on the East Coast differ from those on the West Coast and in the Midwest and Southwest. If an area traditionally turns over its residential rental population in the spring and the fall, ad rates may be higher at those times. Newspapers in small towns are likely to have lower classified rates than those serving large metropolitan areas. Apartment locator magazines' rates may be affected by how frequently they are reprinted (periodicity) and the distribution of each printing (the size of the market they reach). Other types of magazines may vary their rates based on the geographic areas served by an issue, special features in different issues (highly targeted audiences), how frequently they are published (weekly versus monthly versus semiannually), and where an ad appears in a particular issue (on the covers or inside). For broadcast media, audience size may be dependent on programming content (personalities, subject matter, music versus talk versus news) and time of day. Radio stations whose broadcast day is less than 24 hours clear the airwaves and expand the audiences for stations whose frequencies otherwise overlap theirs. Television rates vary for local stations, network affiliates, and cable channels.

the property is not generating sufficient income—i.e., the marketing effort is not achieving your occupancy goals. The key question in this situation is whether the advertising itself is at fault (i.e., the ads and their placement) or whether your expectations of occupancy resulting from it are unrealistic. When budgeting for advertising, it is prudent to include an allowance (reserve or contingency funds) for correcting advertising errors and responding to unanticipated changes in market conditions.

Staff Requirements

One very important aspect of apartment marketing that cannot begin too early is communication with your staff about the marketing plan, specific advertising campaigns, and the leasing goals. Apart from understanding the content of the advertising campaign—positioning statements, images used to convey it, etc.—your leasing personnel and other staff members must become familiar with the advertising schedule (when they should expect heavy traffic in phone calls and visits) and be prepared to respond to prospects' queries generated by the theme of an ad. They must also have an appreciation of the owner's investment in the advertising and make a commitment to accomplishing the goals of the program. Ideally, they will become enthused and share with you their perceptions of the property and their reactions to the advertisements—as well as their perspectives on the success of each ad—all of which will help you fine-tune your campaign. (However, while staff input should be welcomed and carefully considered, it should not be the deciding factor. Management is directly accountable to ownership for the results of the advertising campaign, and the manager must maintain control over its direction and content.)

Once a budget has been set, the next step is to assign roles and responsibilities among the people who will participate in the advertising campaign. Before making specific assignments, the following questions should be answered.

1. Who will have overall responsibility for the advertising?
2. Will the campaign be a team effort? If so, who will be on the team?
3. Who will create the ads?
4. Who will place them?
5. Who will monitor the effectiveness of the advertising campaign and its budgetary consequences?

Few management companies intentionally employ people who have knowledge of or are experienced in advertising. It is common practice to delegate these tasks to novices—bright, creative people with a willingness to learn will find the research activities and the overall marketing activities worthwhile learning experiences—or, alternatively, for the manager to do them.

In small management firms, handling the various advertising tasks tends to be an assignment that is made by default. In a larger firm, there is often a division of labor that typically involves the assistance of some type of advertising consultant. Such an arrangement may be desirable in the smaller company as well. We will discuss the use of an advertising agency first.

Using an Advertising Agency. An advertising agency is potentially beneficial to any management firm. Property managers should investigate and understand how they can take advantage of these benefits. First of all, an advertising agency must be carefully selected, directed, and supervised. Agencies employ professionals who are skilled in the demanding and highly specialized business of advertising—e.g., art directors, copywriters, media buyers, account supervisors, and creative consultants, among others. However, an agency whose reputation has been earned by creating multimedia campaigns for a new brand of potato chip or a monster truck competition may not be the ideal choice to launch an apartment rental ad campaign.

An advertising agency's ability to perform satisfactorily is directly related to the willingness of its staff to learn the business of apartment marketing. At the very least, people at a competent agency will know the advertising business, and that will be helpful to the real estate manager. Many apartment owners and managers, on the other hand, know a great deal about their housing product—they may be very familiar with the complexities of architectural design and HVAC systems, yet know virtually nothing about their markets or the media that can be employed to reach them effectively. They may simply be too close to their products to be creative in marketing them. In such cases, the advertising agency can function as an objective third party, presenting a fresh perspective on the local market or the specific apartment community that will strengthen and vitalize the marketing effort. Advertising agencies help provide a reality check as well as a creative stimulus to the overall marketing effort of the property.

A side benefit of using an advertising agency is that agency personnel can function as intermediaries, saving management staff time and energy. For example, management firms that have made substantial advertising expenditures in the past are likely to be contacted frequently by representatives of the various media in their market areas. In using an agency, their media buyer can handle calls from media representatives and take responsibility for explaining that the advertiser is not buying particular ad space or times.

On the other hand, none of the details of your advertising effort should be delegated to the agency other than the technical aspects of ad production and placement. In this situation, you—not the agency—are the apartment expert. Remember, you are hiring the advertising agency to create and place ads that you will pay for. *It is your responsibility to effectively communicate information about your product and your goals for the ad campaign to the agency people and, furthermore, to approve the art they create, the media in which the ads will appear, and the schedule of their appearance.* Media choices and placement schedules (and their specific costs) will dictate the sizes of the ads and the deadlines for their completion. Because you are ultimately responsible for the success of the overall marketing campaign—your reputation and your contract with the property owner are at stake—you need to take charge at the outset and stay in charge throughout the campaign.

Selecting an Agency. In most metropolitan markets, there are numerous advertising agencies, so it should be possible to select a good one to work with. Several agencies should be interviewed to assure that the right one is selected. The agency you choose will be critically important to the success of your advertising campaign. Take the time to interview representatives from both large and small agencies. Large agencies usually employ more people with specialized talents, but they may also be dedicated to multimillion-dollar clients. A small agency may rely on independent creative talent and be more responsive to an apartment advertiser, perhaps at a lesser cost. However, you should also explore one or two alternative sources. These may be groups of freelance art directors and copywriters represented by an experienced account executive—together they function as an advertising agency. Often such an alternative source will be even less expensive than even a small agency because members of the group work at home, and their overhead costs are lower.

Before you make a decision, ask your primary candidates for the names of two or three clients you can contact—and do check out these references. Ask whether the clients were satisfied with the quality of the agency's work. Were agency personnel responsive to their ideas and concerns? Did they meet the clients' deadlines? Did the agency stay within the client's budget? Also ask the candidate advertising agencies about their workloads and the types and sizes of the other accounts they serve. You want your business to be important to the agency you choose, and it is important to know their typical turnaround times on different kinds of assignments. If you are their smallest account, you could be passed over when the agency sets priorities for projects.

Whomever you interview, be sure you meet the entire advertising team. You might be impressed by the owner of the firm and discover only later that you have some conflict with the copywriter or the art director. You should find out who will be working directly with you and handling the creative aspects of your projects because, more than likely, it will not be the person responsible for acquiring your account. Let the team know what they can expect from you, tell them how you and the owners perceive the apartment community, and gauge their reactions to you and your opinions and feelings.

Interviews usually consist of presentations of examples of the agency's past successes, but be aware that they may show you ads generated for high-budget retail campaigns. They may do this in the hope that you will be overwhelmed and hire their agency on the spot. However, what you want to see is the range of approaches and levels of detail of the work they do so you can determine whether the agency's work is likely to match your needs and expectations. Be sure the work shown to you was produced by the people you will work with—ask for this assurance. You could be seeing work done by others in the firm (people who are no longer there or will have nothing to do with your assignments) or, worse yet, the work may belong to past employers of the individuals you are interviewing—and not be this agency's work (or these peoples' work) at all.

Before you make a commitment, consider a test assignment. Ask the agency to create a small ad or a series of ads for a particular apartment property. An even better test is to request that such creative material be prepared and presented to you at the time of the initial interview. The objective of such a test is for you to be able to evaluate the agency's creativity and copywriting skills as applied to apartment advertising. If they agree, you will likely see one or more small rough sketches and some typewritten copy rather than finished art with typeset copy in place. (The advertising agency's investment in this type of test is minimal and, if you become a client, there may be no charge for it.)

On the basis of the interview and the test assignment, you will be able to tell a great deal about the advertising agency and your ability to work together over time. You can expect that the level of enthusiasm they display on their first assignment will typify your future together. (An agency that is unwilling to do a small test assignment to secure your account should not earn the right to do the larger ones in your campaign.)

One more piece of important advice concerning the interview process: Ask prospective agencies if they are willing to give you "exclusivity of category." You want your ads to be fresh in your marketplace, and that is nearly impossible when an agency is handling a number of residential advertisers—including your competition. Creative people cannot help but let approaches to similar products spill over into one another, in which case your ads will lose their unique quality. (We experienced this with a large agency that had a nationwide clientele.)

Ideally, you will be establishing a long-term relationship with the agency and its personnel. If an agency really wants your business, you will be its only apartment client. If exclusivity of category from the agency as a whole is infeasible, try to arrange for your account executive—or at least your creative team members—to work on your ads exclusively. (We have been fortunate to obtain exclusivity of category within our market area. Advertising agencies are not so numerous there, nor do they have to compete as vigorously as do those in larger metropolitan areas.)

Agency Fees. Just as money is often the cause of strife in personal relationships, billing can be one of the major reasons for a breakdown in the agency-client relationship. How the agency bills its clients should be discussed during the initial interview. As the buyer, you should be sure that you understand what your advertising will cost. You may expect the question, "What will it cost for a new ad?" to yield a response that includes all of the costs involved for ad production, ad placement, and meetings between agency people and your staff. If you receive only a partial answer to this question—one that omits production costs, for example—you will be left with the impression that the ad is much less expensive than it will turn out to be.

Ad production is a complex process encompassing ideas and design, images (photographs or line art or both), copywriting, typesetting, and preparation of finished (camera-ready) art for reproduction. Photography itself entails separate costs for the photographer, film, and processing, plus fees for models if people are shown and, sometimes, travel expenses. The advertiser's wishes also affect the costs. The number of pieces of creative material required, the number of times they have to be revised or modified (or corrected), and the number of meetings agency people are expected to attend will eventually appear on an invoice. You should have an agreement with the agency regarding what they will do and what you will be charged for their services.

Be sure you address the issue of cost-containment with your agency. The two of you should agree at the outset whether the agency will be allowed to add a percentage to production and other costs when they submit invoices to you for payment. (Some advertising agencies mark up the amounts they pay their outside vendors for photography, typesetting, etc., when those costs are passed on to the advertiser, disguising them as fees for account management, account servicing, or some other euphemism.) Most agencies will forego this added income, but you should carefully review the invoices you receive to assure that you are paying only those expenses attributable to your advertising, and that the invoicing conforms to your initial agreement with the agency. As a precaution against excessive handling costs, it may be wise to require that copies of bills for work contracted to others accompany the agency's invoices.

Agencies' billings to their clients include charges for their time in addition to the specific costs of ad production. Advertising agencies also derive some income in the form of discounts from the media in which ads are placed. The type of medium and the geographic location of the market may determine the size of such discounts. Most print media offer a discount to recognized agencies on some or all of the charges they bill for space and frequency (15 percent is common). Many magazine publishers also offer a small discount for prompt payment (one or two percent for payment within ten days is often seen). Depending on the agency's contractual arrangement with an advertiser, the media charges may be billed as the full amounts, or the discounts may be passed along.

Agency-Client Relations. Advertising is not an exact science. If it were, there would be fewer agencies, and advertising would be much less expensive than it is. Once an agency has been chosen, the shared goal of the real estate manager (and owner) and the advertising agency should be to develop creative advertising materials that will break through the copycat mediocrity that typifies apartment marketing.

Success results from trial and error, brainstorming, and a relationship with your agency that is based on honesty and mutual trust. To establish that trust, you will have to share everything you know that will be helpful to the advertising effort. You should provide the agency with ads that you have used in the past, competitors' ads, and the results of your marketing and market research activities. The agency team should visit the property, and they will probably spend time interviewing your staff.

Expect the agency to care about accountability. Your advertising team should want to know how they are doing. Because leasing results are the measure of advertising success, you may want to copy them on traffic reports or arrange for regular telephone calls from your staff. This information will allow the agency to react quickly if an ad is unproductive.

In addition to accountability, the people at the advertising agency need to feel comfortable about taking risks, and you need to be receptive to approaches that may differ from your preconceptions. If you want cutting-edge advertising, your agency team has to feel that the cutting edge is a safe place for them to be. You should be honest in critiquing their work. If it is unsatisfactory in terms of quality, or not appropriate to the image you are creating for the property, you have to be frank in saying so. Ask about elements you do not understand—the creative people may have just misinterpreted your ideas. However, ridiculing their work is nonproductive. Such a response is likely to strain the relationship and stifle the creative input you are seeking. Creative input is why you sought out an advertising agency in the first place.

Advertising on Your Own. We believe the benefits of working with an advertising agency outweigh the costs—especially because of its people's experience and creativity. However, not everyone is as fortunate as we are, and advertising often must be handled in-house. A management company with a large, diversified portfolio may be able to hire one or more communications specialists to handle advertising and marketing tasks. For smaller firms, this is usually not an option. In fact, you or someone in your management firm may be the only person handling your properties' advertising. If that is the case, you have probably already identified media representatives at local publications who are capable of translating your marketing ideas into workable advertising copy.

If you are lucky enough to have several staff members to work with, you might begin by assembling the group and brainstorming. The first task is to determine which assignments are most appealing to particular employees and what tasks they are best able to perform. You may find people in your organization who are intrigued by involvement in the advertising campaign and will work well on their own (or with the agency) and even develop real skills in this area. There may be eloquent writers who would be good at copywriting and natural artists who can try their hands at layout and design. The administrator types will probably be best at gathering information, seeing that it is distributed to all concerned, and managing the billing process. Be prepared to be surprised. Sometimes the most unlikely member of the team will shine when given a new and unusual challenge. At the very least, advertising is interesting—and very different from the routine duties of apartment management.

On the other hand, you may also find that your team does not have the writing and artistic talents to meet the challenge of advertising copy preparation. However, you should be able to train them to accomplish your goals. Such training can start with a discussion of the market research that has been done. The list of property benefits should be reviewed and ranked in order of importance to the marketplace. For example, if the most important benefit on the list is a fireplace, the members of the team should be asked to close their eyes, visualize a fireplace in their minds, and identify the words that come to mind in relation to the image. After a slow start, individuals will probably suggest such words as warmth, home, hearth, glow, coziness, and comfort—these impressions should be written down. The same thing should be repeated for each benefit or amenity on the list. Members of the team will become more adept at visualization and description as they progress through the benefits list. When this exercise is completed, the team should be invited to write copy for an ad for the property that incorporates the words they have listed.

Another key consideration in the development of ad copy is marketing research (discussed in detail in chapter 1). If the market is comprised of young families (adults aged 25–30 with small children) with annual incomes ranging from $20,000 to $35,000, such things as nearby playgrounds, day care facilities, schools, and baby-sitting services might be featured in the ad. Activities expected to appeal to senior citizens (e.g., quilting bees, blood-pressure testing, classes in low-impact aerobics) would not be mentioned.

Market research using focus groups and questionnaires (see chapter 3) allows apartment managers to know the market and test its responses to advertising ideas. Such research will yield most of the information needed to create ads that will attract as many qualified prospects as possible. The same types of research can provide information about the best media to employ in attracting those prospects—great creative ads that appear in the wrong media only waste money and frustrate the apartment manager and the advertising team.

Traffic reports should include spaces to collect information on sources of telephone calls and appointments for showings (see exhibits 2.2–2.5).

They will provide after-the-fact confirmation of the merits of specific ads and media choices or indicate early that changes in ads or media must be made.

Media Selection

The choice of specific advertising media will depend on many different factors relating to the market area and the people in it. It will also depend on the specific media available and their capabilities. Media buying is both an art and a science. A person who has responsibility for an extensive media campaign but is inexperienced in this area should seek the advice of a media-buying consultant. (Advertising agencies employ people who specialize in this esoteric enterprise.) A media buyer presented with basic information such as a specific budget (whether $1,500 or $150,000) and the advertiser's desire to market to prospects within a specific age group (say between 35 and 50 years old) with a particular income level (e.g., in excess of $25,000) will develop a menu of options for reaching that audience within that budget. The larger the audience and the greater the number of ad placements, the more the advertising will cost.

Market Considerations. Prospective residents for particular apartment properties can be characterized by conducting marketing research. If your marketing program is being developed for a property that is in the planning stages, census bureaus, libraries, regional councils, and city planning offices are potential sources of demographic data, which may be available at little or no cost. For an established property, a comparison of the larger local population to the population of your current residents is also appropriate. Demographic characteristics of current residents in an established property can easily be gathered from their lease applications. Information on their incomes, professions, work locations, previous residences, and numbers of children should all be available in this one source.

Psychographic data will also be of assistance in the creation and placement of ads. Market research will identify the buy factors—the features of the apartment community that will be appealing to particular segments of the market. Equally important, information about residents' places of employment and prior residences will facilitate selection of print media that are likely vehicles for apartment advertising. Newspapers in major cities usually feature special sections targeted to neighborhoods or localized areas of the city (published regularly, perhaps, but not every day). Such publications may provide access to a narrowly targeted audience in a part of the city that has yielded prospective residents previously.

Media Considerations. Once the demographic characteristics of the market are known, the media can facilitate the decision regarding where the ad should be placed. Newspapers, magazines, and radio and television stations measure their audiences frequently (readership and listenership, respectively). The size of their audiences determines what they are able to charge for advertising space or time. They also collect demographic data to characterize their audiences for prospective advertisers. In order for apartment rental ads to be successful, they must be placed where they will reach the prospective residents for the property—its market. (This is called guaranteed exposure.) Comparing the demographics of current residents with those of an advertising medium's audience will enable the manager to make intelligent ad placement decisions.

Timing of ad placement should also be considered. Most renters look for apartments on weekends, so Sunday issues of daily newspapers always have large want-ad sections. If a community or suburban newspaper is published only twice a week, the issue closest to the weekend would likely be more productive for advertising apartments. If a metropolitan market has a tradition of maximum apartment turnover at one or two times of the year (usually spring and/or fall), the newspapers may feature special apartment rental sections you can utilize.

In truth, the size of the audience for a particular advertising medium will vary. This is especially true of the broadcast media (radio and television). Although a particular time of day or a regularly scheduled program may have the largest audience, you should advertise at times when your target market is most likely to be listening or watching. You want the audience to be receptive to your message and in a position to act on it.

When selecting media, there are two key elements to consider—in advertising idiom, these are called reach and frequency. *Reach* is the specific audience the medium touches. The reach of the selected medium should be the largest possible number of prospects who mirror the current residents' demographics (i.e., your target market). *Frequency* is the number of times the ad will appear in a particular medium (in print media, each placement is called an *insertion*.)

Reach. When you buy media, you should expect and demand proof that a medium will guarantee certain exposure. The account representative for a particular magazine should be able to state precisely who reads it and the likelihood that a certain number of its readers with certain demographic characteristics will read an ad on the front page, the back page, or in the interior of the publication.

Paid circulation is one way of guaranteeing exposure for an advertisement. An ad placed in a magazine that has paid circulation is more likely to be read by a targeted market than one placed in a magazine that is distributed free. Although free distribution assumes a broad market, that is not always the case. The fact that people are willing to pay to purchase a publication is akin to a commitment on their part to read it.

Sometimes the numbers may appear more impressive than they are. For example, a local radio station may show tremendous reach in the market an apartment advertiser is attempting to penetrate. Advertising will be costly because the station can deliver a huge audience. However, that audience may be spread out over an area of hundreds of square miles that encompasses people living in two or three adjacent states. The reach may be impressive, but the station's listeners are unlikely to be prospects for a particular apartment property. They will not drive for hours to visit an apartment building just because they have heard an ad on the radio.

In addition to newspapers and radio, large metropolitan areas offer a multitude of other advertising media—the insides and outsides of buses, the roofs of taxicabs, panels at rapid transit and commuter train stations as well as inside the trains, and enclosed waiting areas and benches at bus stops. There may be collateral sources in a particular market, and these should be investigated. A telephone hotline that provides current information about community events might be productive for leasing apartments. Display ads in employee newsletters published by large local corporations can be inexpensive and worthwhile. However, display advertising in such unlikely places as shopping malls, supermarkets, and coin-operated laundries typically reflects a fascination with a novel medium or a new technology—or desperation—and is rarely productive or cost-effective.

Retailers and others who have items to sell generally employ certain media—and only those media—to reach their customers. The Sunday newspaper has entire sections devoted to automobiles and homes for sale. Discount and department stores publish discrete advertising sections for distribution inside the Sunday paper. These advertisers know not only that their customers like to shop on Sundays, but that shoppers rely on the newspaper to find out what is available and on sale.

The point has been made before, but it is worth restating. The purpose of advertising in the apartment industry is to convey a message to potential residents. Advertising that reaches beyond potential residents is wasted effort—and wasted money. A full-page ad can be run in the Sunday newspaper—even printed in living color—but if hanging out a "For Rent" sign has been, historically, the most productive advertising technique for that building, then other advertising will only be of marginal benefit.

Apartment advertising should be concentrated in media that are directly related to apartment rentals. Common sense dictates use of those media that prospective residents rely on to find apartments. Publications such as metropolitan newspapers, community newspapers, and apartment locator magazines meet this criterion. The key to the best choice is to find out which media were used by current residents during their searches for housing. This is what makes the use of traffic reports and the honest tracking of prospect sources so vital.

Frequency. The other advertising issue we identified is frequency. It is essential to assure two things—that an ad will be seen and that it will have an impact on the reader. An ad must have a sufficient number of exposures to capture the attention of its intended audience. (Psychologists claim that *an advertisement must be seen or heard three times* in order to consummate a sale or to reach the maximum number of readers or listeners.)

The issue of frequency is not as clear-cut in the multifamily housing industry as it is in retailing because renters' decision-making cycles are typically shorter than those of purchasers of appliances, automobiles, and other consumer goods. It may be logistically impossible to reach prospective renters with an apartment ad three or more times before they make their decisions. They may check the Sunday newspaper or an apartment locator magazine only once before they go out to search for an apartment. Those who make repeated visits to an apartment property before deciding to rent there tend to do so without relying on advertising. For them, the quality of the presentation of the apartment building and the individual apartments, coupled with the performance of the site marketing staff, overwhelms the advertising effort.

In apartment marketing, the frequency of advertising is likely to be less important than the creativity and power of the ad itself. Corny as it sounds, the pop psychologists who say, "You don't get a second chance to make a first impression," are probably right. In advertising apartments, your objective should be to obtain maximum exposure for your ads. Answers to the following questions will help you select the appropriate medium.

1. What is the size and composition of the medium's audience?
2. Does the medium have paid or unpaid circulation?
3. What is the quality and level of its editorial material?
4. What is the relevance or focus of the editorial material it contains?
5. How does the medium guarantee you its audience?

Effectiveness of Print Media. Most of the advertising done in the apartment industry utilizes print media, and there are several fundamental truths that affect the *impact* of print advertising. The following statistics come from the advertising industry.

1. Advertising readership is significantly increased with the addition of color—a two-color ad will attract significantly more readers than a black-and-white ad, and a four-color ad will attract an even larger readership than a two-color or black-and-white ad.
2. The cover position increases readership. For a specialty rental magazine, the preferred positions—in order of readership impact—are front cover, back cover, inside front cover, and inside back cover.
3. The use of separate inserts (i.e., flyers inserted between the pages) significantly increases readership.
4. Price is an important element to include in the copy of an ad—in apartment advertising, it serves as an automatic traffic qualifier.
5. Inclusion of a photograph that shows the product in place or in use significantly increases readership.
6. As ad size increases, readership increases correspondingly.

7. A second ad in the same issue of the publication increases readership by 13 percent.
8. Using a full-page ad as an index, a quarter-page ad reaches 29 percent of the readership; a one-third page ad reaches 33 percent; a half-page ad reaches 44 percent, and a two-thirds page ad reaches 64–75 percent of the readership. By contrast, a two-page ad has only a 39.6 percent greater readership than a one-page ad.
9. The number of inquiries generated by an ad may be greater than its readership would suggest. A quarter-page ad attracts an average of 92 inquiries compared to 119 for a full-page ad, and the *cost per inquiry* for the smaller ad is roughly one-third of that for the larger ad.

Your ads should be created to have the greatest possible impact on your target market. Ad copy should be concise and descriptive, incorporating strong adjectives as appropriate. Features and amenities presented as a bulleted list, in order of their importance based on prospects' presumed "hot buttons," will enhance readability and emphasize the most important buy factors.

Photographs add impact, color photos even more so. However, it is difficult to depict such an abstract concept as "lifestyle." The best efforts will attempt to show the benefits of living in a property—the spectacular view from the windows, the elegantly appointed lobby, etc. Photos must be chosen carefully to match the positioning statement or advertising theme for a property.

Unless an illustration becomes outdated, there is little reason to change the contents of an advertisement. Line art and photos of people may become dated because hairstyles and clothing fashions change over time, but this should not be a problem over the course of a year or two. Unlike consumer products that must appeal to a very broad and diverse universe of consumers (e.g., soft drinks), apartments are marketed to discrete subgroups whose need for this product is occasional. Once a lease is signed, the prospect stops looking at apartment ads. A successful ad—one that draws traffic steadily—should remain in use as long as it is consistent with your campaign goals and positioning statement. Apart from the expense of starting over, it is usually difficult to create a new ad that will have an equivalent impact. As the old adage says: "If it ain't broke, don't fix it!"

Evaluation

Whatever the elements of your campaign, manage your advertising. This is a task that is easily overlooked. Sometimes this task can grow so large that it becomes overwhelming. The important thing is to find a balance that is comfortable and productive. In order to control your advertising efforts, we recommend that you follow this simple plan.

- *Know your competition.* Closely follow their pricing structures and be aware of how they are presenting their product—both physically and in their advertising. Try to determine their level of success.
- *Position your product appropriately.* Your apartment community must appeal to the tastes and needs of the audience to whom you intend to market it. Periodic reassessment of market demographics and your competition is necessary.
- *Evaluate your promotional materials.* Analyze all of the written materials and signage on the property to assure that the message being delivered is consistent with the market positioning of the building.
- *Be creative.* Whether you do the work yourself or hire outsiders to develop your marketing campaign, find creative talent—and manage that talent. Recognize when their work is exciting, fresh, and innovative—and when it is not. Constantly challenge your creative people (whether agency personnel or site staff) to take risks, to outperform the competition, and to dazzle the marketplace with their advertising product. Feel free to be critical, but respect their professionalism.
- *Choose media carefully.* The advertising vehicle should be consistent with the image of your property so that it will enhance your ad. Also, one of the most expensive and complicated parts of your advertising plan is the placement of particular advertisements and their frequency of presentation. Your prospects are busy people. Their environment is cluttered with advertising images and sounds. Your challenge is to break through what they see and hear to present your message clearly and cleanly.
- *Repeat the message.* Humans have difficulty retaining ideas—we retain only one-quarter of a concept that we see once, but our retention increases geometrically with each repetition.

The last two admonitions are extremely important. Mindful of the need to achieve optimal frequency, advertisers tend to adopt a shotgun approach. There are so many advertising media and so many choices available within those media that advertisers create what they believe is the definitive print ad and then run it once in every newspaper and magazine they can imagine. The results are usually disappointing, and the medium is blamed for the results when the advertiser may simply have failed to create an adequate number of impressions in the marketplace to achieve the results that were expected (it did not reach the target market or was ineffective in doing so). If you can only afford to run your advertising once, it is best not to bother. A minimum of three exposures to appropriate print advertising is required to impact readership in a target market. That means three repetitions of the same ad in the same medium (e.g., three postcard mailings, three consecutive issues of a magazine). The same principles apply for broadcast (radio and television) advertising. Because frequency is so critical to success, you must anticipate the number of placements and budget accordingly.

A Practical Example—Experiments with Media

Over the years, we have been privileged to work for a number of clients who have owned extraordinary apartment properties. These communities were elegant and expensive, and some of them had unusually generous marketing budgets. The owners or asset managers had the intestinal fortitude and financial resources to experiment in media with which we had no previous experience. The results were enlightening for us. The following sections describe some of those experiments.

Newspapers. Large cities often have several newspapers. There may be one or more major dailies while others are published weekly, bi-weekly, or on some other schedule. Apartment marketers habitually advertise in the local newspaper without testing its cost-effectiveness. Our research and experience indicate that the productivity of newspapers in apartment marketing varies greatly from community to community.

In many communities in which vacancy rates are high, newspaper ads tend to be of the display type rather than classified. (The two types were illustrated earlier in this chapter, exhibit 4.1). Display ads tend to become progressively larger as the market deteriorates, regardless of whether they are producing traffic. This phenomenon seems to be associated with a need to outsize the competition. However, we have also found that the large size of the ad may impress the developer down the street but actually be met with distrust by the marketplace.

In our experience, apartment renters tend to equate apartment advertising with used-car advertising. Larger ads and more graphic language make the claims less believable. Apartment renters rightly perceive that huge display ads in the newspaper are an indicator that the owner is desperate and that the property itself is in trouble. We have found that a smaller ad (two columns wide by three inches deep)—or a regular classified ad—has just as much impact as a much larger ad (five columns wide by eight inches deep) with the same content.

You have to determine for yourself whether this phenomenon is true in your own market. The traditional wisdom is that the effectiveness of an advertisement is directly proportional to its size. You need to discover whether display ads (the larger the better?) are cost-effective in attracting qualified prospects to your apartment building. If they are not—as our experience indicates—it is counterproductive and inordinately expensive to place them.

In fact, we have found local tabloids are often more effective and far less expensive than the larger newspapers. This proved true in some suburbs of our metropolitan area and in one of our two downtowns (we manage several apartment communities in a major "twin cities" metropolitan area).

The fact that only one of our downtown newspapers is productive illustrates the point that there are no absolutes in apartment marketing. Times change, and marketing approaches must change with them. You must constantly test what you are doing in order to fine-tune your advertising. A certain approach may be effective one season and not the next. What works in one geographic area may be ineffective in another. The style of ad that works for one property may not work at all for the building next door.

There is one invaluable function a newspaper can perform that deserves additional comment, and that is to provide editorial support. In large metropolitan areas, major newspapers may employ editors specifically to inform the community about issues involving housing. If your newspaper does not have such an editor, any newsworthy story may be considered on so-called slow days, and that would be an opportunity to have your apartment community featured. (Some newspapers do editorial pieces on first-time advertisers.) The objective, third-party character of this kind of coverage tends to eliminate any suspicions the public may have about hype in apartment advertising and will generate traffic that paid advertising could never produce.

However, a self-serving approach to this can backfire. We once wrote an article that was a carefully disguised advertisement—called an advertorial in the ad business. We gave it a byline and bought an entire page of our local newspaper in hopes of convincing the public that an objective third party (i.e., the newspaper) really endorsed the apartment community. The full-page advertorial cost $12,000, and while it attracted considerable traffic that resulted in some signed leases, the cost per rental achieved was astronomical. Obviously, the cost did not justify repetition of the experiment, and while we might have persuaded the market that our advertisement was an editorial the first time, repetition would have exposed the fact that it was not.

Magazines. We conducted some research on the topic of renters' preferences about advertising media in our immediate rental market, and we found that some 1,200 respondents utilized the following media sources in making their renting decisions.

> Rental magazines (31.3%)
> Driving by the apartment building (21%)
> Newspaper advertisements (20%)
> Apartment locator services (11%)
> Friends, relatives or business associates (10.8%)
> Radio, television, or billboard advertisements (3.5%)

An additional 2.5 percent indicated "other" sources, including magazine ads and miscellaneous sources.

There are a multitude of magazines that are eager to attract apartment marketing business. Rental magazines seem to be the most productive medium of this type. We found that a four-color 8½ × 11-inch ad consistently produced the highest traffic counts for our middle- and upper-bracket apartment communities.

The same poll also addressed advertising formats, based on different publication page sizes. Among the 1,200 respondents, 57 percent preferred the 8½ × 11-inch format; 15 percent favored a 5½ × 8½-inch format, and 14 percent supported the 4 × 5-inch format. Another 14 percent liked a folded newspaper format. (Many suburban and neighborhood newspapers are distributed in a flat or tabloid format. Those printed on larger sheets and folded for distribution offer the option of positioning ads above and below the fold.) In addition, an overwhelming 96 percent of the respondents preferred color photographs over black and white.

While there are no guarantees, you may find that a glossy apartment magazine produces well for you. If you have more than one publication of this type to choose from, test them against one another. To guarantee a fair test, run the same ad in each publication on several occasions and at different times of the month and year. Carefully monitor all traffic to determine which magazine brings you the greatest numbers of prospects and, more importantly, which one results in the most signed leases.

There are also other kinds of magazines such as glossy monthly publications that bear the city's name or the highly visible in-flight magazines for various airlines. Religious directories from local churches or synagogues are another possibility. The list goes on and on. We have tried them all, and our results never justified their continued use. Whatever the cost—which ranged from $300 to $25,000 per insertion—the return simply did not warrant the expense.

Radio. We have produced dozens of radio ads. Several have won awards. We dearly loved all of them, but they too fell short of our rental expectations. We tried humor, factual delivery (also called brick-and-mortar presentation), testimonials, and sexy voices. We paid well-known disc jockeys and newscasters to tout our properties and bought air time on major and minor radio stations in our market. What usually happened was that we would get only a phone call or two during the first few days that the ad was running—and not much else. (Other managers confirm that radio advertising typically increases the number of lookers but not the number of signed leases.)

We believe what happens in our market is that the ad is heard by some people who are predisposed to the idea of renting. However, once it has attracted a few members of this group, the ad falls on deaf ears. The remaining listeners have no interest in renting at the moment—they tune out the ads—and while they may have an interest at some unspecified future time, it is highly unlikely they will remember the ad indefinitely.

As was mentioned earlier, with radio, you are sometimes paying to reach a market that is hundreds of miles from your property. Some big-city radio stations have such huge markets that advertising on them is excruciatingly expensive and not very productive. On the other hand, we have found the cost of radio advertising in small towns to be extremely low. Their station managers have found that a single disc jockey's voice is monotonous, and they will accept ads that utilize unfamiliar voices just to mix up their programming a little. In this situation, radio advertising may be a superb buy because it reaches only the geographical market you are targeting.

The key to effective radio advertising is to create ads that fit the types of programming aimed at audiences that include your target market. For example, we ran an ad during the morning drive time that characterized the frustrations of commuting to work by car (automobile horns blaring, sounds of traffic passing by at high speeds, etc.). The message was: If you hate driving to work, you should live at our well-located apartment property. The target market was the busy executive. To reach senior citizens, you should advertise during programs directed to them. The same applies throughout the spectrum of your target markets. This is where you can apply the psychographic data you have compiled in your market research.

If you do decide to use radio, be aware of these important considerations. Costs for production in 1990 dollars for a quality ad range from a minimum of $1,600 to several thousand dollars. Script writing, voice talent, and overall production must be of a quality that is consistent with the apartment community that is being sold. You also have to review your traffic results carefully. If one week of each month is consistently productive, you may want to run your radio ads during that particular week every month for an extended period. The radio station ad representative may pressure you to advertise in consecutive weeks, but such repetition tends to be annoying to listeners—radio advertising can be counterproductive for just that reason.

Television. If you have ever thought that television would be a great way to advertise your apartment community, you are not alone. While our experience with television advertising is not extensive, we had the opportunity to produce quality television ads and to test their productivity. We were able to hire a Hollywood director, and we had an original piece of music composed for one ad. We also had available some terrific scriptwriting talent and an excellent advertising agency to pull it all together.

Our first ad was designed to promote the unusual amenities of the apartment community and the vast array of concierge services that were offered. It ran on all local stations in time slots that were appropriate for our demographics. It cost approximately $25,000 to produce the ad and approximately $50,000 to run it over a three-month period. The ad resulted in 12 leases—at a cost of slightly more than $6,000 each.

Reviews from the marketing team were mixed—the advertising agency loved it; we had mixed emotions, and the owner hated it. What amazed us about the ad was its ability to stay in people's minds—three years later, when we mentioned the ad or the catchy jazz background music, people remembered it. In retrospect, the fact that the owner disliked the ad so vehemently (which limited its exposure) may have compromised its effectiveness. The owner loved his property—to him, the somewhat light-hearted focus of the ad was almost sacrilegious. In deference to his wishes, we produced an elegant factual (brick-and-mortar) ad with a spectacular voiceover. It cost only $10,000 to produce, but the owner demanded an extended and very expensive media run. In contrast to the jazzy ad, it produced neither traffic nor rentals.

As with radio, television advertising should be presented at the times and be consistent with the programming aimed at your target market. In many large cities, there are television programs dedicated to the sale of single-family homes. These may consist of paid programming (e.g., one-half hour or longer time spans, purchased by developers of new subdivisions) and are often shown on Sunday mornings or at other times of day when so-called public service programming is scheduled—the times that consumer product advertisers do not buy. Some stations have begun to offer the same type of service to rental properties. We tried them in our marketplace, where they are scheduled late at night, and found them unproductive. The lack of response can probably be attributed to the times and days the programs were broadcast. (Usually the number of viewers is lower than for other types of programming, and the late-night audience is likely composed of people for whom television provides companionship when they cannot sleep rather than a source for information about apartments.)

Although television advertising has not been productive for us to date, that may not always be so. Television advertising may work very well in your market area. You have to explore it to find out.

Billboards. Today, billboard advertising is essentially dominated by the tobacco industry, which is forbidden to advertise in most other media. Various tobacco companies spend millions of dollars bombarding consumers with the dubious pleasures of their products; their ads are frequently seen by people driving through residential neighborhoods. In many areas, the fact that this industry spends an exorbitant amount of money on billboards virtually prevents other advertisers from securing long-term usage of high-visibility billboards in close proximity to apartment communities. (Local zoning ordinances sometimes preclude billboard advertising altogether.)

However, you may be able to contract for a specific location if you are willing to commit to a long-term contract and pay a premium rate—standard contracts often rotate ads among locations, usually at the billboard owner's discretion. Even if you are successful, it is highly likely that the billboard location you prefer will be available to you for less than one-fourth of the contract period; in the remaining time, your ad will appear in areas that are much less desirable. This situation is unfortunate because *billboards can be extraordinarily effective in providing directional signage*. We have managed properties that were difficult to find, in communities in which city ordinances made signage permits impossible to acquire. The use of a billboard that merely gives simple directions to the apartment community—even for a short time—can be invaluable. *Exhibit 4.2* shows two examples of directional billboards that were successful.

At times, road construction has also been extremely detrimental to our rental traffic—it diminished the flow of prospects to a trickle. Billboards helped break through the confusion of this situation as no other medium could.

Direct Mail. In our experience, the effectiveness of direct mail for apartment advertising is mixed. The results seem to depend on the reliability of the mailing lists that are used. Lists must be absolutely targeted and up-to-date, or your direct mail campaign will not be worthwhile. As an example, we know of one owner locally whose retired father painstakingly copied the names of all renters on the mailboxes in competitive buildings, returning frequently to update his lists. He sent monthly newsletters, postcards, and letters to these prospects and experienced real leasing success.

Our own experiments with direct mail have been somewhat disappointing. On several occasions, we purchased lists from mailing list brokers (the leading houses in the United States). We have bought lists of the names of people of certain ages and incomes who are living in small geographic areas. On a few of these occasions, we have been even more specific. Having noted that the cars in the underground garage at a particular apartment community were generally less than three years old and cost more than $35,000 when new, we paid a premium for a very specific mailing list of individuals who owned vehicles of this type. The returns on all of these lists were discouraging.

As a point of reference, one to three percent is considered a normal return on a direct mail piece—we were getting much less than one percent. We followed up our direct mail with telemarketing and discovered in the process that the lists we had purchased were not what we were promised. Less than 15 percent of the names on the lists actually had all of the characteristics we had specified.

It is apparent that direct mail has several limitations. Continually escalating postage costs and revisions to postal regulations regarding mass mailings have made direct mail more costly and risky than it was just a few years ago. Success requires a massive audience—you have to mail 1,000 pieces to obtain a one-percent return of 10 prospects—and it costs a lot more (per prospect) to reach the ones who will respond.

A narrowly focused list is essential for marketing apartments. One source for creating such lists is a reverse directory from the telephone company. These directories are organized by street address, and they list the names and phone numbers of all the people who live at apartment buildings. They also

EXHIBIT 4.2
Directional Signs Using Billboards

These examples were very successful. One included the property name and specific directions *(top)*; the other had no property identification, just an arrow and a phone number *(bottom)*.
Photographs courtesy of Belgrade Enterprises, Minneapolis, Minnesota *(top)*, and Stuart Management Corporation, Saint Paul, Minnesota *(bottom)*.

list the names and phone numbers of personnel employed by businesses at a specific address. However, such directories are usually compiled at the end of the calendar year, which means they become dated quickly in an increasingly mobile society. They are also expensive, and the cost may be prohibitive for use at a single apartment community. On the other hand, a management company with responsibility for marketing several properties within a major city or otherwise limited geographic area may find a reverse directory a worthwhile investment. When we were marketing to corporate transferees, a reverse directory helped us find the right person in the company to contact. The position in the organization (e.g., human resources director) and the phone number assigned to it did not change, regardless of how many people held that position over a period of time.

Other Types of Media. Apartment marketers in our particular market area have a veritable smorgasbord of advertising media to choose from. In addition to the usual daily and Sunday large-circulation newspapers plus signage and banners on the property, there are glossy apartment locator magazines, specialty publications directed to businesses and senior citizens, billboards, enclosed bus stop waiting areas (transtops), radio and television with large audiences, and a host of others, most of which routinely feature apartment advertising.

We have obtained good results using bus stop enclosures near our properties as directional signage—we showed a picture of the building, a property name, and an address. Ad benches are ubiquitous in many large metropolitan areas. One we see everyday shows a property name (not one of ours), an arrow, and directions to get there (right, three blocks). In areas where local ordinances limit or prohibit billboards, bus shelters and ad benches located near a property can be wonderful directional signs. They are as effective as billboards and much less expensive.

Other real estate managers in our market utilize side panels on buses, and they may advertise inside buses as well, but we do not. Something to keep in mind regarding bus and transit advertising in general is that rolling stock may be deployed anywhere in the transit service area. Scheduled operations as well as necessary maintenance will determine where and how often your ad will be seen. The likelihood that your ad will be exposed within a defined geographic area—and therefore reach your specific target market—will diminish as the size of the metropolitan area increases and its transit services are more widely distributed. The larger the area served by a transit company, the more diluted the impact of your advertising.

We offer this additional caution about outdoor advertising: Advertising copy exposed to the elements (rain, snow, etc.) is subject to surface wear and accumulation of soil and, sometimes, graffiti, all of which can reduce its impact due to illegibility. These factors can also have a negative effect if you want to present a wholly pristine image for, say, an upscale apartment community. Before signing a contract for outdoor advertising, you should ask whether and how often the surfaces are cleaned, ad benches are repainted, or printed ads on bus panels will be replaced during the term of a contract.

As you can see, we have had some very challenging opportunities to learn about different advertising media. We hope the lessons we learned will encourage you to explore your market more thoroughly and ultimately help you find which medium works best for advertising your apartment properties.

CHAPTER

5

Build a Professional Staff

While *location, location, (and) location* are generally considered the three most important determinants of the success of a real estate venture, *people, people, (and) people* are the most critical factors in the prosperity of the multifamily housing industry. Prospects are people—they rent apartments from other people. Apartments are cleaned and maintained by still other people, and it is people who advertise the availability of apartments, account for the rental income they generate, pay the bills, and attend to the multitude of other tasks that characterize apartment ownership and management. The apartment business is extraordinarily labor-intensive, and labor means people. Obviously, the human component of the apartment industry is crucial to its success. While the broad subject of property management staffing is beyond the scope of this book, we consider it important to devote a chapter to the selection, training, and motivation of those personnel who will be responsible for leasing your apartments.

Hiring Leasing Personnel

Only a few very large apartment communities have employees whose exclusive ongoing job responsibility is leasing. Except during lease-up or when move-outs are especially high, leasing is often likely to be only one facet of a multifaceted job. The position may be titled Resident Manager or Assistant Manager; sometimes this work is delegated to the single person who handles on-site housekeeping or maintenance. However, the title of the person responsible for renting the apartments should not disguise the importance of this job. Only when an apartment is rented does it produce income, and income is what keeps an apartment community functioning.

It is axiomatic that the key to achieving a high level of occupancy in an apartment community is a capable on-site staff. Prospects rent apartments from people who sell them well. The leasing staff establishes the first linkage between the apartment community and the prospect—and initiates the long-term relationship with those who become residents. Consequently, hiring quality professional sales personnel, training them thoroughly, motivating them, and rewarding excellent performance by means of financial and other incentives—i.e., compensating them adequately—are priorities in apartment management.

Define the Job. The first step in the hiring process is to define the job. The staffing of an apartment building will require preliminary evaluation of the tasks to be performed and the skills that will be sought in the employment marketplace. The importance of the leasing effort—and the personnel hired to accomplish it—will depend on the characteristics, needs, and competitive situation of the apartment community itself. Take, for example, a property consisting of 100 or more units in a city in which there is very little competition. While occupancy levels may remain high, the residents themselves may be demanding and difficult to please. Leasing is likely to be handled directly by the site manager who may not have to have a stellar sales personality. It may be more important to hire someone who will do a terrific job of supervising maintenance and housekeeping personnel and respond appropriately to residents' requests. On the other hand, the leasing effort at a property with numerous vacancies and constant turnover of residents will require concentration on this activity. Someone whose sole responsibility is leasing apartments will have to be more personable and have excellent selling skills.

In our experience, selling skills and management skills tend to be mutually exclusive. Because leasing results in a "sale" of sorts, we will focus here on suggestions for hiring people with the best combination of skills for a particular leasing job. In this context, the search for the perfect employee will be to some extent theoretical—unaffected by the stresses (deadlines and short-notice resignations or dismissals) that are typical of the real world of apartment management. However, we recognize that such factors do have an impact on personnel selection and management. We have been affected by them ourselves, and we know that such pressures sometimes frustrate and delay our purpose. Rather, our goal here is to help you design an efficient system of personnel selection that can be implemented even when other constraints temporarily intervene.

In hiring someone who will be responsible for the leasing of an apartment community, the property itself and the characteristics of its current residents must be given appropriate consideration. People responsible for leasing must be comfortable with their role and the prospective residents with whom they will interact.

Key questions to be answered regarding the job itself can be identified as follows.

- How large is the leasing task? Will more than one person be required to accomplish it?
- Will leasing personnel have duties related solely to leasing? If not, what other duties will they be expected to perform?
- To whom will leasing personnel report?
- Exactly what will this individual (or group) be expected to accomplish?

A brand-new high-rise apartment building with several hundred units to rent will need a larger staff than an established property with a low turnover rate. When several people will be involved in the leasing effort, it may be appropriate to hire a leasing director who will report to the property manager. This individual would then be responsible for hiring and supervising a leasing staff (one or more leasing agents). The time frame for the leasing activity will also be a determining factor. Expectations of 80-percent occupancy within six months of opening a new building will require a more intensive leasing effort than a similar occupancy goal to be accomplished over a two-year period.

Once you have determined what you want this person to do, the next step is to identify what skills are required to succeed in the job and, from them, what personal characteristics candidates must have.

Identify Requisite Skills. As noted earlier, good selling skills are imperative for a successful leasing effort. Inherent in the job of leasing is the ability to interact well with prospective residents in order to match their housing needs with a specific apartment product. This suggests that it is important to identify the particular skills and abilities you want your leasing personnel to have and the personality characteristics you will want them to exhibit. A good way to begin this process is to write the name of the job at the top of a sheet of paper and then divide the area of the page into two columns labeled "skills" (left) and "characteristics" (right). The example we will develop here will be for a position titled "leasing director." Because such a position has a broad range of responsibilities and skill requirements, we will be able to address a larger array of job skills and personal characteristics. Apart from the requisites that relate exclusively to supervisory responsibilities, those related to selling will apply directly to a position of leasing agent, as will many of the ones related to interpersonal interaction.

Thus, the skills list for a leasing director might include such things as selling skills, supervisory skills (ability to manage people under normal conditions and in a stressful environment), negotiation skills, and motivational skills (in addition to organizational skills and communication skills). Another important requisite is expertise in directive listening, that is, the ability to uncover a prospective resident's "hot buttons" (those features of the apartment product that will determine whether a sale will be made) without making the prospect feel that he or she is being interrogated.

The characteristics list is likely to be longer. It might include the following attributes: personable, outgoing, honest, punctual, loyal, fun, self-motivated, creative, optimistic, hard-working, dedicated, dramatic, enthusiastic, nurturing. Other personal elements such as community involvement and service orientation may also be important. For example, a prime candidate for leasing director will already have established a network of local contacts that will expedite the leasing effort.

Once drafted, these lists should be set aside to let your thoughts settle. However, you should return to the list several times over the next day or so and examine it for content. Try to determine priorities within the skills and characteristics inventories. Such a review process may reduce the lists somewhat although they are just as likely to grow. The important thing is to decide which skills and which characteristics are absolutely essential. (Some may turn out to be unnecessary, and you may have to compromise on some qualities that you initially considered indispensable.) The skills and characteristics inventories form the basis for the questions you will ask each applicant during an interview.

Develop Interview Questions. Job interviews generally provide only a short time in which to determine whether the person sitting across from you is a likely candidate for your leasing position. To get the information you need with a minimum of discomfort to interviewer and interviewee, the questions must be probing yet subtle. Questions that can be answered yes or no will not yield a full assessment of the candidate's capabilities. The questions you ask should be open-ended, preferably requiring the job candidate to talk about ways he or she would respond to particular situations. One approach that works well incorporates a form of role-play into the interview process. *Exhibit 5.1* provides some examples of role-play scenarios that relate to skills noted in the previous section. The interview you conduct should be tailored to the requirements of the position you are trying to fill. Specifics should be relevant to the responsibilities this person will be expected to assume and the personal attributes you think are important to getting the job done.

In exploring personal attributes as such, a less direct approach may be used. Here again, open-ended questions are preferable. Specific questions should be designed to discover how the candidate would behave in different types of situations. The subject of the question and the candidate's response should characterize as nearly as possible his or her actual behavior in a hypothetical situation that calls for, say, honesty, punctuality, or loyalty. Honesty might be addressed in the context of an opportunity to benefit at another's expense (e.g., receiving a ten-dollar bill in change when one dollar was due or a substantial undercharge on a restaurant check). Punctuality may be ad-

EXHIBIT 5.1
Examples of Role-Play Scenarios

Sales Ability—I: Describe the demographic and personal characteristics of a prospective resident in sufficient detail so that the leasing agent candidate could make reasonable assumptions about a potential leasing transaction. The objective would be to have the candidate cite two examples of closing techniques that he or she would employ in the situation.

Sales Ability—II: An alternative scenario would be one in which the prospect has been shown two apartments and indicated a preference for the second one. All of the prospect's questions about the building, the amount of rent, the security deposit, etc., have been answered. The prospect has indicated very clearly a desire to live at this property. The objective would be to have the candidate attempt to close this sale in a single sentence.

Ability to Manage People: Suggest a situation where the candidate supervises several employees, two of whom appear not to get along (frequent quarrelling about job responsibilities or working hours could be cited). The problem is affecting the entire group, and while the two have been productive, their performances have been slipping. The objective would be for the candidate to describe what he or she would do to resolve the situation.

Ability to Negotiate: This skill could be addressed in the context of a request for bids from contractors for a particular item (e.g., an expensive neon sign). The scenario should indicate the parameters of the situation (e.g., reputations of the contractors, schedule, budget) and cite the bidding results. Example bids could provide a challenge related to cost or time or both. The objective would be for the candidate to relate how he or she would deal with the contractor of choice and attempt to bargain for a better price.

Ability to Motivate Staff: To set the scene, the property might be characterized as three years old, with all of its prime units already rented. Because of that fact, leasing efforts appear to be stalled. The objective would be for the candidate to suggest incentives to keep the leasing staff enthused about their jobs.

Managing Personnel in a Stressful Situation: Describe a large apartment community that is owned by someone who is financially strapped. The owner's behavior (e.g., coming to the leasing office several times a day and expressing dissatisfaction with the condition of the property and the quality of the staff) is creating a stressful work environment for leasing agents. The objective would be for the candidate to describe how he or she would deal with the owner and, more importantly, how he or she would handle the staff's reactions to this behavior.

Directive Listening: Describe a hypothetical prospective resident for the candidate. An example might be a newlywed couple, both of whom are professionals. Include some personal information regarding hobbies, recreational activities, or cultural pursuits that might have been elicited during a walk to the model apartment—e.g., he plays handball regularly and she likes to swim. The objective would be for the candidate to suggest specific "hot buttons" for the hypothetical prospect and, further, to indicate why the first apartment shown to this prospect will provide a perfect lifestyle for him or her.

dressed by asking what the candidate's former boss would report about his or her record of being on time for work. Loyalty can be presented in the context of conversations criticizing one's employer or the owner of the apartment property (e.g., how would you react to a co-worker's claims that your boss exhibits favoritism?). Examples related to the new job or to the candidate's prior experiences are likely to generate more meaningful responses.

It is also important to assess the candidate's enthusiasm, creativity, and motivation. The following questions are likely to elicit varied answers from different candidates.

1. What is the most spontaneous thing you have ever done?
2. What do you consider to be your greatest accomplishment?
3. What goals do you have for yourself over the next five years, and what have you done during the past three months toward achieving them?
4. If you were responsible for putting together a bonus plan for your employees but had no money in your budget, what other kinds of 'perks' would you provide and how would you allocate them?

Direct answers to such questions as: "What kind of work schedule did you maintain at your last job?" and "Did you work after hours and on weekends?" will help the manager determine the candidate's level of dedication. Finally, the best way to find out what someone expects from the job—if he or she is hired—is to ask very specific questions: What do you expect to accomplish in this job? What do you expect to gain from it?

Apart from having the requisite job skills and personal attributes, leasing personnel must be knowledgeable about the community at large. They must be able to answer questions that prospective residents may have about the neighborhood. Candidates' community and neighborhood awareness can also be explored with direct questions (e.g., How many shopping areas are there in this suburb?). They should know locations of nearby supermarkets and department stores, services such as dry cleaning and shoe repairs, churches and synagogues, day care facilities, and governmental agencies, among others. Highway entrances and exits, public transportation, schools, and recreational facilities are other items prospects often ask about. (In some situations, especially in large metropolitan areas, the best job candidate may come from outside the property's neighborhood, in which case that individual's on-the-job training must include learning the benefits of the neighborhood.)

Prospect for Candidates. Once your interview questions have been formulated, the next step is to find sources for prospective employees. The focus and intensity of this search will depend on whether you intend to hire an experienced leasing agent or prefer someone with a general background in real estate, sales, or service. Requirements for prior experience should be a consideration in budgeting for compensation for the position. Real estate experience might be considered a plus and apartment leasing experience of even greater benefit.

Aptitude may be found in many places, some of which may not have been anticipated. It is not always necessary to seek only experienced candidates. Today more and more, individuals from outside the housing industry are being hired and trained for apartment leasing jobs. Employers of leasing agents reason that the multifamily housing business does not have a monopoly on bright, attractive, personable, honest people. Moreover, they recognize that sales skills can be learned and that the performance of novices may surpass that of experienced leasing agents. Some even believe it is more important to be able to hire motivated salespeople (i.e., people from other industries who have supported themselves by selling on commission or have been successful working in fields where success depends on customer service).

It has been our experience that quality salespeople hired from outside the housing industry, when properly trained, motivated, and supervised, can actually out-perform veterans. However, there is a risk involved. The novice lacks experience, and his or her potential may or may not blossom in the role of leasing agent. Conversely, the experienced leasing agent has a proven track record for which he or she must be appropriately compensated in salary or commissions and bonuses. Often the true leasing stars in a community have priced themselves out of the market—their salary range exceeds what many property owners can afford.

One method of finding candidates with extensive experience is by *networking* with other people in the apartment industry. Let friends and associates know that you are in the market for a leasing director and ask for their assistance. Perhaps they have recently advertised for a position and have on file promising applications. Like most businesses, management companies are constantly seeking top-flight people. However, people in the industry are often hesitant to commend individuals who applied for jobs with them—they may want to approach those prior applicants again when similar jobs become available at their firms. Given this natural hesitancy, you may want to proceed with caution if they are willing to refer one of their applicants—such a recommendation should not override your normal procedures for evaluating job candidates.

It is also true that people who are well qualified for a particular type of work sometimes apply for the wrong job. In fact, we benefited from someone else's experience along this line. A few years ago, we did some consulting work for the owner of a new apartment property in Florida. We traveled to the city every week and would accomplish specific tasks on each visit. As the opening of the complex approached, we decided to advertise the availability of site positions in the local newspaper on Sundays and conduct interviews on Mondays and Tuesdays. In the first several weeks, no likely candidates applied. Forty-five days before the grand opening, we arrived in the city and discovered that the newspaper had failed to run our ad—an entire trip was potentially wasted. In near desperation, we attempted to network with local CERTIFIED PROPERTY MANAGER® (CPM®) members of the Institute of Real Estate Management (IREM), to which we belong. Unfortunately, none of the names in the local directory was familiar to either of us. We called each one and explained our dilemma. All were cordial, and some offered names of possible candidates. However, we struck gold with one CPM member who was a vice president of a national firm headquartered in the city. He had recently advertised for a commercial property manager, and many of the applicants did not have the qualifications essential for the position (he received 30 resumes from people who had no commercial experience). Many of those nonqualified applicants did have extensive backgrounds in residential leasing and management. This CPM member was kind enough to share their applications with us; he even called the people to assure that they would be willing to interview for the positions we had available. Because of his generosity, the trip turned out to be a huge success—we were able to find well-qualified people for all of our staff positions at the property.

That particular experience leads us to make a recommendation: Membership in professional organizations affords excellent opportunities for this type of networking. One such is IREM, which has more than 100 local chapters throughout the United States and Canada. There are also numerous local and national apartment associations. Often these organizations provide job listings as a service to their members. Let your colleagues know that you have jobs available; they can be of immeasurable help. Referrals from other professionals can save you valuable time, energy, and money.

If all attempts at networking fail—sometimes they do—more traditional search methods such as newspaper advertisements may have to be used. Your ad should describe the perfect candidate for the job, based on the skills and characteristics you listed earlier. Also, the ad should be carefully thought out so that the language used will in no way discriminate against certain "protected classes" of individuals (i.e., minorities). We have found that the account representatives who do the actual advertising placement are sensitive to issues related to equal employment opportunity, and they will help you avoid mistakes.

Time spent in composing the ad and money spent for extra lines of type (so that all of those extra personality traits can be delineated) will pay off. You will receive more inquiries from better-qualified individuals and, consequently, spend less time interviewing candidates and deciding which one to hire.

Another possible source for job candidates is an employment agency. Use of an agency spares the employer the time required for screening applicants—the employer need only interview the most qualified candidates. To identify those candidates, the agency must have a detailed job description and a list of the requisite skills and experience. There is a fee involved, and it can be substantial (equivalent to one month's salary or a percentage of the annual salary its candidate will be paid). For this reason, use of an agency may be cost-prohibitive.

Interview Applicants. The interview is a very important step because it is the prime opportunity for evaluating the job candidate. Having defined the job and developed interview questions, it is imperative that all job candidates receive the same treatment. Setting hiring policies, implementing specific procedures, and following them faithfully will assure compliance with laws regulating fair employment practices and equal employment opportunity. Such factors as age, race, religion, national origin, sex, or disability must *not* enter into the hiring decision, influence the compensation offered for a job, or affect employment longevity after hiring. (Such discrimination is prohibited under Title VII of the Civil Rights Act, which is enforced by the U.S. Equal Employment Opportunity Commission, as well as under various state and local laws.) In some locales, discrimination based on sexual orientation is prohibited as well. Reference to applicable laws and legal counsel will help you establish appropriate procedures.

However you prospect for leasing personnel, the likelihood of having only one applicant and of that one person being perfect for your job are extremely rare. Newspaper ads often include a request that applicants send a resume to a blind box number. Such a blind ad can attract 50 or more responses, and additional prospects may be generated from networking or other sources. As a result, the number of prospects for a leasing job can be very large, and you will probably not want to interview all of them.

To make the number of prospects more manageable, it may be appropriate to devise an intermediate qualifying test. For example, one of the attributes that is usually considered indispensible for leasing personnel is a cheerful, professional telephone personality, and that requirement can be used to further screen prospects. A brief telephone conversation will allow you to grade an applicant's telephone skills on a simple scale of excellent, good, average, or poor.

Some or all of those called may be invited to complete an application for the job. This is not intended to be the interview but rather to help you make a reasonable decision whether to interview the prospect. You should use a standard application form and require all applicants to complete it. A standard form allows you to collect the same kinds of information from every single prospect and will facilitate your evaluation of their qualifications. (Resumes can be attached to the application forms.) In particular, the completed application will demonstrate whether a candidate has previously held responsible positions for periods of time that you consider acceptable and whether his or her education, skills, and experience are appropriate for your job (i.e., how they compare with what you are seeking).

This application step will also give you an opportunity to see how these candidates present themselves in general. What you are looking for is a good "fit" between the candidate's "persona" and the image you want to project for your apartment community. Compliance with an established "dress code" is one way to help assure such a match up. (The nature of the leasing activity can require compliance with a dress code that sets parameters for apparel and grooming of personnel who meet and interact with the public directly.) Ideally, a leasing agent will come to work dressed in acceptable business attire and appropriately groomed. Prospective residents' interest in the property could be turned off by a leasing agent's attire or behavior because people respond automatically to such nonverbal cues. Putting prospective customers at ease is as vital to successful leasing as it is to selling.

Along these same lines, most job candidates will come to a formal interview dressed and groomed to present themselves in the best possible light; they may not be quite so polished just to fill out an application. However, someone who appears in dirty, torn jeans and a T-shirt with mustard stains on it may be saying: "I don't care enough about myself—or your job—to present myself in an appropriate business-like manner." (A word of caution: One reason that we recommend inviting job candidates to apply in person is to see whether their grooming and general presentation skills are appropriate for the job. It is a fact of life that some of the reasons for selecting one job candidate over another are subjective. However, job-related skills and ability must be the only criteria for employment.)

Having eliminated from consideration those who are obviously *not qualified for the job,* you can narrow the field further by sorting through the applications and identifying the ten or fifteen best ones. Compare how you graded each one on the basis of his or her qualifications (education, skills, experience) and telephone skills, and reduce the field to the top five. These are the applicants you will actually interview.

In making appointments, be sure to allow sufficient time for each interview. If possible, spread the interviews over two or three days so that you will be fresh for each one. Hiring a leasing agent is an important decision—if too little time is spent with the job applicants, the chances of making a good decision will be reduced.

The first interviews should narrow the field to one or two candidates who will be interviewed a second time—at the apartment site. If time allows, ask each one to arrive at the property early for a walking tour. Pay particular attention to how the candidates behave in this environment. Listen carefully to their comments about what they see and to the questions they ask. From their remarks, you should be able to gauge their enthusiasm and whether their interest in the job is genuine.

This can also be an opportunity to test their selling skills and techniques. For example, you might comment on the shortcomings of the common areas or the apartments and see if the candidates instinctively perceive your remarks as objections to be overcome and respond to them accordingly. Note their body language. Do they smile? Do they use their hands? Is the enthusiasm in their speech matched by their expressions and their body movements? (Enthusiasm is contagious, and it is an essential characteristic of a leasing agent; however, someone who is overly spirited may repel prospective residents.)

In addition to specific selling skills, your observations should encompass the candidates' attitudes toward rental housing, renters, and rents. Candidates for a leasing position should be comfortable with the types of apartments they will be showing, the types of people they will be showing them to, and the rental rates they will be quoting to prospective residents. Someone who is uncomfortable in your particular economic milieu is less likely to be effective as your leasing agent.

The real test in hiring a salesperson in the apartment business is based essentially on common sense. Just as we recommended asking yourself "Would I want to live in this apartment?" as part of your evaluation of whether a unit is ready to be rented, you can similarly ask yourself "Would I be likely to rent an apartment from this person?" in evaluating candidates for a leasing position. The criteria at issue are the candidate's credibility and acceptance by your prospective residents. The chosen candidate should be the one who will do the best job of accomplishing the leasing and occupancy goals that have been set for the property.

Another, perhaps secondary, consideration in the selection may be a potential for advancement within your company. You may be in the market for a skilled leasing agent now, but at some point, you may want to promote that person to a supervisory role or to another property management position. Your ultimate decision should be to hire the candidate you believe will be able to work best for you in the environment of your firm.

Training Leasing Personnel

Once leasing personnel are hired, they should be given every opportunity to be successful on the job. New employees should be made comfortable in their environment. Introduce them to all of the other employees with whom they will be interacting. They should meet several times with their supervisor. In addition, someone hired into a supervisory position (e.g., a leasing director) should meet with whomever he or she will be supervising. An organizational chart showing personnel names, job titles, and working relationships will help new employees become familiar with the lines of communication and authority within the organization and their own place within it.

It is important to minimize the risks of employees failing. To this end, job descriptions should be written down and incorporated into an operations manual. The employee should have a copy of his or her job description and be given an opportunity to discuss it or ask questions. A thorough understanding of the scope of one's job responsibilities and the specific tasks one will be required to perform is essential to a good start in a new job.

Specific job duties (tasks) are best explained by someone who is familiar with them or, better yet, someone who actually does the work or has done it successfully in the past. The ideal situation is to have current employees in good standing train their successors. In the real world, however, it is more likely that a departing employee gave short notice or was discharged, or a new employee may have been hired only after the former employee had moved away or taken another job. Someone who has been promoted within the organization may be encouraged to train his or her replacement or a newcomer to a job he or she has mastered. Often, though, the promoted employee is busy learning new job responsibilities and unavailable to train a successor. Sometimes a job is brand new, and there is no experienced employee to do the training. In fact, most of the time, the manager is required to train new leasing agents personally in order to teach them how he or she wants the job done.

Apart from learning how to do their jobs, employees should be encouraged to continue learning for their own benefit as well as their employer's. Local universities and community colleges frequently offer evening or weekend classes in subjects related to real estate and business, and there may be seminars or other classroom-type opportunities to learn (or polish) selling and supervisory skills. Training should not stop with an assessment that the employee is capable of doing the job for which he or she was hired. Often continued learning is necessary for job or career advancement.

Individualized Learning. Human beings learn in different ways. The most prominent are reading, listening, and imitation of others. For each individual, one of these three methods is dominant, and it will facilitate training if each new employee can, within reason, utilize the technique that best suits his or her learning style.

New employees will often provide clues about which of the approaches works best for them. Those who learn from the written word may offer to take the procedures manual home for the evening and, the next morning, ask probing questions about what they read. Others may have difficulty learning a particular task until they are shown exactly how to do it. After a demonstration, they will have what appears to be a stroke of brilliance and move forward with the work with no further difficulty. In apartment leasing, it is important to listen—not only to prospective residents' needs and wants but to what employees are saying as well. In the latter case, listening has to begin during their initial training.

Training should be practical. Leasing is a hands-on job, and no amount of reading or classroom listening can substitute for direct experience. Despite the variability of individuals' learning strategies, we have found that demonstrations and one-on-one instruction are generally effective means of

> **Training Adjuncts and Alternatives**
> When one-on-one training and skills evaluation is not a viable option, alternatives must be considered. A highly skilled leasing agent may need only to develop knowledge about the product (apartment features), the property as a whole, and the community at large in the context of his or her new position. This can be facilitated with something as simple as an opportunity to walk around using a checklist. For new personnel who need to develop or polish leasing and selling skills in particular, a training videotape or role-play session may be the answer. Such opportunities may be welcome adjuncts for established employees as well. A large staff to be trained, as for lease-up of a new building, may justify hiring a training consultant or having a professional trainer speak to the group. The efficiency and effectiveness of such measures will depend on how compatible they are with the leasing policies and procedures established for the property. The latter should be spelled out in an operations manual. New hires should be required to learn and adhere to those policies and procedures. Veteran leasing agents may rightly be expected to contribute their experience and expertise toward reworking the policies and practices to increase their effectiveness.

training leasing personnel. It is always worthwhile for a neophyte to watch a skilled veteran in action and, conversely, for a veteran to constructively critique the new employee's techniques during an early apartment showing. (Selling techniques are detailed in later chapters. The emphasis here is on the fact that both initial and ongoing training are indispensable to success in leasing.)

Ongoing training is essential to the development of individual employees and to the vitality of a company. Some employers are concerned about investing in training that their employees will take away with them when they go to work for someone else; they see training as wasted money. However, it is more likely that the investment in employee training will be paid back many times over in the form of improved performance as a reflection of the employees' appreciation for their employer's faith in them. Those employees most likely to go to work for the competition where they believe they will be appreciated more are the ones who are not trained.

Job Parameters. Regardless of how the specifics of job training will be handled, the manager should take some time to talk with newly hired staff members about the parameters of their jobs, performance expectations and rewards, and responsibility and authority. Employees must understand their objectives—in this case, the leasing of apartments. They must know precisely what they are expected to accomplish—how many units leased, at what rental rates, by what date—and how their accomplishments will be measured and rewarded (any special commissions or bonuses for exceeding expectations). The manager will be reporting to the owners regularly about operations in general and leasing in particular; new employees have to know what they are expected to contribute to such reports and how often. Perhaps most important of all, employees must know and understand the extent of their responsibilities and the limits of their authority—what they can do on their own and when they need guidance or permission from others before proceeding.

Such discussions are healthy for both employer and employee. Generally, managers have no difficulty delegating responsibility to others; however, they sometimes fail to provide employees with the authority essential to getting the job done. A fledgling leasing director might be assigned the responsibility for lease-up of a 200-unit apartment property within a specific time period—e.g., from the point at which the certificate of occupancy is issued to greater than 90-percent leased in an 18-month period. At the same time, he or she may be expected to accomplish this with insufficient funds for signage and advertising, an inadequate staff, and a building that is lagging behind its construction schedule—all of which make it virtually impossible to meet the established goal and deadline. Apartment owners and managers often seek miracles and, when they do not occur, assign blame where none is warranted. In many instances, they are the ones at fault because they have not provided their employees with the tools they need to succeed. The most important of these is authority. The leasing director in this example might be able to circumvent the stated limitations if his or her responsibility includes specific authority to act—for example, to exceed budgeted spending (within certain dollar limits), to hire additional personnel on a temporary or part-time basis or reassign tasks to increase group productivity, to adjust move-in dates or prorate rents as an accommodation to construction delays, etc.

Training should be designed to teach the employee to succeed. Like winning a game, success in the job requires more than an understanding of responsibilities. The employee must understand the rules (behavioral and other standards) by which he or she is expected to play the game of apartment leasing. The initial training period is the time when the employee learns about the mores of the company—the requirements for behavior, performance, creativity, loyalty, etc., that must be followed in order to win the game and succeed in the job. Today, most employers conduct formal evaluations of their employees' job performance; it is unfair to evaluate job performance against standards the employee does not know about.

Motivating Employees

The apartment manager or leasing director must know how to motivate leasing personnel. The simplest formula for retaining and motivating good employees is to create an environment in which they can succeed, pay them fairly, praise them when they succeed, and help them when they do not.

The work environment extends beyond the cubicle or the corner office in which an employee may sit at a desk for eight hours a day. It encompasses people and personalities, communication and support, physical property, and belief systems. Many of these are intangibles, but if they are present they can be perceived; if they are lacking, they will surely be missed. The best way to guarantee that the work environment you create is barrier-free and nurturing is to ask the employees who function in it to comment on it. Employees need to feel that they can make constructive criticisms without fear of reprisals. An atmosphere that fosters comments and suggestions will allow problems with the work environment to surface quickly and be solved painlessly. Even in a relatively problem-free work environment, there is always the challenge of helping employees improve their productivity. The key is to discover what motivates each individual employee and find ways to provide that motivation.

Studies have found that individuals respond to some degree to one of three types of motivators—ego, power, or money. However, a manager may not know which one will stimulate a particular employee. Members of the leasing team may be motivated temporarily by their supervisor or by other team members—they will want to be accepted (and respected) by their peers and to keep up with them—but the individual's basic drive for success comes from within. All that an employer can do is create an atmosphere in which the employee's internal motivation can flourish.

One way to begin this process is by writing down the names of the leasing team members and trying to assign one of the three motivators to each of the names on the list. If you conducted the initial interviews, your interview notes may reveal clues about motivators. You may have asked job candidates about factors that stir their productivity or about their proudest accomplishments. Some candidates may have revealed motivators when asked what they liked (or disliked) about their previous supervisor. Because questions of this type often produce useful insights, they are an important part of employment interviews.

Your own observations of team members' behavior in different situations will provide additional clues. The *ego*-motivated employee responds best to praise. Awards, contests, plaques, letters of recognition, public acknowledgments (e.g., in the company newsletter), and job titles are all stimulants for this type of employee. The *power*-motivated employee thrives on challenge. This type of individual will readily assume increasing amounts of responsibility—in doing so, there is a presumption that he or she will also receive authority commensurate with the new accountability. Promotions, a larger staff to supervise, and greater access to lines of authority within the company are ways to keep this employee motivated. The *money*-motivated employee is inspired by financial success. He or she will be motivated by salary increases based on performance, as well as bonus and incentive plans determined by team accomplishments.

It is important to offer a word of caution about trying to satisfy the money-motivated employee. Financial rewards are the way that most employers stimulate productivity, and results are often disappointing. Typically, bonus plans are offered by employers who are anxious to achieve particular results (e.g., greater conversion ratios or increased occupancy), and once those goals have been achieved, the incentive is no longer available and employees tend to become bitter. It is only human to want to rely on such bonuses. Some employees even consider them to be a different form of compensation to which they are entitled over the long term. Thus, when the bonuses disappear, the standard of living previously enjoyed by the employees suddenly disappears.

Sometimes employees are insulted by the amount of the bonus that is offered. We know of one instance in which a team of leasing consultants was offered $200 apiece if they achieved a net gain in occupancy of 20 residents in each of three consecutive one-month periods. These employees calculated that the net financial gain to their employer if they achieved this goal would be between $18,000 and $20,000 per month—an amount approaching a quarter of a million dollars annually—and, consequently, they were offended and angry about the bonus amounts, and their productivity actually diminished.

Despite the potential difficulties, monetary rewards cannot be ignored because they are strong motivators. An important consideration, of course, is available funding. In lieu of specific bonuses, it might be worthwhile to create a structured series of awards using a point system related to leasing success as the measure of value. The awards themselves could take the form of "gift certificates" of varying face values earned by accumulation of a certain number of points within a discrete time period (e.g., one month, three months, etc.). The forms of the individual awards could vary widely. One possibility is actual gift certificates from a department store redeemable for merchandise. Another is arrangements for dinner for two, the "value" depending on the restaurant (or choice of restaurants). A third possibility is tickets for an entertainment—this offers the widest range of "values" because of the differences among ticket prices for such things as sporting events, rock concerts, plays, etc. A major award might be a weekend getaway package at a prominent local hotel. This type of program can be ongoing and would be limited only by available activities in your market area. It could offer a way to foster healthy competition among leasing agents and provide an opportunity to reward everyone according to his or her individual success without breaking the bank. In fact, presentation of the "awards" in a ceremony that all competitors attend could itself add to the benefits of such a program.

Building a Leasing Team

The success of a leasing organization depends on the staff members having a shared commitment to individual accomplishments and unified goals. However, the "team" that we call the leasing staff is a delicate organism, one that can easily be sidetracked from its mission. The notion of team-building is helpful in understanding where individual members are in terms of their development and orientation—and, more importantly, how they can get back on track when their performance slips.

Apartment community owners and management companies are often perplexed by slackening effectiveness or, sometimes, a precipitous drop in productivity. Based on our experiences consulting for various members of these two groups, we have arrived at a theory that seeks to explain the development of teamwork among the members of a leasing staff—the staff seems to progress through four evolutionary phases: form, storm, norm, and perform.

At the *form* stage, team members exhibit hesitancy, dependence, anxiety, politeness, and discovery. The team appears tentative about their behavior—they are unsure about what they are expected to do. They may seek to disguise their insecurity by boasting about their credentials to other members of the team.

We have occasionally found leasing teams that are mired in this stage because either the goals that have been set for them are too high, or the team members believe that they are. The team can proceed to the next stage only after they have decided (1) what their goals are and (2) that these goals are actually attainable.

The *storm* phase is typified by team members exhibiting their worst qualities. At this stage, individual behaviors change—jealousy, over-zealousness, hostility, resistance to working together, frequent conflicts, struggles for leadership, and rigidity are displayed. Newly formed teams typically find this stage extremely difficult to overcome because they have never encountered the level of tension that characterizes it.

During the storm period, the team is focused on which member will be in control. The leader who emerges is frequently perceived as too restrictive or too arbitrary. Fortunately, such conflict is often beneficial because it leads to the development of several important things—an organizational system, a coordinated way to formulate general rules, and overall strategies for accomplishing the group's purpose. Members of groups need to feel needed, and the storm phase leads to participants feeling comfortable with their own levels of control and satisfaction in achieving the goals of the team.

Organizationally, however, the storm period is problematic—most groups tend to become stalled in this phase, and members are inclined to drop out because the work environment is so disagreeable. Until the group resolves the conflicts that are characteristic of this phase, the leasing office is seen as a place where there is constant struggle for position and survival. When the members agree about how work will be allocated and how everyone will benefit from working together, the team can move on.

The *norm* phase is typical of maturation—team members exhibit acceptance, cohesiveness, sharing, harmony, and intimacy. There is give-and-take and constructive feedback; members are sufficiently relaxed with one another to reveal their vulnerability and their weaknesses.

For some, this period can be uncomfortable because certain behaviors may be mistaken as flirtation (signals may be misinterpreted and mistakes made). Some team members may become overly affectionate with the team in general. Others may mask their discomfort with humor. Still others may busy themselves with housekeeping tasks (emptying ashtrays, making coffee, filing papers). Because the team has come together, the leader is less important, and that may lead to his or her uneasiness. However, this period allows for unexpected talents to be displayed—team members tend to take more risks and are supportive of one another when they do so. New knowledge is gained, and the team learns to respect and appreciate the contributions that each one has made. They are clearly focused on the team goals: the group works closely together, and the players are interdependent. They move forward when their ultimate goal is in sight.

The *perform* phase is rarely achieved. Team members who reach this stage actually finish the task that they had set out to accomplish—they find themselves reaching personal peaks (in productivity, problem-solving, decision-making), and there is a generalized sense of accomplishment and well-being.

One of the major reasons for the disenchantment felt by many apartment marketing professionals is that ultimate goals are so difficult to attain or, once attained, they are immediately succeeded by other, more-challenging goals. The feeling of triumph that can be achieved in the perform phase is fleeting. Often it is replaced by the discomforts of a storm phase when new members are added to the group. Depending on the strengths and experiences of these new participants—and the group's willingness to admit them as equal partners—this storm phase can be relatively short, or the group may become dysfunctional.

Team-building should be ongoing. Our best advice, when considering the formation of your team, is to concentrate on the various personalities and skills available to your team. Who are the players? Do they appear to like each other? Do any of them show signs of insecurity? Have they worked together successfully in the past? If not, have any or all of them been members of teams that progressed past the storm stage?

The stresses of team-building, while unavoidable, are also desirable. Leasing professionals are developed as a by-product of this dynamic. Those who survive will be valuable assets to your company into the future, continuing to serve either on the front lines of apartment marketing or in increasingly responsible professional capacities.

Maintaining Staff Morale

A leasing staff can be likened to a stable of racehorses—they are a magnificent breed, extraordinarily talented and high-spirited, and they require an inordinate amount of care and nurturing. To a large extent, people's ability to function well is related to their level of contentment—i.e., their morale.

Once again, we caution you to pay careful attention to the daily drama in your leasing office. Notice whether and how much staff members are supportive of each other. Listen to what they say. Observe how they look, how they act (and react), and how much they smile and laugh. Their happiness and contentment are the insurance policy for the success of your properties. One of the ways that you can determine the morale of the group is to ask the members whether they feel appreciated and, if not, what would help them obtain that feeling.

To observe your leasing staff in action and measure their performance, you must monitor their success, first in translating telephone inquiries into visits to the property and then in converting those visits into signed leases. Your monitoring systems can take whatever form your capabilities and interests allow. At the very least, you should track incoming phone calls and prospect traffic at the site. The efficiency and effectiveness of your advertising programs in producing telephone inquiries, site visits, and signed leases, and the productivity of your site staff in converting phone calls into visits can be measured using traffic report forms and guest cards. (Example traffic reports are presented in chapter 2; the guest card is discussed in chapter 6.)

Computers offer a more sophisticated approach. There are many types of spreadsheet software that will allow you to develop programs for accumulating and evaluating such data. It is also common practice to calculate the cost of each signed lease derived from a particular advertising source. (We show examples of such costs in chapter 4.)

It is essential to know how each individual employee is doing. No employee should be judged solely on his or her productivity on a particular day. Reviewing several weeks of activity will equip both employer and employee to rate strengths and weaknesses and focus on areas that need improvement. Reports from "shoppers" (see chapter 1) can provide some insights into how leasing personnel are perceived by prospects.

Concentrated and consistent attention to performance over time will also serve to identify the employee who has suddenly (or gradually) become less productive than he or she was previously. Such discovery will facilitate corrective action before the productivity problem becomes too great or spreads to others on the team. While direct feedback may not be possible or practical on a day-by-day basis, specific areas of concern should be acknowledged as promptly as possible. This is important both to prevent problems from recurring or growing and to reinforce particularly successful results.

A new leasing agent's performance should be evaluated formally at the conclusion of the training period or within a short time after that. Subsequently, periodic reviews serve to keep both employer and employee apprised of progress and problems. The period between such reviews is likely to vary with the workload, the employer's expectations, and the employee's experience and growth in the job. Most employers review performance minimally at one-year intervals, and periodic salary adjustments often depend on the outcome of the review.

Although no single program for monitoring leasing performance and success is perfect, the important thing is to have and use such a program. You will be much more successful if you track information about the productivity of those who work with and for you because you will be collecting data that can be measured and compared. Not only will a monitoring system help you measure leasing progress and advertising success, it will allow you to take corrective action at an early stage and provide a tangible basis for team members to take an occasional bow (or receive a pat on the back) for their achievements.

CHAPTER 6

Strategize Leasing Activities

Selling is the conversion of potential buyers into actual buyers through a series of actions or operations conducive to a desired end—the sales process. Selling is hard work. Those who are most successful at it think through their approaches in exquisite detail long before they greet their customers. In other words, they strategize the sales process.

In apartment marketing, the actions required to effect a lease are neither random nor accidental. Every leasing agent is challenged to discover particular strategies that produce optimum results. Not everyone is comfortable with the same methodology. Nor do the same approaches work equally well in every situation.

In the first part of this chapter, we outline what might best be called traditional leasing methods—tactics that we have found productive in leasing apartments at lower-end and mid-range rental rates and when the supply of apartments in the market is limited. However, a different approach is more productive in leasing high-end properties and when apartment product is plentiful. Our strategies for these types of properties conclude the chapter. (See also the discussions of concessions and soft markets in chapters 1 and 2.)

Leasing is essentially stylistic, and personal preference on the part of the participants is a key factor in determining whether a lease will result from the interaction between the leasing agent and the prospective resident. To demonstrate this, we have defined the leasing process as a drama in three acts: (1) getting acquainted with the prospect, (2) showing the property, and (3) closing the sale. Whether you subscribe to the drama analogy or use another approach altogether, this chapter will help you train your leasing personnel in the best ways to achieve your leasing goals.

Strategies for Getting Acquainted

The first act in the leasing drama begins as a response to your advertising—an ad that appeared in a newspaper or rental magazine or on a billboard or simply the signage on your property. Whatever the source of the response, the leasing drama will most likely be initiated with a telephone call.

The Telephone. Communication between human beings is extremely intricate and sophisticated, especially when one of the speakers has a specific purpose in mind. In the case of apartment rentals, the leasing agent's purpose is to obtain the prospect's commitment to visit the apartment community and be shown an apartment. The first telephone call, the one with which the prospect makes contact with the leasing agent, is crucial to the eventual "sale" of the apartment. All of your advertising dollars have been spent for the sole purpose of getting that call.

Try to visualize that first telephone call as if your prospect were walking through the front door of your property. The way you handle the conversation will either move the deal forward or frustrate the sale. Be aware that *the voice is a sales tool.* We achieve our communication goals by being persuasive, and tone of voice is one means of being convincing. Imagine the various tones of voice that you might use to communicate anger, boredom, glee, suspicion, or sadness—then think about the reactions they will generate. Now, think of the tone of voice you would use to greet an old and dear friend you have not seen for months. That warm, welcoming tone is the one your prospects will find most inviting.

How you sound is crucial. Insincerity can be sensed as easily over the telephone as it is in person. The old trick of smiling while you are talking really works. (A small mirror kept near the phone will allow you to check on your smile and practice as often as necessary.) You may feel silly at first, but people will hear the smile in your voice.

What you say is equally important. Evaluate the elements of your greeting. Our personal favorite is: "Good morning! The Highlands Apartments. This is Kathy. How may I help you?" Its tone imparts a friendly and helpful attitude. Its content welcomes the prospect, provides reassurance that he or she has indeed called the right number, and lets the caller know that the person answering the phone wants to help.

Decide what greeting you will use. Practice the greeting until you are comfortable with it, then tape record yourself answering the telephone, and critique your tone and delivery. Repeat the process from time to time as a safeguard and to be sure that you have not lapsed into a monotone. If different people will be answering the phone, it may be helpful to suggest several acceptable greetings they can use and indicate your preference. Then, everyone should practice and have their answering techniques tape recorded.

During the initial telephone call, be sure you obtain the prospect's name and telephone number. You will need that information if you have to reschedule the appointment. Sometime during your initial telephone conversations, you will have to decide whether to address your prospects by their first names or by their surnames with the appropriate form of address (Mr., Ms., etc.). Some people welcome informality; others are offended by it. Your approach will vary according to your estimate of the prospect's willingness to be informal during the sales process. If you use your own first name in answering the phone, the prospect may respond in kind. On the other hand, it may be appropriate to start out more formally. A caller may identify herself up-front, "This is Theresa Jones calling about your ad." In that case, you may greet her, "How may I help you, Ms. Jones?" She may correct you, "This is *Mrs.* Jones"—or she may say, "Please just call me Theresa," and your problem is solved. In every instance, you should let the prospect be your guide.

The sales process is basically the creation of a personal bond between buyer and seller. Applied to apartment leasing, such a personal bond must be created between the prospect and the leasing agent. This bond is indispensable to the leasing drama and to the long-term relationship between the apartment property and the resident. Use of the prospect's name is one means of initiating that bond. People love to hear their names; being remembered on such a personal level makes them feel important. When the prospect arrives for the appointment, greet him or her cordially by name, and repeat your own. The most crucial bit of information you will have acquired so far is the prospect's name. Use it frequently during your conversations. People remember the people who remember them.

Different property management firms have developed successful techniques for using the telephone. It is important to develop methods that will work for you and help you achieve your leasing goals. Remember that you have an agenda for each call—you want to bring the caller to the apartment community for a showing. The caller probably has an agenda as well, and it likely includes obtaining answers to several questions about the apartments you have available. The amount of rent (and any deposits), the size of the apartment (number of rooms and, perhaps, square footage), and the terms and conditions of a lease are common questions, so have this information ready. Answer the caller's questions as thoroughly as you can and then "close" the telephone call. In this case, *closing* means making an appointment (date and time) for an apartment showing. Here are some tips for closing.

- Have the prospect write down the directions for reaching the apartment community.
- Agree on an appointment date and time.
- Set the appointment as soon after the telephone call as possible; later the same day is preferable.

> **Answer Each Question with a Question**
>
> The objective of the initial conversation between prospect and leasing agent is to arrange an appointment for a showing. If the leasing agent only answers the prospect's specific questions, that is not likely to happen, as can be seen from the following example.
>
> *Leasing Agent:* "Highlands Apartments."
> *Prospect:* "Do you have any one-bedroom apartments?"
> *Leasing Agent:* "Yes."
> *Prospect:* "How much are they?"
> *Leasing Agent:* "$550 a month."
> *Prospect:* "Thank you." (Prospect hangs up.)
>
> The preceding is an extreme example of how answering a prospect's questions can go nowhere. Ideally, the leasing agent will answer each question and then pose a question in turn until an appointment is made.
>
> *Leasing Agent:* "Good morning. You've reached The Highlands Apartments. How may I help you?"
> *Prospect:* "Do you have any one-bedroom apartments?"
> *Leasing Agent:* "Yes, we have several. Rents begin at $550—depending on size and view. Would you prefer a city view or a river view?"
> *Prospect:* "I think I'd like to overlook the city. Do you have exercise facilities?"
> *Leasing Agent:* "Yes, we do. We have a brand new exercise room with all the latest equipment. Would you like to come out right away or would after work be more convenient for you?"

Prospects will not rent apartments they cannot find easily. The directions you give must be accurate, and the prospect must understand them. Repeat the information, if necessary. Ask where the prospect will be coming from, and suggest a direct route if you can. (Remember, too, that a scenic route can show off the features of the neighborhood.) You want the caller to write down the directions for two reasons.

1. Once people agree to do something verbally, they have made a commitment. The commitment becomes stronger when they write down what it is they have agreed to do.
2. Written directions give you an edge over your competition. The prospect is probably looking at the Sunday newspaper or a dog-eared rental magazine. The written directions will place you at the top of the list of apartment buildings to visit because your property will be easy to find.

Be specific in setting the appointment time—but not so precise that the caller is intimidated. If a prospect feels embarrassed about not being able to arrive on the minute, he or she might decide not to come at all. Ideally, you want to agree to a convenient time for an appointment on the same day the prospect calls. Your prospect is motivated—the call itself tells you that. Further-

EXHIBIT 6.1

Example Guest Card

GUEST CARD

Agent _____ Date _____
Appointment _____
      Date   Time   Day of Week
Name _____ Phone _____
                      Home
Present Address _____
_____ Phone _____
 City   State Zip Code   Office
Company Name _____ Occupation _____
Occupants (No.) _____ Date Needed _____ Desired Rent _____
Apt Desired _____
    No. Bedrooms No. Bathrooms Need Parking?
Why Moving _____
Special Needs _____
Source of Traffic
_____ Newspaper Ad _____ Daily _____ Sunday
_____ Apartment/Living Guide
_____ Radio _____ Television
_____ Resident Referral _____ Drive By _____ Transtop Poster
_____ Other: _____

---

more, an appointment for the following day or later in the week (or the next weekend) may not be kept. Something could come up that would make the meeting unnecessary (in particular, the prospect could rent somewhere else and not even bother to cancel the appointment with you). So, if the appointment must be made for another day, you should confirm it by phone beforehand. If the prospect has decided not to come, your phone call will save time, and if the prospect intends to keep the appointment, your phone call will strengthen the relationship.

There is more to this first telephone call than a greeting and a closing. The prospect's questions provide the substance for the conversation in between. To better serve that prospect during the showing, you should begin to complete a guest card during the telephone call.

The Guest Card. The guest card is a vital tool in the leasing transaction. It creates a sales biography of your prospect—a working document to which you will add information as your interview progresses. When you have completed the guest card, it will contain all of the information you need to lease a particular apartment to your prospect. *Exhibit 6.1* shows a sample guest card format.

Whatever form your guest card takes, it should provide spaces for the

EXHIBIT 6.1 *(continued)*
Example Guest Card—Back

NOTES			
Call Back	Date	Scheduled Visit	Comments

prospect's name, occupation, current home address, home and work telephone numbers, how he or she learned about your property (newspaper or magazine ads, signage), the size or type of apartment desired, and any special needs that must be addressed (e.g., special parking or access because of a handicap). The back of the card can be used to list the apartments shown to the prospect, note the leasing agent's comments about the showing, and record details of follow-up efforts.

Completing the Guest Card. During the prospect's initial telephone call, you should have obtained his or her name and written it onto a guest card. Also, during that initial conversation, you should have made notes about what the prospect told you about himself or herself—while the information was fresh. What size apartment does the prospect need or want? (How many bedrooms? How many bathrooms?) How many people will be living there? Did the prospect ask about rental rates? When is he or she planning to move? Did the prospect say where he or she worked? Was a pet mentioned? A waterbed? Were any specific desires or preferences expressed (e.g., for a particular view, a special carpet or wall color)? Were any needs stated (schools, day care, special accommodation for a handicap)?

Pay close attention to your prospect's first two questions. These are his or her "hot buttons"—the factors this prospect considers essential to the sale.

The Guest Card As a Sales Tool

According to Anne Sadovsky, one of the leading experts in apartment marketing, too many leasing agents simply have prospects fill out a guest card and then interrogate them. In the December 1990 issue of *MinniMag*, she recommends giving some thought up front to the way prospect qualifying is handled. She strikes a comparison with buying an automobile. Imagine how you would react if you were eyeing a red convertible, and the salesman approached you and wanted to know if you had a job or asked for your phone number—without any preliminary conversation. Sadovsky thinks most people would be turned off by such an approach, and she's right. If you think about it, most automobile salespeople are interested in getting the customer excited about the car. They want the customer to sit in it, to drive it, to fall in love with it. Because of this, their qualifying questions will be subtle, expressing an interest in the customer. Their efforts are directed to increasing the customer's interest in the benefits of owning the car and intensifying the customer's emotions.

You can take a cue from that example. Start qualifying your prospects with statements that will put them at ease. You might say something like this: "I know renting an apartment is a big decision for you. I want to make that decision easier for you by helping you find the perfect place to live. To do that, I need your help. Is it okay if I ask you some questions to get us started?" In other words, put yourself in the prospect's position and try for an approach that would work on you.

The sole purpose of the guest card is to help you identify those cues that will lead to a match between a particular apartment in your inventory and the prospect's needs and preferences. You want to know, in as much detail as possible, what the prospect considers inadequate or unfavorable about his or her current living situation. If the address entry indicates that the prospect is currently renting an apartment, you will want to find out what it is about his or her present situation that has led to the decision to move. Is the apartment too expensive? Is it too small? Is the building deteriorating? Is the location too far away from work or recreation? Any or all of these factors as well as many others may be at work. In exploring the prospect's objections to his or her current situation, you will be creating opportunities to sell the specific features and qualities of your apartment community.

This exercise has dual significance: First, the guest card should reveal enough information to enable you to know what has gone wrong with the prospect's current living situation. Second, having discovered the problem or set of problems, you can begin to sell the advantages of your apartment product as "benefits" that will overcome those "objections." Without this information, you will be giving the prospect a "tour" of your property, when what you really want to do is "show" the prospect an apartment that is likely to fit his or her needs. Before you can show the prospect an apartment, however, you will have to work together to find a match between his or her particular requirements and the apartments you have available. In other words, the issues of apartment size, room layout, and location in the building have to be addressed.

The first question usually involves price or availability, suggesting a sensitivity about the cost of the apartment or the fact of an active search for housing. The second question lets you know that there are certain factors the prospect considers to be so vital that they will have to be satisfied if you are going to make the sale. *Write the prospect's questions down!*

The apartment leasing process requires you to establish a "buying temperature" in each prospect that you will artfully raise, step by step, until he or she is overwhelmed by the desire to rent. Although some "hot buttons" may be partially disguised, we believe the sample guest card will allow you to collect all of the information you need to achieve the sale. The beginning of your contact with the prospect is the best opportunity to gather this vital information. Be precise and accurate in recording the information on the guest card, and the results will be reflected in your leasing velocity.

Using the Information to Sell. It is crucial to explore the reasons why the prospect's current home—whether an apartment or something else—is no longer satisfactory. Understanding the prospect's reason or motivation for moving will help you tailor your apartment presentation. If this person has opted for apartment living because the pressures of single-family home ownership are too burdensome and time-consuming, you will want to stress the carefree lifestyle of your apartment community during your sales presentation. On the other hand, if he or she is living in an apartment or a property that has undesirable characteristics (e.g., too noisy, too small, poorly maintained), your sales presentation should emphasize the attributes of your apartment community that will meet—and exceed—the prospect's requirements. (However, you must make certain—through good management—that those claims are real. Otherwise, if that prospect becomes a resident, you will soon lose him or her to a competitor, who may be told the same things about you.)

Effective use of the guest card requires asking questions that will uncover the keys to your prospect's satisfaction, things that you can match with features of your apartment community. By discovering what your prospect needs—and how his or her current living environment fails to meet those needs—you will be able to do *targeted benefit selling*.

The guest card is a selling tool. Its utility is maximized when leasing personnel use it properly. We have found that the weakest points in the leasing process are at the beginning and end of the leasing agent's contact with a prospect. It is a natural human tendency to be somewhat shy in our dealings with strangers, and that is a problem. We have seen leasing agents hand their prospects a guest card, ask them to complete it, and then retrieve it before all the blanks are filled. They glance at the card to determine what size apartment is desired and start for the model unit. The prospect is then given a tour of the model rather than a showing of the particular benefits of the apartment community. A lease may result from such a haphazard process, but the leasing agent has not really transacted a sale.

The reason for this behavior pattern among leasing agents may be that they are most comfortable with what they know. If they are permitted to tour prospects around the apartment community, they need only memorize their so-called sales pitch. On the other hand, interactive conferences with prospects will require the leasing agent to improvise—if a prospect's comments divert the leasing agent from the memorized script, he or she may panic.

The best strategy is for the leasing agent to complete the guest card during an interview with the prospect when he or she arrives. This protocol requires the leasing agent to have a conversation with the prospect, ask gently probing questions designed to obtain precise information, and write down the prospect's answers. The interview questions might follow these examples.

> Where are you living now?
> Is that an apartment or a single-family home?
> When does your lease expire?
> Why have you decided to move?
> What particular features are you looking for in your new apartment?

The answers to these open-ended questions will tell you exactly what it will take to sell the prospect an apartment. Other questions should be asked to obtain specific information: How many people will be living in the apartment? How much rent do you expect to pay? Because price (i.e., the amount of rent) is a real concern for many people, it may be prudent to ask a subtle question about income. Prospects may underestimate or overestimate what they can pay for rent, and an income figure will suggest a range of affordability and, therefore, a range of apartments to be shown. (A rule of thumb often used is that income should be approximately four times the amount of the rent. Thus, an apartment that rents for $600 per month would require income of $2,400 monthly or $28,800 annually.)

When interviewing a prospect, listen carefully to what he or she says—and does not say. Most people conduct conversations without listening very well. They tend to be thinking about their own responses while the other person is talking, then they interrupt the conversation trying to make their own points. What would otherwise be a dialogue soon becomes a monologue because each person is concentrating on the message he or she wants to convey to the other.

The best conversationalists say very little, but they listen intently. Then they ask sensitive questions that clarify or add to the information the speaker has conveyed. Train your leasing personnel in the art of listening. As they become more skilled at listening, they will recognize that the sale can be closed *only* after they have obtained enough information to be able to make a reasoned interpretation of a prospect's housing needs. They will eventually feel comfortable about guest card interviews. When they take the time to determine prospects' needs, their leasing performance will improve dramatically.

Strategies for Showing Apartments

The second act in the apartment leasing drama—the actual showing of apartments—has five components, all beginning with the letter P.

1. *Product* is the condition of the property—its curb appeal. This is what will create that all-important first—and lasting—impression on your prospects. A good way to evaluate your product is to ask yourself some questions, such as the following: Have the hallways been vacuumed? Are the windows sparkling clean? Is the exterior free of trash? Are the apartments in showable condition? (No apartment should be shown unless it is ready for someone to move into it.) In short, does the apartment community, both inside and out, look as though someone really cares about it and the people who live there? To be sure that it does, you must walk the property every day *before* you open for business. During this inspection, imagine that you are a prospect who will be looking critically at your property through your eyes, and ask yourself: "What will they see?" The best test, of course, is to assume the role of a prospective renter and ask yourself whether you would want to live in the apartments you are going to show to your prospects. (Curb appeal and apartment market-readiness are discussed in chapter 1.)
2. *Pride* is what you should feel about your apartment community, your job, and your employer. People who are proud of themselves, what they do, and whom they work for invariably do a better job than those who are not. Pride creates enthusiasm, and enthusiasm is indispensable to the salesperson—in this case, the leasing agent. We believe that apartment leases result from the transfer of enthusiasm from leasing agent to prospective resident.
3. *Personnel* are all the staff members your prospects are likely to encounter during their visit to your property. Leasing personnel as well as other staff members must present themselves in the "image" of the property. Their attire and appearance should be appropriate for their positions. Appearance affects one's ability to conduct business. If a leasing agent's appearance is inappropriate, prospects can be distracted by it, concentrating on the person making the presentation rather than on the business of renting.
4. *Presentation* is the manner in which the prospect is greeted and the apartments are shown. Traditionally, presentation meant a guided tour of the property and selected apartments. Features and amenities might as well have been ticked off on a checklist; each would be named, located, and given a quick inspection, and the tour would move on to the next item. Using this methodology, leasing agents would often memorize a script and then become flustered if a prospect interrupted with a question or comment.

The key to apartment leasing today is to determine the prospective resident's needs, identify apartments that should meet those needs, and then characterize the features of those apartments as benefits that address the prospect's specific needs and will enhance his or her lifestyle. The pride mentioned earlier, the enthusiasm of the leasing agent, should be put to use in preparing for each apartment showing. You need to know about your product so you can sell it convincingly. You need to listen to a prospect's responses to your presentation so you can gauge your success—or modify your presentation so that it will be productive. Presentation is the focused application of the leasing agent's selling skills.

5. *Productivity* is the successful conversion of prospects into residents. The leasing agent's skill is measurable by its results—the acquisition of signed leases.

The main component of showing apartments is presentation, and that requires selling skills. In the next sections, we will demonstrate the elements of presentation: preparation, benefit selling, personalization, and handling of objections. (These steps presume that all apartments in the community that are available to be leased are, indeed, ready to be shown and occupied.)

Preparing to Sell. Assume that you have an appointment at ten o'clock this morning for an apartment showing that will be your first of the day. You should prepare for this activity by tidying the office. Put away the packages that were delivered this morning; stash the loose plumbing supplies in the closet, and neatly stack the papers on your desk. Now you can get down to the business of strategizing your sales process.

Review the information on the guest card you prepared during the telephone call that resulted in this appointment. It will guide your selection of apartments to show. If you have one, take a copy of the site plan map that shows how the building or buildings are laid out on the property, and draw a line from your office to the first apartment you expect to show your prospect. Now, retrace that line, beginning at your office, and indicate the stops you intend to make along the way by writing a series of numbers next to the line. Each number should correspond to a feature of the property (e.g., laundry facilities, mailbox area, party room, sauna, pool, storage lockers, etc.) that you will identify and describe. Then, list the numbers on a separate sheet of paper and indicate what you expect to tell the prospect about them.

What you write depends on how much prompting you think you will need. The laundry area might be characterized with a few words (e.g., ten washers and dryers, gentle, refund lost money, wine and cheese parties) or with several descriptive sentences (i.e., a script): "We have a lovely laundry area with ten washers and dryers. The machines are especially gentle on clothes, and we've set the timing on the dryers so that there is more than adequate time to dry a full load. And if you ever lose your money in one of the machines—it happens only a couple of times a year—we'll refund it on the spot. But the best part about doing your wash is that we have wine and cheese parties every few weeks right here in the laundry room. Our residents can wash their clothes and get to know each other at the same time. It's really fun!"

Bear in mind, however, that your purpose is to show apartments. The discussions that you have during your sales presentation should be focused on the *benefits* that your property offers. In this context, being a wonderful conversationalist can be a disadvantage. If a prospect is more impressed with you than with the apartment, you will have raised his or her "buying temperature" for the wrong product. The following examples illustrate the difference.

> One of the best leasing agents we have ever known was a young lady named Karen. Karen always directed conversations to the product she was selling. If her prospect said, "I have children who visit from California every few months," Karen would respond, "After you move in, you can reserve the guest suite for them. It's beautiful. The guest suite will give your visitors some privacy, and it can serve as your extra bedroom at minimal cost when you need it. Let me show it to you."
>
> Another leasing agent, Linda, was equally adept at putting her prospects at ease. However, if her prospect said, "I have children who visit from California every few months," Linda would reply, "Really? I went to college in Santa Barbara. I loved being so close to the beach. We used to drive up to see the redwoods every Fall. Where do your children live?" The conversation would then spin off into children's activities and the various tourist attractions in Southern California.
>
> Karen's prospects rented apartments; Linda's did not.

Remember: In the leasing environment, it is important to guard against idle chitchat. Each statement you make and every question you answer should refer to your apartment community and how one of its benefits will enhance your prospect's lifestyle. If you do not keep this in mind, you will not succeed in leasing apartments.

Selling Benefits. Having drawn the line to the first apartment you intend to show your prospect, take a floor plan of that unit (if you have one), and plan your presentation. Sketch out for yourself how you will present the apartment. At each point where you intend to highlight a particular feature, place a number and, on a corresponding sheet of paper, write down the statement you intend to make about it.

Selling features requires you to illustrate how various attributes of your apartment community and the apartments you show your prospects will enhance their lives. Simply pointing out a feature is discourteous to your prospect. If you say, "In here we have the walk-in closet," you would be noting the obvious. On the other hand, you might say, "In the master bedroom, we provide an unusually large walk-in closet. There are five extra linear feet of hanging space and twelve additional square feet of shelving compared with other apartments in our market. Our residents are just delighted with the spaciousness of these closets." Factual information, provided enthusiastically, will lead to a constructive conclusion about how the feature improves lifestyle. It sells the feature of the apartment as a specific benefit—this is what you should strive to achieve.

Remember: Buying is partly an emotional process. Creating positive emotions or feelings about the apartment and community will increase your ability to sell. Try to make your benefit statements powerful reasons for your prospects to move into your apartment community.

Personalized Selling. Salespeople correctly believe that buyers who like them personally are more apt to make a purchase. Recognizing that sellers are working hard and doing their best to please their customers, buyers accordingly make supportive statements, thus indirectly indicating that they do like the salesperson. Buyers tend to agree with what the salesperson tells them. This human tendency to please one another has both good and bad consequences, as we shall see later in this chapter.

There is a distinct psychological component to the interaction between buyer and seller. Personalization is just one of its many facets. In this section, we will consider how this personal psychological aspect helps the selling process. Stated as a rule, it might be presented as follows: *If the rental agent and the prospect like one another, and if the rental agent indicates a liking for a particular feature of the apartment, the prospect will also like it.* This rule can be extended further: *If the rental agent likes the feature because of his or her own experience with it, the prospect will like it even better.*

You can employ the psychology of buyer and seller to advantage by including in your presentation as many illustrations of your favorable impressions of the features of your apartments as you can. This will personalize your sales process. (The following examples assume the leasing agent lives in the apartment community.)

> If your building has skylights in the corridors, or in the units themselves, you might say, "I really love natural light. Even on the rainiest day, my apartment is bathed in it. I like to sit back and look at the moon and stars shining through on a clear night. I just can't resist the beauty of nature!"

If your building features large balconies, you might say, "Look how spacious this balcony is! I put my recliner out on my balcony and enjoy the sunshine on my days off. My husband and I have our little barbecue out there, and we broil steaks. When we have guests, we use the large gas barbecue and the wrought iron table and chairs by the pool. I'll show those to you when we walk around the grounds."

This technique can also be used to sell such routine features as the appliances in the apartments. "You know, when I lived in my first apartment, my roommate and I didn't have a dishwasher. When we finally got one, we could stash eight place settings inside it before we had to wash the dishes. I have the same type of dishwasher in my apartment, and it's terrific! It gets our glassware absolutely spotless. It uses only half as much water and a third less electricity than the models we had just three years ago."

If you learn during the initial interview that a prospect family has two small children and that facilities for youngsters are exceedingly important to them, your presentation should concentrate on the children and their happiness. Point out the benefits of the local school district and nearby parks, and indicate the availability of day care. (You might mention whether there are reliable baby-sitters in the area or if youngsters of similar ages already live in the building.) You can allude to the warmth of the wading pool and how much your own children enjoy playing in it.

Remember: If you plan where you will take your prospect and what you will probably say at various points during your demonstration, you will be better prepared to conduct a successful showing. However, planning also means allowing for flexibility in your presentation; you must resist the temptation to map out your presentation so thoroughly as to squelch spontaneity. Too much preparation and memorization can make your presentation sound as though it has been tape-recorded and placed in a can on the shelf, where it can be retrieved and played for every prospect regardless of his or her circumstances. Such a "canned" approach absolutely discourages targeted benefit selling. The leasing agent who relies on this strategy will occasionally enjoy some success because the type of prospect for whom that technique works will drift into the leasing office now and again. However, in our experience, a canned approach is ineffective.

Overcoming Prospects' Objections. However diligently you try to match the needs of your prospects with the apartments in your inventory, objections are certain to arise. There are two ways to regard objections: First, you can consider them as negative judgments about your product and simply disregard them because otherwise they will frustrate sales. Alternatively, however, you can welcome them as indications of a prospect's continuing interest in your apartment community. In truth, objections are useful evidence that your targeted benefit selling style is actually working, and you should handle each objection as it arises.

We recommend that you listen carefully to objections—ask for them, in fact—and use them as sales tools. Objections are merely another way your prospect has of telling you about his or her "hot buttons." The following example epitomizes the importance of objections in the apartment-selling process and illustrates once again the ramifications of the psychology of the buyer-seller interaction.

> We were hired to assist with the lease-up of an upscale suburban apartment community whose potential for success was in doubt. We found that the advertising campaign was generating telephone calls and that the leasing staff were converting those calls into site visits. However, prospects were not becoming residents—despite what appeared to be effective sales presentations by the leasing agents.
>
> During one-on-one training sessions with the leasing staff, we assumed the roles of prospects. The leasing agents completed the guest card phase of the rental drama with us, demonstrated the various features of the common areas and individual apartments, and attempted to close sales with us. We critiqued their performances at the conclusion of each act of the drama and suggested ways to improve their presentations.
>
> At one point, a leasing agent remarked, "I think my clients are all going to rent. They nod a lot and seem to like everything I show them, but they never ask questions. Then, when I ask them to fill out a rental application, they just mumble and thank me and go out to their cars and leave. What am I doing wrong?"
>
> What was wrong was that their sales techniques were canned, and it affected the entire staff. The leasing agents were literally overwhelming their prospects with the myriad features of the apartment community. The prospects never got an opportunity to ask questions or even to share their expectations about apartment living with the leasing personnel—the staff never gave them the chance.

Remember: Leasing agents are hired by apartment communities to lease apartments to prospects. This means that the purpose of their business is to give a personal presentation or showing of a property rather than merely a tour. The best way to assure this result is to train on-site leasing personnel to concentrate on matching the benefits of the property to the needs of their prospects.

Prospective apartment residents need to be active participants in the apartment sale. The sales process has to accommodate their questions and

> **Showing Apartments versus Giving a Tour of the Property**
> We define a property *showing* as a demonstration of how the apartment building in general and a specific apartment in particular meet the prospect's expressed needs and preferences. As such, a showing is a specific, individualized sales presentation of all of the ways that the benefits of the property meet the requirements of the prospective resident as articulated and explored during completion of the guest card. By contrast, a *tour* of an apartment property consists of nothing more than walking through it and pointing out the features. There is no attempt to sell advantages to the prospect. The session typically concludes with an exchange of business cards and a perfunctory invitation to the prospect to call if he or she has any questions—this is a substitute for closing the sale. If a lease were to ensue from a tour, it would be entirely accidental—i.e., a result of the prospect having demanded one.

concerns. If the process does not do that, your prospects will politely walk away and search for an apartment at another property where the leasing agent will try to *meet their needs* by finding out what those needs are.

Think of your own experiences. How often do you say, "I'm just looking," when a salesperson approaches you in a department store? How often do you try to find an item yourself rather than allow a salesperson to help you? We would guess this happens most of the time. Ask yourself why you prefer to search for the right department or the right aisle and sort through mountains of merchandise instead of asking for help. Most likely this is because you are afraid of the "hard" sell. A lifetime of encounters with salespeople has convinced you that they will try to sell you something you do not want or cannot afford, and then you will have to go to the trouble of exchanging it. To avoid the hassle, you choose to do it yourself rather than enlist the assistance of the one person who is most likely to help you.

We have found that leasing agents are generally afraid of objections (this despite their own history as consumers). Sometimes they take the objections personally and feel hurt. They may respond in a negative way—or not at all. What they have forgotten is that objections are a productive prelude to a sale—their own fears about being coerced into buying something they do not want should alert them to their prospects' expressions of concern. Receptivity, rather than indifference or defensiveness, is the key to overcoming objections.

The most difficult aspect of overcoming prospects' objections is evaluating what they mean in the first place. Is the prospect simply asking a question or camouflaging a real concern? What appears to be an objection may actually be something more fundamental: The prospect is unwilling to be completely honest because he or she is worried that you—someone the prospect likes—will be offended.

We have found that the best way to approach objections is to be forthright. You should handle them as they come up during your sales presentation and even provide opportunities for your prospect to be critical. If you can make prospects feel comfortable about asking questions, you will find that their underlying apprehensions, if any, will surface as well. In truth, objections generally arise in three areas: Price, amenities, and the decision to rent.

Objections related to price are something many leasing agents dread. Suppose you have indicated to your prospect that you have several different apartment layouts, noting the prices for each unit type, and your prospect asks, "You mean your 800-square-foot apartment costs $750 a month? I saw a larger two-bedroom apartment down the block for $675, and they were offering a month's free rent."

This objection raises the two most common issues related to price—competing apartments that have lower rents and the availability of concessions. While they are separate matters, these issues can be handled in the same way.

> "You're absolutely right, Theresa. Their apartments are less expensive than ours. They offer move-in concessions, and we don't. I'd like you to give me an opportunity to show you our two-bedroom apartment. We'll start out by looking at a model apartment that displays the features we talked about. As you'll see, it has a full-size washer and dryer. That's really convenient for families like yours where there are small children. At (the competition), they have only a small laundry room in the basement.
>
> "What we really offer is *value*. Most of our residents have been with us since the building was built. A lot of them have children, and we have a supervised swimming program for the youngsters every afternoon. I think John and Eric will love it.
>
> "As we're walking around the community, please ask me any questions you have. I'm really proud of our apartments. My family has lived here since it opened, and we're very happy. Please look carefully at the condition of the apartments I show you and the common areas—the hallways, the exercise room and all the rest. Compare our quality with what you've seen elsewhere.
>
> "One other thing, Theresa. We've never offered concessions or rent discounts. We haven't had to. What we've found is that our residents appreciate the value they get at our property, and that leads to high-quality residents. When we're finished, I think you'll agree that living here is worth at least as much as we're charging."

This example is intended to highlight several points. First, the leasing agent met the objections head-on. She did not apologize for the amount of rent being charged. She compared some of the amenities of her building with those of the competition—without being derogatory—and invited her prospect to do the same; she also solicited questions during the showing. She sold two of the amenities—the in-unit laundry appliances and the swimming program—directly to the needs of the prospect. She used her prospect's name appropriately. She mentioned her own satisfaction with her apartment in the building. Finally, she justified the rent on the basis of quality.

A price objection can be a deal-killer unless it is handled candidly. We have found that the only effective way to address it is to set it in a context of value—the resident will be paying for higher quality. Prospects are often anxious about price. They are hungry for a deal but distrustful of giveaways. The assumption is that if an owner has to give part of the product away, there must be something wrong with it. This particular suspicion frequently arises in the housing context, yet prospective renters are willing to pay more for apartments if they are convinced that the value they will receive is commensurate with the price.

Objections involving amenities are also common. Prospects may want particular features that your community does not offer, or they may want *more* of a feature that you do have. They may want in-unit washers and dryers, but you have centralized laundry facilities. They may want an indoor swimming pool, and you offer only an outdoor pool. They may prefer dark-colored carpeting with a clipped pile, and the carpeting in your apartments is light-colored and has a deep pile. Most leasing agents treat such objections with disdain. They say, "Sorry," but in effect they mean, "Take it or leave it." In doing this, they transform a simple statement of interest—"It would be nice if I could have a washer and dryer in my apartment"—into an absolute prerequisite for signing the lease. In other words, what may have been just the expression of a wish becomes a potential lease-killer.

There are at least two constructive responses to this type of objection. First, you can actually provide the feature if it is physically possible to do so—for example, remove the light-colored, deep-pile carpeting and install it in another apartment, and buy and install the color and style of carpeting that the prospect prefers. Such a decision, of course, depends on your assessment of whether meeting the request is an absolute requirement for a lease, whether it can actually be accomplished, and whether you have the authority to grant it. Often the feature noted in an objection is merely something considered desirable, and there is a completely satisfactory alternative. The following is an example.

> *Prospect:* "I want a washer and dryer in my apartment. I think it would be too inconvenient to haul all of our dirty clothes downstairs to the laundry room. A family of five accumulates so much laundry. You can't imagine!"
>
> *Leasing agent:* "You know, when we first moved into the building, I would have preferred to have laundry facilities in our apartment, too. When our second baby was born, I was washing diapers and baby clothes almost every day. Then the owners installed six new sets of

appliances in the laundry room, put in the large table and comfortable chairs, and redecorated the entire room. My husband likes the place so much that he's taken over the laundry duties! He can do six loads at once and get the job done in an hour—not the six-hour ordeal I used to endure. Then, too, with all the magazines and paperback books down there, it's almost like a library. Come on, I'll show you."

When faced with an objection, the best approach is to convert it into a benefit by persuasively selling the advantages of the existing feature. To be prepared to meet objections head-on, you have to anticipate them. Identify potential objections to the features and amenities of your apartments and your building. Then, on the basis of your own experiences with them, write down all of the positive qualities that each one offers. Being prepared to handle the objection before it arises will help you make better use of the personalized selling psychology noted earlier. The following example uses this same technique.

Prospect: "I don't like those window air conditioners. They don't cool the entire apartment. And they're so noisy! I definitely want central air conditioning in the apartment."

Leasing agent: "I used to feel the same way. The first apartment building we lived in had central air, and I thought I would really like it. But on the hottest summer days, there would be an energy emergency or the system would be down, and we couldn't even open the windows to let in some fresh air. Then, too, we often forgot to turn the air conditioning off when we left for the day. Our electric bills were a nightmare! We like the window units because we can cool just what we need, and it's energy-efficient and so much less expensive. You know, the window air conditioners actually lull us to sleep."

The third common objection concerns the decision-making process itself. This may appear as the unavailability of a player who has to agree with the prospect's decision before a lease can be signed—a roommate or a spouse has to be consulted or some other absent decision-maker has to approve the choice. There are also other restrictions that may make a decision impossible or infeasible (e.g., the prospect's current lease may not expire for 90 days or more, and he or she cannot afford to pay rent on two apartments; or the prospect believes he or she has to see three other buildings before making a decision). In these types of situations, the leasing agent should plan to follow up with the prospect by phone in a day or two. (This can even be announced in the closing: "I'll follow up with you on Wednesday morning, okay?") For the prospect who is still looking, the extra effort may encourage a favorable decision. If the prospect has signed elsewhere, the call is a way for the agent to find out why his or her property was not chosen and, perhaps, learn how the property or the showing could be improved.

Although there are several ways to handle decision-making objections, the most common approach—and one that is generally misguided—is an attempt to coerce the lease by creating a false sense of urgency: "Mark, this is the last vacant two-bedroom apartment I have. I can't just take it off the market while you try to make up your mind. In fact, I have an appointment in twenty minutes with a nice young couple who are moving here from out of state, and they need an apartment right away. So, if you don't sign a lease now, I'm certain this apartment won't be available when you need it. Just go ahead and write me a check for the security deposit and the first month's rent, and you'll be all set."

Frankly, creating a sense of urgency is part of the sales process, and it does have merit. Human beings tend to delay important decisions until they cannot be avoided—unless forced to make up their minds, they prefer to preserve as many options as possible. Consequently, if it is true that a particular apartment a prospect wants is in short supply, common sense dictates that your prospect should be made aware of that fact. It would be unfair not to disclose something essential about the availability of an apartment that is preferred. However, using coercion to acquire a signed lease typically has two results: The prospect usually cancels the transaction by stopping payment on the check, and an otherwise marketable apartment is removed from the market temporarily. Sometimes coercion results in the prospect feeling that the leasing agent is desperate—that the property is in trouble—and all of the bonding that has occurred between the leasing agent and the prospect will be destroyed. *Closing a lease by coercion is just not good practice.*

Strategies for Closing

A product is sold only when the sale has been closed. The closing is the seller's explicit invitation to the buyer to make a purchase—or, as is the case in the apartment environment, to sign an application and a lease. We mentioned earlier that most leasing agents have the greatest difficulties at the beginning *and the conclusion* of the selling process.

The closing is what determines a successful sale. There may be many scenes in this third act of the leasing drama—or only one. Some people in retailing believe that it takes a minimum of five closings before the average customer makes a purchase. In apartment leasing, there are those who claim that senior citizens typically visit an apartment property at least sixteen times before deciding to rent. We believe that the success or failure of apartment communities is directly related to the ability of their leasing agents to close sales. We believe further that the ability to close leasing sales is directly related to the strategies the agents use.

Closing is a challenge. It requires the leasing agent to ask the prospect to make a decision—in effect, to judge the agent's presentation and the quality of the apartment product. Because of this, leasing agents are reluctant to attempt the closing. Instead, they will try to postpone it by saying, for example, "Call me when you have made your decision." Others may try to shift responsibility for closing to the prospect. They will create an uncomfortable silence at the end of the showing and, finally, ask, "Well, what are you going to do?" Even worse, they may simply avoid closing altogether. They may hand prospects their business card at the end of the apartment showing and tell them, "Call me if you have any questions."

The reluctance to close the sale, while understandable, is misguided. The slogan, "you don't get what you don't ask for," is particularly apt. You cannot obtain signed applications or leases if you do not ask for them. The sole purpose of interviewing prospective residents and showing them apartments is to prepare them to rent one. If, as we have suggested, interviewing and showing can be likened to successive acts in a drama, then closing is the last act of that drama—and failing to close the sale is akin to dropping the curtain after the second act of a three-act play.

We also noted earlier in this chapter that apartment leasing is stylistic. The leasing agent should employ closing techniques that match his or her own unique style. Some closing methods are direct, others are subtle; some are complicated while others are easy. Because the leasing process is utterly dependent on the closing—and leasing agents are often weak closers—it is vital to develop strategies for the closing and to plan for it throughout your sales presentation. As is the case with other strategies in the leasing process, you should not only plan for the close, but also practice your technique. Practice will enable you to tailor your closing statements to your perception of the prospects' receptivity to a particular closing technique. The following discussion opens with an example of an obvious closing that you may have observed in everyday life; we will then consider examples related to apartment leasing.

> Suppose you are having dinner in a restaurant, and you are seated next to a family with a toddler in a highchair. It is taking too long for the food to arrive, and the baby is bored. While mom and dad are engaged in a rare conversation, the child spies a spoon across the table and decides he wants it. He attempts to get his parents' attention by stretching and grunting in the direction of the spoon. Mom, distracted, responds with an angry, "No!" Whining ensues. The mother repeats, "No, sweetheart!" and a tantrum follows. What do the parents do? They give the baby the spoon, of course. Why? Because the baby closed—*he refused to take no for an answer.*

Closing need not involve obnoxious behavior—only persistence—and it can be accomplished in a matter of minutes. For example, your prospect may seem to be in a hurry during your presentation. In effect, he or she may direct the apartment showing process by saying, "Don't bother to show me the exercise room or the fitness area. I want to see a two-bedroom on the first floor that is close to the lake."

When you have shown such an apartment and answered whatever questions the prospect had about it, you should try to close the sale immediately: "We've found the apartment that is just right for you. Let's go back to the office and fill out the application." Such a summary close—a simple statement acknowledging that the prospect is ready to sign a lease and inviting him or her to do so—is an effective strategy for concluding the leasing drama. A silent close is equally effective in this situation, and much more dramatic: Simply hand the prospect a clipboard with a rental application and a pen.

On the other hand, many prospects consider the renting decision to be an important matter in their lives. They tend to be particularly thoughtful in evaluating apartment features, and they may compare the advantages of each unit you show them and want to return to several apartments they have seen to determine which has the larger living room or the better view of downtown. Closing the sale in this situation requires you to help your prospect weigh the pros and cons of the apartment candidates: "Remember the first apartment I showed you, Theresa? That one had bedrooms on either side of the living room and the huge walk-in closets. I remember that you liked the room layout, and the light-blue carpet color is perfect for your furniture. The second one I showed you is a little smaller, you'll recall, and a bit less expensive. But it has the separate dining room that is just the right size for your dining room furniture. Which one would you prefer?" This type of summary close is a more scholarly approach, and it can be varied to allow the prospect to write down the advantages of the various apartments and then arrive at a decision independently.

Whether the advantages of apartments are balanced against each other orally or in writing, you are performing a vital service—you are giving your prospect the confidence to make a decision. You are saying, in effect, "Theresa, both of the apartments I showed you are beautiful. You'll get terrific value from either one. Whichever one you select will meet your needs. Now, let's concentrate our attention on which of these two great alternatives will be the better one for you." Inspiring confidence in the prospect is often a useful strategy.

In an earlier discussion about buyers who say they are "just looking" to fend off aggressive salespeople, we hypothesized that shoppers tend to reject help from sales clerks because they are afraid they will be pressured into buying something they do not really want or paying more than they can afford. The opposite is also true. Buyers almost invariably seek approval from someone else—a spouse, a shopping partner, or even a salesperson—before purchasing something, especially something expensive. This is yet another component of the psychology of the buyer-seller interaction: Buyers need independent validation of their buying decisions. The savvy leasing agent can provide that validation. You ought to help your prospects have confidence in their decision-making ability. Validation is an additional closing strategy.

Some leasing agents prefer to rely on their personality strengths, and they are often very effective. We knew one particularly productive agent who asked her prospects to sit down in the middle of the living room of the apartment when she had concluded her presentation. Mary would inquire, "Well, how did I do?" The prospect, somewhat confused, would ask what she meant, and Mary would explain, "I'd like to rent you this apartment. My job is to lease apartments. How did I do?" Faced with the choice of telling Mary that she had done poorly or that she had done just fine and they would rent the apartment, most of her prospects rented on the spot. Those who were not convinced would articulate their reasons for not renting, and Mary would proceed to handle these objections. In this way, she eventually rented apartments to virtually all of her prospects. While this may seem overly aggressive, all Mary did was uncover objections that had not been identified or stated previously. In overcoming those objections, she removed any obstacles to a decision to rent.

In truth, many closing techniques require the leasing agent to be aggressive in seeking the sale. They demand that the leasing agent assume the prospect will rent—i.e., that there are only insignificant details that remain to be finalized. In the following example closings, the scenario is the same: The leasing agent and the prospect return to the leasing office after the apartment presentation. Shortly after they are seated—and without further discussion—the leasing agent hands the prospect the application and a pen. From this silent action vignette, the leasing agent can reinforce the closing verbally using different types of statements.

> "Will a move-in date of the twentieth be best, or is the weekend before more convenient for you?"
>
> "Theresa, would you prefer to pay the first month's rent, plus deposit, right now—or would you rather just put down the deposit?"
>
> "You've decided on the two-bedroom apartment with side-by-side bedrooms. Would you prefer to live on the second floor, or would a first-floor apartment be better for you?"

However you close the sale, there are three steps in effecting a closing. They will all be part of the closing strategy that you employ.

First, write down several closing statements, in words that are comfortable for you, then practice saying them aloud. Role-play the closing statements with someone else—another leasing agent or a friend—until you feel comfortable making them. Remember: You may have to use several statements with one prospect—perhaps as many as seven or eight—so be prepared with a number of them.

Second, your prospect may signal readiness to buy during the apartment presentation. If the prospect says, for example, "Can I get Seamist green carpeting in this type of two-bedroom apartment? I really like that color," you will have to resist the temptation to continue your presentation until it is finished; instead, you should proceed directly to the close. You might say, "I can get Seamist carpet for you. Would you like to move in this weekend?" Remember: Buying signals can occur seemingly spontaneously—at any time during your presentation. You will want to decide which summary closing statement will work best when that situation arises.

The third and final step in closing is to incorporate foreshadowing statements—the "if, then" aspect of a closing—into your apartment presentation. For example, after completing the first act of the leasing drama (the interview prelude to the showing), you might say, "Maggie, if we can find a one-bedroom apartment on the first floor with a terrific view of the lake, are you prepared to sign a lease today?" If you are comfortable with such a conditional closing statement—i.e., an acknowledgment up front that you have to fully satisfy the requirements your prospect has told you are most important—then your sales presentation will focus on those requirements. Once you have fulfilled the stated requirements, you can simply hand the application to your prospect.

A Practical Example— The Retailing Comparison

We have found that personal selling is absolutely essential when leasing apartments in upscale properties and when there are large numbers of vacancies, as during initial lease-up (or in a soft market). However, the traditional leasing techniques we have already described are not always effective in these circumstances. Because prospects can be selective based on considerations other than immediate need and the limits of what is available, they can choose their housing based on what they do *not* want. This calls for a different strategy altogether.

We were also aware that personal selling is a cornerstone of successful retailing. The components of a retail sale are attention, interest, desire, and action—all on the part of the customer. To complete a sale, the salesperson must approach the customer, determine his or her needs, present specific merchandise, answer the customer's objections, and close the sale, perhaps suggesting additional merchandise to complement what the customer has already selected. These steps may not seem all that different from what we have already described in this chapter, but we think the retailing perspective has implications for significantly improving apartment leasing success.

To demonstrate the application of a retailing-oriented strategy, we will use the example of a particular retail sale—the purchase of a blue suit. The description of the transaction will allow us to point out similarities and dif-

Basic "Selling" Techniques

The "step theory" of selling requires the salesperson to gain the customer's attention, arouse his or her interest, stimulate a desire to own the product, and complete the transaction. The sales transaction begins the moment the customer walks in the door, and personal contact should be initiated as soon after that as possible.

Approaches to the customer vary. One is to use a simple welcoming greeting such as "good morning." A service-oriented approach might be initiated with, "How may I help you?" These two approaches are usable in any context. A third possibility is to focus on the product—in a store, the customer may have picked up an item of merchandise, and that action can be used to initiate contact. In apartment leasing, all three approaches might be employed. When the leasing agent is the initiator, "Good morning. How may I help you?" is a natural opener. Discussion of particular apartments will grow out of that. However, if a prospect enters and immediately states a desire to see a particular style of apartment, the agent may initiate contact using a product-oriented approach, perhaps characterizing all of the available units—e.g., "Our available apartments all have marvelous river views."

In retailing, a customer's "needs" are determined by asking questions about what, when, how, and how much. In apartment leasing, such questions might take the form of, "How large an apartment are you looking for?" and "When do you want to move in?" A wide array of such preliminary questions may be needed to find out the specific needs of the individual prospect.

Interest in a particular item is generated when the customer is able to touch it. In apartment marketing, a particular unit (or floor plan) is shown, and the leasing agent sells it by describing how its features will benefit the prospective resident. The features-benefits assessment can only grow out of a prior determination of needs.

Inherent in the selling process is a certain resistance on the part of the buyer. Specific objections can often be converted into "reasons to buy." First, however, concerns about quality and/or price have to be separated from "excuses not to buy." To accomplish this, the agent may have to ask specific questions—e.g., "What exactly don't you like about . . . ?" or "What rent were you expecting to pay?" It may also be necessary or appropriate to reassure the prospect with factual information about quality, durability, or care requirements (e.g., "These new self-cleaning ovens are a real time-saver").

Savvy salespeople use their customers' objections as steps toward closing the sale. As each objection is met, the customer is invited to complete the sale. For example, suppose a prospect hesitatingly expressed concern that an apartment on the west side of the building would cost more to air condition. This could be met with, "We have the same apartment plan on the east side of the building, where it is cooler in the evening. If that unit is satisfactory, are you ready to sign a lease today?" Sometimes the most effective close is a straightforward request made at an opportune moment: "Shall we return to the leasing center and complete your application?"

ferences between retail selling and apartment marketing. Then, based on these comparisons, we will suggest strategies that you can use to create an effective leasing process for your apartment community.

The Concept of "Need." As we have stated earlier in this chapter, there is a certain psychology involved in buying. The purchase of any item begins with an idea—the notion of having a particular need. While this need may be utilitarian, there are elements of desire, fantasy, and status-seeking that are likely to be considered in the decision to buy. The market price of the item (affordability) is also a consideration. The shopper may act on impulse and buy additional items such as coordinated accessories. Thus, in the final analysis, the purchase may take on a larger dimension. It is these psychological aspects of buying that will form the basis for our comparison of apartment leasing and retail selling—the evaluation of the blue-suit purchase scenario.

> Assume you are in the market for a new suit. Your attention may have been caught by advertisements for blue suits in newspapers or magazines—or catalogs—or you may have seen blue suits displayed in store windows when you were shopping. Perhaps your friends or business associates have been wearing blue suits. After looking over your current wardrobe, you decide that a summer-weight blue suit is the one addition that is absolutely necessary.
>
> However you arrived at the decision, you have become a potential customer—you are predisposed to buying a blue suit. Like most people, you probably have a particular shade of blue in mind as well as a particular cut and style. If you are somewhat imaginative, you may fantasize about how you will look in the blue suit. You may decide that you will need a new shirt or blouse to wear with your new suit and, perhaps, a pair of shoes and a belt to create a complete outfit to wear to work or to a particular social function. The blue suit increases in desirability, progressing naturally from a mere idea into a feeling of need.
>
> How you go about satisfying that need will depend on your personal shopping style. You may choose to look in the local paper for stores that are advertising blue suits on sale, or you may leaf through mail-order catalogs. You want to know how much you will have to spend to fulfill your blue-suit fantasy and whether you can, indeed, "afford" to buy it. Perhaps you will telephone a friend and plan a shopping excursion. Your friend may have some ideas about where to shop and where you might find a bargain.
>
> To develop this example, we will assume that you will go shopping for your suit, either alone or with someone else. You may want to shop at a particular clothing store because a salesperson there has helped you in the past, or you may drive to a nearby shopping mall.

Regardless of any special sales, you have chosen a store that is likely to have a selection of blue suits that are in your price range and will appeal to you. (Presumably, at least for the present, you have decided against buying a cable-knit sweater or a set of soft-sided luggage or suits of other colors that are being offered at other stores—in addition to or instead of the blue suit. Unless the store does not have what you want, or they cannot convince you that what they do have in stock—a beige corduroy blazer, perhaps, or a paisley skirt—will be superior to your blue-suit fantasy, you are likely to be the proud owner of a blue suit before you leave the store.)

At this point, you have become an active consumer of blue suits. The purchase will take place unless your reaction to the store or to something the salespeople did—or failed to do—keeps it from happening. Equally important, you are likely to walk out of the store having bought not only the blue suit but also a good deal more. You probably will buy the shirt or blouse or the shoes and belt that you had earlier envisioned as necessary complements to the suit. (You were only slightly less predisposed to purchasing them than you were to buying the blue suit.) Because you are in the store and predisposed to buying, you may also pick out a smart gray skirt or a pair of slacks to go with a jacket that you had purchased previously.

However the sales transaction proceeds, it is highly unlikely that you would leave the store having spent only what you believed was the maximum amount you had available to spend for the blue suit when you drove to the mall.

Here we will stop for a moment and consider the significance of what has transpired in the retail purchase scenario and its implications for apartment marketing.

First, you established the need for a new blue suit. You had in mind what shade and style it would be, and you had some idea of how much the suit was likely to cost. For want of a better word, you had a fantasy about your new blue suit—you knew what it would look and feel like to wear it and how others would react to your appearance in it. In psychological terms, you developed a perception that your status would be improved when you wore your new blue suit. Fantasy is an important motivator in retail buying.

The same elements apply to a search for housing. The first consideration is also a characterization of need. The need for shelter is a strong one. In psychological terms, it is virtually equivalent to the need for air to breathe and food to eat. You create a need for your apartment product first by advertising and then by the interaction between the prospect and the leasing agent. Advertising is your means of gaining the renter's attention and creating interest in how your apartments will meet his or her particular need for housing.

Your prospects have a perceived need for your product for reasons that you will explore with them in great detail. As with the desire for a blue suit, some elements of this need will be positive in nature. A career woman living in a studio apartment may decide that her recent raise means she can afford a one-bedroom apartment. When a young couple learns they are about to become parents, they begin to think about having more living space. Roommates may decide they would like to have separate bedrooms. Like retail shoppers, prospective residents also fantasize about where they would like to live and the types of amenities they would like to have available. They may think about having a separate dining room and a nice set of furniture in it, or they may decide that a building with a swimming pool is their ideal. Whenever they are out for a drive, they look at apartment buildings and make notes of "For Rent" signs. If their lease is due for renewal soon, they are already scanning the want ads. They may do a great deal of looking and comparing—and fantasizing about living in a particular apartment—because they, too, want to achieve a good "fit" with a new apartment. Status and image are also components of this fantasy. So, too, is the sense of home.

Think of all of the slogans and phrases that have been devised to link home to feelings of comfort and fulfillment. Some examples are home cooking, home is where the heart is, hearth and home, home for the holidays, and there's no place like home. The last two are also song titles, and many other songs have been written that capitalize on the warm, fuzzy sensations that the concept of "home" awakens: "The Green, Green Grass of Home," "Take Me Home, Country Roads," and "I'll be Home for Christmas" are just a few.

In contrast to these positive images and feelings are the often dominant reasons for seeking different housing. When people perceive that their housing is somehow inadequate to meet their needs—e.g., too small, too noisy, too dirty—or when their social situations change radically because of divorce, squabbles between roommates, or similar situations, the result is a feeling of profound discomfort. Whatever made their previous housing situation comfortable, safe, and enjoyable has evaporated and been replaced by an emotion that is best characterized as anxiety. They no longer have the sense of security in their home. They no longer have a sanctuary.

The threat of the loss of sanctuary—and its accompanying anxiety—are feelings that people seek to avoid. A person who is homeless experiences a feeling of intense need to make that sense of loss go away. Often the search for replacement housing is itself anxiety-provoking. Apartment hunting is not most people's idea of a good way to spend leisure time. Anyone who chooses to spend time looking for an apartment is doing it because he or she needs one. It is precisely because apartment-hunting is both necessary to existence and potentially unpleasant that people are inclined to spend as little time as possible on the process and welcome the assistance of anyone who will take an active role in reestablishing their sense of sanctuary.

Prospects are likely consumers of apartments because they do not look for housing until they have an immediate need for it. Whether your prospects are seeking to fulfill a lifestyle fantasy or to overcome a current housing situation that is deficient in some way, this need has overcome whatever unpleasantness they may attribute to the search for housing and literally driven them to your door. By whatever means they have arrived, your prospects are active, potential consumers of your apartment product. It is your job to match their needs and preferences with what you have to offer. Only if you cannot meet their needs is there a good reason for them to leave without having signed a lease.

Issues of Value. As noted in the blue-suit scenario, active consumers who need to purchase a product, or who are motivated to do so, tend to purchase more of that product or a different type of that product than they had planned. If they consider that product to be inherently valuable—or if it can be demonstrated to be more valuable than the product they had originally planned to purchase—they may spend more than they had intended.

The implications of these ideas about consumer spending are also extremely significant in apartment marketing and should not be ignored. When prospects walk through the front door of your apartment community, they are not just window-shopping. They are active, potential customers who are predisposed to renting apartments and should do so if you strategize the sales process correctly. In addition, prospects often underestimate what they can afford to pay for rent. While many people will make extreme financial sacrifices for desirable extras to be included in a new house—because they perceive a long-term benefit in homeownership—such sacrifices are not all that common when people are renting apartments. However, there are people who do not want to own their own homes and are willing—and able—to afford higher rents for special features and amenities. If you show them an apartment that fulfills their fantasy—i.e., offers a spectacular view or a separate dining room, a fireplace, or some other feature they consider particularly desirable—they may be quite willing to accept a higher rent even though they had thought it was out of their reach. A predisposition to rent and a lifestyle fantasy are strong motivators of prospective residents.

These days, the act of purchasing food, clothing, and many other items is largely one of selecting a prepackaged item from a shelf or rack and paying for it. Such "self-service" is common in all kinds of retail stores. Shoppers can be "just looking" regardless of whether or not they buy anything, and salespeople may be sought out only if a customer needs assistance in finding a particular item or if something that is on display cannot be sold. The store of the future may even permit customers to check out their own purchases. The technology for this already exists (bar codes on products, magnetic strips on credit cards, etc.).

However, self-service can never prevail in apartment leasing. The fact that prospects must be shown a particular apartment is a primary reason for this—the prospect cannot see an apartment without being taken to it. Also, many of the benefits to the renter are not immediately apparent. For example, in-unit laundry equipment might be enclosed in a closet; the swimming pool might be at the other end of the building. Besides, a property with good security is generally *not* accessible to nonresidents.

The notion that prospective residents are "just looking" is a hard one to accept—even if that is their explanation for the visit. (We believe that property owners and real estate managers are justifiably skeptical when this notation appears on a traffic log as a reason for not renting.) Your prospects have gone through a selection process prior to driving into your parking lot—it is no accident that they are there. Perhaps they have seen your ads in the newspaper or heard them on the radio. They may have discussed their needs with a friend or relative who is one of your residents. They may have consulted with an apartment-referral agent who described your apartment community and recommended it to them. *Most importantly, they have chosen you.* At least for the moment, they have ruled-out the building down the block, the one across town, and all of the other housing alternatives that might be available—e.g., single-family homes, townhouses, condominiums, etc. Even if a prospect only saw your property while driving by and stopped in to ask about availability of apartments, he or she is responding to a need. As with the purchase of the blue suit, the sale should take place unless something beyond your control happens.

The Importance of Service. The service component of apartment leasing is grounded in an understanding of the difference between "selling" and "helping people to buy." Selling is perceived as manipulative. This implies that an inferior product is being foisted on a gullible consumer. Helping people to buy is the exact opposite. It requires the leasing agent to (1) determine the prospect's needs and (2) try to match those needs with available apartment product. Only if a match is achieved will a rental result. Having captured the prospect's attention and attracted him or her to the property, your immediate objective is to hold this person's interest while you sort through the inventory of available apartments together.

Those apartment marketers who focus on what their prospects want and need, help them find it, and assure their satisfaction after the sale will have a definite competitive advantage. Another look at the blue-suit scenario will reinforce the distinction we are trying to make.

> The retail sales transaction begins when the customer walks in the door. In a well-run store, a salesperson approaches and greets the customer, saying, "What can we do for you today?" or, "How may I help you?" Those are the words, but the connotation is, "Why are you here?" or, "How do I begin to sort through the inventory in my store so that I can provide for your needs and make you feel satisfied with your purchase?" Whatever the greeting, its effect is to permit

the salesperson to begin to filter-out product, to focus on the subject of the sale that he or she is confident is about to happen. The implicit assumption is that the shopper has come to that specific store for a reason. The salesperson will do what is required to learn what that reason is and match it to one or more items in the store.

After learning that you want a blue suit, the salesperson will pique your interest by gently guiding you to racks of suits. Thus begins the process of finding out about size and cut, color preference, and price sensitivity. The salesperson will assist you in fulfilling your fantasy of owning a blue suit by selecting blue suits from a rack. You participate by trying them on until you find the one that you had in mind all along, the one that fulfills your fantasy of blue-suit ownership.

The greeting, "How may I help you?" is also a way of getting down to business in apartment marketing. It should convey that the prospect has come for a very specific reason—to find housing—and that the leasing agent (the "I" in the greeting) has housing available in various shapes and sizes at an assortment of prices. It should imply understanding that the prospect may be feeling some discomfort about finding a place to live and probably wants to make the correct selection right away. It should also suggest confidence that the agent's available inventory includes appropriate housing to meet the prospect's needs. All you need is a place to start. The prospect's response to your greeting will tell you where.

It is at this point that selling apartments differs from selling clothing because you cannot take apartments from a rack and ask prospective residents to try them on. Prospects have to see apartments in person in order to determine whether they fit. In this context, fit means not only that the prospect's furniture, clothing, pots and pans, and all the rest of his or her "stuff" can be accommodated by the apartment, but also that the place feels like home. You cannot explore that in the sales office. However, before the two of you examine actual apartments, you will do the next best thing—begin to sort through your inventory by showing the prospect floor plans that you think may fulfill the prospect's needs as the two of you have defined them in completing the guest card. (The guest card was discussed in detail earlier in this chapter.)

In helping people to lease apartments, the floor plan is an absolutely vital tool. Floor plans perform three major functions.

1. They are a means of detecting price sensitivity.
2. They permit display and comparison of available options—and prospects' reactions to them.
3. These comparisons allow the leasing agent to determine the prospect's needs—before an apartment is actually shown.

All three are aspects of the psychology of buying.

Buyers are often reluctant to let sellers know that they cannot afford to buy the product. It may be mostly a matter of pride, but this should not be disregarded. The subject of price is so important to the sale that it is worth consideration at the point in the sales process when it first arises. Prospective renters may have no idea what apartments cost when they walk through the front door of an apartment community, or they may want a more expensive apartment than they can afford. Because there are no price tags on your apartments, the only way prospects can find out what they cost is for you to tell them. This can be handled painlessly—and delicately—at the beginning of the sales process. As you show the prospect various floor plans, you can write down the rental amounts on the ones in which they show interest.

For example, suppose you have available three different styles of two-bedroom apartments. (From the guest card interview, you have determined that the prospect needs a two-bedroom unit.) One floor plan offers 900 square feet of living space and rents for $720 per month; a second has 1,000 square feet and rents for $750, and the third and largest floor plan has 1,200 square feet and rents for $925. As you show the prospect floor plans for the three types, point out the advantages of each style and write the rental rate on the floor plan as you conclude your remarks. You can then ask, "Which one of these apartments shall we look at first?" A prospect who is price-sensitive will probably ask to be shown the least expensive apartment. Knowing in advance that price is important to a prospect will guide you in showing apartments within a narrow range of rents. This will save you going through the entire sales process before discovering a cost objection that could easily have been detected at the outset—and thus avoided.

In addition, your prospects probably believe that you, the leasing agent, are the apartment-renting expert. If you show prospects only one apartment—usually there is only one model—they may assume that you have only one unit type available and that it has to be rented as is (i.e., fully furnished). If the model does not appeal, a prospect may decide to look elsewhere. Prospects who are shown floor plans for all of the styles you have available will soon realize that they have a choice, and they will be in a better position to select the one they want to see first. This initial determination of preference involves prospects directly in the sales process. That is a technique that should permeate your entire presentation. By letting you present an array of apartment types to prospects so that they can make choices up front, floor plans are also important time-saving devices.

Finally, floor plans can help you convey to prospects that you are genuinely interested in meeting their needs. By painstakingly describing the various features of the available unit types, comparing them with one another, and asking prospects whether they find particular features desirable, you begin to raise their "buying temperature" and create a bond with them. Floor plans allow you to get better acquainted with your prospects by discovering their preferences—their likes and dislikes. Your purpose is to separate out for your prospects' consideration those apartments or apartment types that are most likely to meet their needs. Your ultimate goal is to get as close as possible to *the one best apartment* for your prospect. Unlike a retail store, where you can take items down from a shelf and show them until your customers find the ones they like, apartment leasing requires you to travel to one apartment after another until you eventually locate the one that is just right. Floor plans are crucial in determining where to start looking.

While the examination of floor plans is an opportunity to determine price sensitivity, it is not the only one. As we noted in chapter 4, inclusion of the rent in your print ads serves as a preliminary qualifying technique. Usually, people will not seek an apartment they know for fact they cannot afford. If your display advertising has included rents, it is usually not expensive to have the ad enlarged and mounted. It can then be displayed in or near your rental center as a point of information for prospects who were not drawn to the property by the advertising itself—i.e., those attracted by signage, word of mouth, etc. (Many restaurants similarly save customers potential embarrassment by showing prices on menus in display cases at their front entrances.)

Issues of Desirability. The prospect's interest in renting has been increased as different floor plans were shown. By now, the inventory-sorting process has identified one or more specific apartments to be shown. Properly done, the demonstration of the apartments and the benefits of living in your apartment community will stimulate the desire to live there.

When the leasing agent and the prospect leave the rental center, it will be to travel to the first apartment that the agent will show the prospect. If the apartment is some distance away, they may travel to it in the rental agent's personal car or, perhaps, in a golf cart. More likely, however, they will walk to the apartment, chatting amiably as they stroll along. This time should be used to learn more about the particular prospect, to find out additional "hot buttons" that were not revealed during the completion of the guest card.

Typically, this involves an exploration of the prospect's preferences for leisure-time activities as well as other information that might be helpful in the sales process. For example, the leasing agent might discover that the prospect is a former swimming champion who loves to spend free time in an outdoor pool. Undoubtedly they will linger in the pool area en route to the apartment showing. Alternatively, the agent may find out that the prospect enjoys playing cards or bowling or some other recreational activity. The agent may know of other residents who have similar interests or a formal recreation program in the area that might be appropriate to mention to the prospect. Perhaps the prospect works at the same nearby company as a number of current residents, and that could present the possibility of carpooling and informal get-togethers.

What the leasing agent is trying to do is identify linkages between the prospect and the property. Such linkages are made-to-order sales opportunities: They have the inherent potential to make the apartment community feel like home for this prospective resident. If prospects learn during the sales presentation that other residents of the apartment community have similar interests or comparable occupations, or if there are attractive recreational activities on site, then there is the potential of forging a bond between the prospective resident and your community. A corollary to this point is that if such a linkage does not exist, an attempt to establish one not only wastes the valuable time of both prospect and leasing agent, but also creates the likelihood that the showing of the property will deteriorate into a tour.

The Nature of "Objections." Demonstration of the product is intended to increase the customer's desire sufficiently to complete the sale. Questions raised by the customer or indications of opposition to something about the item or to the item itself are the substance of "objections." The customer's objections must be overcome before the sale can take place. Successful salespeople actively encourage customers' objections and use them to move the transaction forward.

Objections are by definition negatives. Most people are not used to or comfortable with trying to elicit negative responses. As we noted earlier in this chapter, it is only human to seek out affirmations from others. The desire for approval and the need to be liked are so strong that if others provide appropriate indicators of approval or acceptance, they are believed. People in the sales milieu have been taught that the more yes answers they hear from their customers, and the more positive examples of body language they elicit, the closer they are to making a sale.

Salespeople's longing for yeses is reinforced by their customers' behavior—affirmative responses to questions about the appearance, quality, and price of goods and appreciative nods when they are asked whether a product is to their liking. In this situation, the consumer continues to say yes until he or she departs the store—empty-handed. Until and unless the "cycle of yeses" is interrupted, either by the salesperson or by the customer, the purchase transaction is not likely to occur.

In studying a number of retail salespeople, we have concluded that the most effective ones are those who assertively seek to assist their prospective customers. They smash through the cycle of yeses to discover the flaws in each successive piece of inventory they show in order to satisfy the customer in the product they show next. They consummate a sale only after all of the customer's objections have evaporated, and they close the deal in no more than two short sentences.

At this point, we can return to the blue-suit scenario to illustrate the closing of the sale.

You have entered the clothing store with a fantasy about purchasing a blue suit. You know what the suit itself will look and feel like and how you will look when you wear it, and you have some idea about what it will cost. If these expectations are met—i.e., if your fantasy is fulfilled—you will most likely buy the suit.

The sales process will be stimulated *if* you accept assistance from a salesperson, and *if* you become actively involved in helping him or her sift through the available inventory. This requires that you articulate specific reasons for your displeasure with each suit that you see or try on. You will be more likely to purchase the blue suit that you have in mind if you let your salesperson know, item-by-item, how the blue suits shown to you do *not* fulfill your fantasy.

Having moved among the clothing racks in the store, you are now standing in front of a three-way mirror. You and the salesperson have selected a number of blue suits in your size, and you are presented one for inspection.

The salesperson asks, "How do you like it?"

You answer, "The fabric's too heavy. I really want a summer suit."

You are handed a lighter-weight suit. "How about this one?"

"Well, I like the material," you reply, "but I prefer the single-breasted style."

The salesperson picks out another blue suit, and another, and still another, each one meeting your most recent objection. The suits you appraise and try on are all summer-weight and single-breasted. You consider a variety of pinstripes and chalk stripes; you look at lighter and darker shades of blue. By a process of elimination, you end up with a blue suit that satisfies all of your requirements and fulfills your fantasy.

By breaking through the "cycle of yeses," the clerk has made the sale inevitable. What happens next is simple—the salesperson closes the sale: "Will that be cash or check? Or will you be using your credit card?" There are no fancy closing techniques because none are needed.

Similarly, the showing of apartments is the heart of the leasing process. It is at this stage that the prospect is transformed into a resident. Thus far, the leasing agent has collaborated with the prospect in a determination of needs, and as a result, a certain amount of the available apartment inventory in the community has been *excluded* as likely targets for the lease that will follow. The leasing agent has focused on one particular apartment as the most suitable candidate to be shown to the prospect, and the two of them have traveled to the apartment. During the trip, they have isolated physical features and social factors of the apartment community that are especially attractive to the prospect. In short, they have found some linkages that are forerunners of the sale.

When they arrive at the door of the target apartment, the leasing agent opens the door and either precedes or follows the prospect into the unit. The

EXHIBIT 6.2
Beware the Hidden Negatives in the Cycle of Yeses

Example I—The Carpeting is Wrong
Agent: "Don't you just *love* this carpet? This tobacco-brown color just came on the market!"
Prospect: "It's very nice."
What the prospect really thinks: "My furniture is mauve and peach; it would look terrible in here. If this is what they're selling, I'd better get this over with as soon as possible!"

Example I—A Better Approach
Agent: "How do you like the color and quality of this carpet? How would it go with your furniture?"
Prospect: "My couch, loveseat, and all the rest of my living room furniture are mauve and peach. Do you have a more neutral color?"
Agent: "Sure. I have the same apartment layout—the two-bedroom townhouse-style that you prefer—down the hall. It has new carpet in a color they call sandstone. Shall we look at that one?"
Prospect thinks: "This person is interested in my satisfaction. I think this might be the right place for me."

---

agent's first statement upon entering should be intended to convey to the prospect the most memorable and desirable feature of the apartment. In other words, his or her voice should provide an exclamation point at the end of the sentence. If at all possible, the exclamation should address a particular "hot button" for the prospect. In any case, it should be the most emphatic statement that is made during the entire sales presentation. The following are some examples.

> "Just look at that *marvelous* view of downtown!"
> "Can you *believe* the size of this living room?"
> "Have you ever seen such an *enormous* kitchen?"

The idea of entering an apartment and making an exclamatory statement is to counteract the all-too-common tendency among leasing agents to simply identify the obvious: "This is our two-bedroom model." or, even worse, "Here's apartment 203." By contrast, that first statement should be *un*forgettable—the singular impression which the prospect will excitedly convey to family and friends after signing the lease. You want to build upon the prospect's growing excitement by expressing enthusiasm.

From this point on, the leasing agent's task is simply to show apartments to the prospect and elicit objections to each one until all of the prospect's concerns have been eliminated, and there is nothing left but to sign the lease.

The Fallacy of the "Cycle of Yeses." We believe that the "cycle of yeses" has the potential to obstruct virtually every commercial transaction, including apartment leasing. Leasing agents are no less susceptible than any

EXHIBIT 6.2 *(continued)*

Beware the Hidden Negatives in the Cycle of Yeses

Example II—The Location is Wrong
Agent: "Your apartment looks down over the outdoor pool. It's really beautiful in the summertime!"
Prospect: "That's great!"
What the prospect really thinks: "I'll bet it's really noisy in the afternoons and evenings. How am I going to get work done at home if there's going to be all this racket? This place isn't going to be right for me at all."

Example II—A Better Approach
Agent: "Is there anything that you *don't like* about this apartment?"
Prospect: "Well, I like the layout, but I really would prefer not to be so close to the swimming pool. You see, I work sometimes during the day, and I think it might be too noisy here."
Agent: "I'm glad you told me that. Sometimes it *does* get a bit loud when the kids are out of school. I didn't know that you might want an apartment you could also use as an office. Let's walk over to the east side of the building. We have a one-bedroom apartment there that has a huge den with a view of the skyline."
Prospect thinks: "This person really cares about helping me find the right apartment. I'll bet the management in this building feels the same way."

---

other salespeople to the need for validation—i.e., having their prospects approve of the product they show them. As a matter of fact, leasing agents are generally taught to be proud of their properties, to represent them positively in the market, and to respond to their prospects' objections by making constructive comments. Much of this training is beneficial, but we believe that some of it is mistaken and impedes deals. By emphasizing features of the apartment that the leasing agent believes are their positive characteristics, he or she may unconsciously stimulate a *negative* reaction in the prospect. Moreover, the manner in which a feature has been emphasized can make it difficult for the prospect to say what he or she really thinks. (*Exhibit 6.2* provides two examples of this.) Because both buyers and sellers want others to like them, they are more apt to camouflage their reactions when telling the truth might threaten another person's ego.

The lesson should be clear: Uncovering objections to product is the key to sales success. You can find out those objections only by asking your prospects what they are. Then, having shattered the cycle of yeses, you continue to show apartments until all of the objections are overcome.

CHAPTER

7

Enhance the Leasing Activities

The prospect's decision to live in your apartment community may be the climax of your marketing and leasing efforts, but it is not the conclusion of the leasing process. There are numerous details that must be wrapped up before the prospect becomes a resident—i.e., actually signs a lease—and moves into an apartment.

Rent affordability is one such detail that is addressed very early in the leasing process. In determining which apartments to show, the leasing agent should have already discovered whether the rental rates at the property are affordable for its prospects. As noted in earlier chapters, inclusion of rent information in advertisements is a means of prequalifying prospects (most people will not consider apartments that are beyond their reach), as is a discussion of apartment layouts and attendant rents during the initial interview. In fact, a prospect's initial call may include an inquiry about the rent (e.g., "Do you have any two-bedroom apartments renting at $500–$550?"). While a stated range may be below your starting rents, a response from the leasing agent that puts your rates into perspective can facilitate an agreement to proceed with a showing. Ideally, a prospect will be shown those apartments that are affordable for him or her.

Once a prospect decides to rent at your property, the next step is to determine that he or she is qualified to lease the chosen apartment. This means that the applicant will meet minimum standards of financial responsibility, employment, stability, and other criteria that you establish for a particular rental property. It is prudent for the real estate manager to establish such qualification standards in writing and require that they be applied uniformly to all applicants. (Equal treatment is mandated under fair housing laws, as noted later in this chapter, and practices that can be interpreted as discriminatory must be avoided.)

In addition to qualification of prospects, this chapter will also discuss security deposits, the contents of the lease document, and renewal leases. While not obviously part of apartment marketing, these are nevertheless important aspects of leasing, especially because of their legal implications. The chapter concludes with another look at some marketing tools available to leasing agents and their applications to market research.

Qualifying Prospects

Prospect qualification involves two issues—the prospect's ability to pay the rent and his or her prior performance as a renter. Both of these issues pertain to *risk*. The owner, as landlord, is entitled to the assurance that a prospect has both adequate financial resources and a track record as a responsible resident.

The real estate manager's duty to the property owner is to maximize net operating income. This is accomplished by renting apartments to people who can afford to pay the rents specified in the leases and by ascertaining that they will abide by the rules and regulations that are in place at the property. Failure to make sure that a prospective resident will perform under the lease will defeat the owner's objectives. As a consequence, rent may be paid late (if at all); the new resident's behavior may antagonize others; and there may arise potential for litigation. These consequences can be minimized, but only if the manager establishes a tenant screening procedure that is rigorously applied to every prospective resident.

Resident qualifying is so important that some people in the apartment industry think it should be an integral part of the sales process—i.e., that prospects should be prequalified when they telephone to inquire about apartment availability. Their leasing personnel are instructed to interrogate prospects about their income and employment history and to ask for personal and professional references that can be checked—all of this during prospects' initial telephone calls, before they are shown an apartment.

Our approach is just the opposite. We believe prospects occasionally ask questions that may indicate our rents are beyond their means, but we also believe that a leasing agent's suspicions about a prospect's financial resources should never be used as justification for not showing that person an apartment. Prospects often attempt to camouflage their ability to pay—they may ask pointed questions about rental rates, or their appearance or manner of dress may suggest a low level of income when the opposite is actually true. We further contend that allowing or encouraging leasing personnel to prequalify prospects leads to a reduction in productivity as well as to screening that is unrelated to a prospect's financial means. Leasing agents who prequalify prospects tend to treat their apartment communities as if they are exclusive social clubs into which only a select few can be admitted. Their decisions are likely to be based solely on a prospect's appearance, and that can be disastrous. This is demonstrated in the following example.

> A major high-end apartment community in our metropolitan area had failed after a prolonged period of lease-up. A new management company was hired, and the property began to prosper almost immediately—it achieved nearly 95 percent occupancy within a few months. We asked the manager about the reasons behind her startling success. "Did you drop the rents?" "Did you start offering leasing concessions?" "What about other concessions?"
>
> She chuckled. "I didn't do any of that. I discovered that the leasing staff were making decisions about prospects when they walked through the door. If prospects weren't wearing designer clothes, or if they didn't drive expensive cars, their applications were denied. Sometimes the staff simply refused to show apartments to people they thought wouldn't qualify. I told them to stop making snap judgments, and I reviewed the applications myself.
>
> "You know," she continued, "people around here don't like to show off. Blue jeans, T-shirts, and sandals reflect personal tastes and, very often, have nothing to do with people's incomes. I solved the problem just by using common sense!"

A screening process that is based on personal preferences of staff members almost certainly will destroy the leasing effort. Worse, still, it can lead to discrimination against "protected classes" of individuals—a practice that is illegal as well as unethical. (Fair housing issues are discussed later in this chapter.)

The Application Form. Prospective apartment residents should be qualified by verifying specific financial and other data that are provided on a standardized rental application form. To be most useful, a rental application form should require identification of the space to be rented, the rental rate, the term of the lease, and the amount of the security deposit and any fees to be paid. It should call for such personal information as the name, driver's license, and social security number of every adult who will be responsible for the lease—plus the names of all other occupants including minor children. If pets are allowed, the application may require a description of the animal including type or breed, size, age, etc. (Many properties that permit pets establish a separate policy regarding them, with additional specific requirements that must be met.)

Information about applicants' current and prior residences is typically requested, including their address and phone number and the name and phone number of the landlord, how long they lived at that location, how much rent they paid, and their reasons for leaving.

Also critical are applicants' employment data—company name, address, and telephone number of current and prior employers, plus job titles, names of immediate supervisors, duration of employment, and salary levels. Other sources of income such as disability benefit programs, governmental allotments, etc., should also be identified. The names and account numbers for institutions where the applicants have checking and savings accounts, automobile loans, and credit cards are important sources of credit information. Automobile ownership and licensing information is often included as well. Most application forms also require one or more personal references and the name of someone to contact in case of an emergency. It is a good idea to include a statement of authenticity—i.e., that the applicant has provided true and accurate information and grants the landlord permission to verify it—and places for signatures of at least two persons.

Exhibit 7.1 is an example of a form that we use. Note that it lists an application processing fee and calls for unmarried applicants to complete separate forms. These types of requirements are among those that local (municipal, county) jurisdictions often regulate in housing ordinances. State and/or local landlord-tenant laws will also affect the contents of an application form and of a lease. The example form also indicates how payment of fees and deposits was made. Personal checks will likely be the most common form of payment. Checks are negotiable, replaceable, and convenient. Only money orders and cashier's checks are better—they represent guaranteed cash. However, their having to be purchased separately (for a fee) makes them inconvenient. Cash, on the other hand, is legal tender in the United States. It also poses several problems—large amounts of cash create a risk of theft and require frequent (daily or more often) trips to the bank to make deposits. Yet, refusal to accept cash may void the right of collection. Apartment managers should establish policies and procedures for collecting deposits, application fees, and rents and for handling the various negotiable entities (cash, checks, money orders). In this context, it is proper to state a preference for payment by check or money order.

Resident Selection Standards. While prequalification of residents is an unsound practice, selectivity is indispensable. It is crucial to the success of your apartment community that you establish minimum standards to be met in a tenant selection process—documented in writing—and that all prospects are measured against these standards before their applications are approved. Standards for resident selection should include at least the following.

1. A minimum age requirement so that the applicant can legally sign the lease.
2. A ratio of rent to household income.
3. A minimum period of employment with a current employer.

EXHIBIT 7.1
Example Apartment Rental Application

RENTAL APPLICATION FORM

Apartment Community _____ Date _____
Street Address _____ Apartment No. _____
City/State/Zip Code _____ Date of Move-In _____
Rent $ _____ Deposit $ _____ Paid _____ Cash _____ Check # _____
Application Processing Fee $ _____ Paid _____ Cash _____ Check # _____
(Fee is non-refundable.)

Insert "N/A" for non-applicable items. Unmarried applicants please complete separate applications.

APPLICANT (Please print clearly.)	Date of Birth	Driver's License No.	Social Security No.	Dependents
Applicant #1 (Complete Legal Name)				
Applicant #2 (Complete Legal Name)			**DO NOT WRITE BELOW** To Be Checked By Leasing Agent	
Present Address		Apt #	How Long?	
City	State	Zip Code	Home Phone	
Present Landlord		Rent Paid	Phone	
Previous Address		Apt #	How Long?	
Previous Landlord		Rent Paid	Phone	

SOURCE OF INCOME (Employment If Employed)

For Applicant #1	Salary	Position	Phone	
Address		Supervisor's Name	How Long?	
Previous Employer			Phone	
Address		Reason for Leaving	How Long?	
For Applicant #2	Salary	Position	Phone	
Address		Supervisor's Name	How Long?	

Enhance the Leasing Activities 181

ADDITIONAL SOURCES OF INCOME (Part Time Job, Assistance, etc.)

Source	Amount	Phone

BANK ACCOUNT (Indicate Branch and Services Used)

Name	Account No.	Phone	— Savings
Address		Zip	— Checking
			— Loan

AUTO(S)

Make	Year	License Plate #	Model & Color
Monthly Auto Payment $		Paid to Whom (Even if paid in full)	
Make	Year	License Plate #	Model & Color
Monthly Auto Payment $		Paid to Whom (Even if paid in full)	

REFERENCES   **PETS** — No — Yes   Kind

Name of Father and/or Mother (Applicant #1)		Phone
Address	City State	Zip
Name of Father and/or Mother (Applicant #2)		Phone
Address	City State	Zip
Personal Reference (No Relatives Please)		Phone
Address	City State	Zip

IN CASE OF EMERGENCY PLEASE CONTACT

		Phone
Address	City State	Zip

EXHIBIT 7.1 (continued)

CREDIT REFERENCES (Be Specific)

Account Name	Address	Account #
Account Name	Address	Account #
Account Name	Address	Account #

List All Occupants (Names)	Relationship	Age

The foregoing information is supplied to the management to induce them to rent to (me/us) and is true and correct in all respects. (I/We) authorize whatever credit investigation may be considered appropriate. Such investigation may include the exchange of information and a report from a credit-reporting agency. If a credit-reporting agency furnishes a report, its name and address will be furnished upon (my/our) request.

_____   _____
Signature (Applicant #1)   Signature (Applicant #2)

This form is provided as an example only. Requirements for collection and disposition of security deposits, handling of a credit check, and applicants' signatures and authorization may vary. Guidance of appropriate professional counsel is advised to assure that a rental application conforms to state and local laws.

4. Satisfactory references from one or more prior landlords regarding payment of rent and behavior as a resident.
5. Satisfactory references regarding creditworthiness (from financial institutions, credit card companies, etc.)
6. An appropriate ratio of occupants to apartment size.

Residents must have attained the age of majority before they can sign a lease. (Depending on state law, the age of majority may be 18, 19, or 21.) This is because a lease is a contract—a legal document—and only adults can be bound by such a contract. (Sometimes minors may be exempted from this limitation in regard to signing a lease because housing is a necessity; real estate managers can accommodate an exceptional situation by having a parent or guardian sign the lease as guarantor for an underage prospect.)

A criterion relating rent and household income will assure the applicant's ability to meet the obligation of regular rental payments. The proportion may vary, but when there is such a policy, it is often stated that the monthly household income for residents must be at least four times the amount of the rent.

A reasonable period of employment is a measure of stability and financial security. Often the requirement is that each resident must have been employed by the same employer for at least twelve months during the past two years. This time span will accommodate recent job changes or relocations. If an applicant has been with his or her current employer for less than six months, it is likely that he or she worked at least a year for a prior employer. The exception to this might be a young adult who is new to the work force or a prospect whose primary employment is seasonal (e.g., construction).

Typically, residents are required to have satisfactory reports of rental payment and behavior from two previous landlords. Checking with the current landlord and the one immediately before that should verify that the applicant always paid the rent promptly and behaved responsibly as a resident. (Those who have not previously been renters should have a record of on-time mortgage payments.) It is especially important to contact both of these landlords. The current one may comment favorably to encourage your acceptance of an applicant who has posed problems at the property, while the previous landlord no longer has to deal with that person and is therefore likely to comment more frankly.

It is also important to verify other specific credit references. This will indicate what and how much additional debt the prospect is carrying. If at all possible, each credit source should be contacted. Some people pay their credit card charges in full each month while others allow a substantial balance to be carried forward. Many individuals are paying off loans for one or more automobiles. Credit bureaus, while helpful, cannot always provide a complete picture—state and local laws may limit the information you can obtain from credit bureaus, and their records may not be absolutely up to date. What you really want to know is whether the applicant is creditworthy.

The absence of a credit record may indicate that someone always pays cash, but that does not preclude a poor credit record. Large outstanding credit card balances (as opposed to credit limits granted by the issuer) and other debt amounts can impinge on a resident's ability to pay rent.

Real estate managers sometimes set limits on the number of persons permitted to live in an apartment, usually based on the number of bedrooms. Such a criterion is aimed at assuring a quality lifestyle for their residents (i.e., levels of privacy and comfort) as well as preventing excessive wear and tear on the property. Various real estate associations have from time to time suggested guidelines. However, local jurisdictions may set maximum occupancy limitations which may be higher than those preferred by the property owner. With this in mind, you may set a minimum standard that no more than one person will be allowed to live in a studio apartment, no more than two persons may occupy a one-bedroom unit, and no more than four persons may live in a two- or three-bedroom apartment. Note, however, that limitations on occupancy by children may be affected by federal or state law. It is therefore wise to check with an attorney before establishing specific occupancy limitations.

Such *minimum standards* guarantee that applicants selected to become residents will be financially responsible—i.e., that they can meet their obligations under the lease and are willing to do so—and that they will behave responsibly in caring for their apartments and interacting with others who live in the building. Employing a selection program has several benefits.

- It assures that you will be admitting people into your community who can afford to pay the rent you are charging.
- People whose applications are approved will be creditworthy.
- Your residents will be reliable and stable.

Such a clientele will insure the continued growth and permanence of your apartment community.

Compliance with Fair Housing Laws. A variety of federal laws, state statutes, and local ordinances prohibit discrimination against certain "protected classes" in multifamily housing. Discrimination on the basis of race, color, sex, religion, or national origin or because of physical or mental handicap or familial status (children under age 18 living with parents or legal guardians, pregnant women, or people seeking custody of children under age 18) is expressly forbidden. Under state statutes or local ordinances, protected classes may include other groups such as people who are unmarried, people who are receiving public assistance, or those who have certain lifestyle or sexual preferences. Protection is also extended to persons who associate with members of protected classes—i.e., roommates. *To assure compliance with fair housing laws, the real estate manager should draft specific* *policies, have them reviewed and approved by legal counsel, and train leasing personnel to apply them uniformly to all applicants.*

It is important to establish and adhere to a policy of nondiscrimination in advertising apartments for rent, showing specific units, qualifying applicants, and selecting residents. Violations of fair housing laws can result in civil lawsuits, with the possibility of punitive damages having to be paid. These can even involve administrative proceedings in which the government acts as both investigator and prosecutor. Violations of fair housing laws can be expensive. Claimants may be awarded actual damages, damages for pain and suffering, punitive damages, attorneys' fees and court costs, and civil penalties. Several of these categories may result in the awarding of multiple damages, and claimants may seek injunctions prohibiting future discriminatory conduct. Subsequent violation of the injunction may subject a landlord to higher damages and even criminal liability.

A discrimination lawsuit is probably the most serious and complex legal situation a landlord can face. Consequently, it is imperative to hire an attorney to defend you against such claims. (It is wise to seek the advice of an attorney whenever a legal issue arises in the multifamily apartment business.) Discrimination lawsuits are frequently instituted against landlords, and they often involve claims of discrimination based on the actions of a property owner's agents—i.e., the real estate manager and the leasing staff. It is important to note that claims of discrimination may be made regardless of whether a rental application was completed or the fact that no lease was ever signed. Such claims may be made by people whom you have never met, and they may arise because of the conduct of virtually any employee on the property. For this reason, it is important for you and all of your employees to understand the scope of fair housing requirements and, even more importantly, to avoid any type of conduct that may result in such claims. While there are some exemptions under these laws, the exemptions generally pertain to the renting of rooms in an owner's single-family home under particular circumstances. It is best to assume that fair housing laws apply in every situation and to avoid discrimination in apartment marketing and renting by following both the letter and the spirit of the law.

It should be evident from the preceding that violation of fair housing laws can have severe consequences. What should you do to avoid claims of discrimination? First, be certain that practices and attitudes throughout your company are nondiscriminatory. Remember: Nondiscrimination in housing—both initially and at renewal—encompasses marketing and advertising programs, apartment-showing and screening procedures, and acceptance and subsequent treatment of protected classes as residents.

You can begin by scrutinizing the content of your advertising campaign. Words have implications, and some specific words can create problems. For example, it is illegal to use the words "adults only" or "seniors welcome" in your advertising unless the property complies with very stringent statutory requirements including the availability of certain specific amenities for the elderly such as congregate dining. Apartment properties generally must be available to prospects regardless of their age. In this circumstance, you may be faced with complaints from elderly residents who were promised when they moved in that the apartment community would be occupied by seniors only. (Senior citizens making housing choices often are influenced by the fact that children will not be allowed except, perhaps, as short-term visitors.) Leasing personnel who made such promises may have been acting in good faith and in accordance with then-existing law. However, the Fair Housing Amendments Act of 1988 severely restricted housing intended for seniors only. Those who object to living in an apartment community that admits children have to be made aware that landlords are legally precluded from offering a child-free environment.

However you decide to market your property, whether it is undergoing lease-up or merely seeking residents to fill turnover vacancies, you must satisfy affirmative marketing regulations. What this means is that prospective residents who can be identified as members of any protected class—by race, color, religion, sex, national origin, or any other characteristic on the basis of which discrimination is prohibited by a federal, state, or local fair housing law—cannot be subjected to discrimination in rental housing. Note that these protected groups are referred to as minorities even though their absolute numbers in a particular community may be greater than those of so-called majorities.

There are two types of discrimination—different treatment and different impact. The first may arise when members of protected classes are treated differently than others who are not members of that class—e.g., charged a higher security deposit or a higher rental rate. The second results when prospects are treated equally, but the impact of the treatment is different because of the prospect's minority status, as when physically handicapped persons do not have the same access as those who are not handicapped. (The Fair Housing Amendments Act of 1988 spells out requirements for accommodating residents who are handicapped. Compliance with the Americans with Disabilities Act requires modification of public accommodations for access by handicapped individuals, and this law may apply to the "common areas" of a residential property.)

It is imperative that you guarantee that there are no discriminatory practices in the operations at your property. You can test yourself, your employees, and your procedures by asking questions such as these.

- Am I treating this applicant any differently because he or she is a member of a minority group?
- Am I acting in any way that will potentially exclude as residents a higher number of minorities?

- Does what I am doing have a valid, nondiscriminatory business purpose? Even if it does, is there any other way of accomplishing this business purpose that would have less impact on a protected class?
- Are there any instructions from an owner or other person in authority, whether written or not, that make it explicit or understood that apartments should be unavailable for rental to minorities or that showing an apartment to a member of a protected class should be avoided?
- Do I or any of my employees falsely tell prospects that an apartment is unavailable? Is it conceivable that this misrepresentation is based on a prospect's minority status?
- Do I or any of my employees delay, hinder, avoid, obstruct, or in any way discourage renting an apartment because of an applicant's minority status?

A more general test, because it has wider implications, is this: Are all prospects shown all available apartments they are qualified to rent?

Fair housing law also addresses advertising specifically. In advertising the availability of apartments, it is unlawful to do any of the following:

1. Make, print, or publish, or cause to be made, printed, or published, any notice, statement, or advertisement concerning the rental of housing that indicates (a) any preference, limitation, or discrimination because of minority status or (b) any intention to make such preference, limitation, or discrimination.
2. Use words, phrases, sentences, or visual aids that have a discriminatory effect in any such notice, statement, or advertisement.
3. Selectively use, place, or design any such notice, statement, or advertisement with the effect of discriminatorily limiting or enhancing its appeal.

Furthermore, the law sets out those actions that are required for compliance with the law and those that are forbidden because they are discriminatory.

Remember: Discriminatory marketing practices are unlawful. You cannot refuse or fail to (1) show an apartment, (2) provide information about it, or (3) rent an apartment after a bona fide offer has been made to negotiate for the apartment because of the prospect's protected status. Further, you cannot discriminate (1) in the terms, conditions, or privileges of the rental of an apartment or (2) in providing services or facilities in connection with an apartment rental because of the resident's minority status.

Whether you are developing policies and procedures for marketing a new apartment community or revising an established marketing and leasing program, it is a good idea to have the components of your marketing program reviewed from time to time by an attorney who can advise you regarding compliance with fair housing laws. Given the current propensity for initiating lawsuits, it is preferable to have a policy of accepting applications from all prospects who wish to make them and hiring a third party (e.g., a credit bureau) to evaluate whether an applicant is qualified to lease the particular apartment. This can avert potential lawsuits based on violation of fair housing law because the screening process is largely shifted to a third party which assumes liability for the accuracy of the information.

Security Deposits. It is standard practice in residential leasing to require payment of a security deposit to guarantee the resident's performance of the lease. The purpose of the deposit is to provide funds to defray the cost of extensive cleaning and repairs when the resident moves out. Because most apartments are occupied literally around the clock, they are subject to more wear and tear than other types of properties, and that is understood. The deposit is intended to pay for repairing such things as holes in wallboard, breaks or other damage to wood doorframes, repairs to appliances, etc.— work that exceeds the ordinary repairs needed to restore the unit to the landlord's move-in standard. The resident is expected to have cleaned the unit thoroughly and generally to have returned the apartment to the condition it was in when he or she moved into it, ordinary wear and tear excepted. Such things as kitchen and bathroom cleaning not done by the departing resident are examples of charges that are properly debited from a security deposit.

The security deposit may be collected in part or in full at the time the rental application is signed. Any amount not paid would be due at the time the lease is signed or when the first month's rent is collected (in any event, before the resident moves in). If the applicant does not qualify or a lease does not result for any other reason, any security deposit monies usually must be returned to the applicant. (This deposit should be separate from any fee for processing the application or conducting the credit check; "application fees" are usually nonrefundable. Retention of part or all of a "security deposit" when a resident does not move in may be permissible under certain circumstances. Legal counsel should clarify when and whether such is possible and advise on policies and practices in this regard.)

The amount of the security deposit is often set equivalent to one month's rent although other amounts are used. The argument favoring a full month's rent is that if the resident skips out before the lease term ends, at least the landlord has a final month's rent. Such a policy demands that a renewal lease include provision for collecting additional security deposit funds to maintain the rent equivalency when the rent is raised. On the other hand, a security deposit *not* equal to one month's rent tends to discourage a departing resident from trying to use it as the last month's rent under the lease.

In general, it is a good idea to have a policy requiring a security deposit and to establish an amount that will permit recovery of extraordinary repair and cleaning expenses. Factors to consider are the property itself and the caliber of your residents. A more substantial deposit is necessary and appropriate where there is a history of residents skipping out on a lease or where damage to apartments is frequent and extensive. In such situations, *the same security deposit requirement must apply to all rental applicants.* (Higher security deposits must not be used as a subterfuge for discriminating against protected classes.) Checking with the prior landlord as part of the qualification of prospective residents is intended to assure that they are not likely to cause extensive damage or skip out.

Apartment owners and managers must be aware that state and local laws may regulate security deposits. Apart from any limitations on the amount of the deposit and how long it can be held after a resident moves out, there may be requirements for the landlord to pay the resident interest on the deposit for the period it is held. Regardless of such requirements, it is imperative that you maintain accurate and complete records of security deposit collections, account for deductions from the deposit when it is returned, and assure that the funds are kept separate from operating funds so that they are available for disposition. (The best practice is to hold them in an escrow account, preferably interest-bearing.)

Security deposits can become part of your apartment marketing strategy. When every other competing property in the market is charging a full month's rent, setting security deposits at a lesser amount can be a marketing and leasing advantage. Also, a schedule for prorated return of the security deposit amount can be used as a lease renewal strategy (as discussed later in this chapter). Such a program is an expression of confidence in your residents and appreciation for their continued occupancy. It also puts cash back into the resident's pocket well *before* move-out, which will make the later cash outlay to lease a new apartment—i.e., rent plus security deposit—an even greater burden and thus a disincentive to moving. (Ordinarily, return of the deposit from a prior lease cancels most of the amount of the security deposit on the subsequent apartment.)

Documenting the Residential Lease

The contractual agreement between landlord and apartment tenant is a residential lease. It provides the resident the right to occupy a private dwelling in exchange for regular payment of rent to the landlord. A properly prepared written lease will protect the interests of both parties. (The specific contents of a lease are beyond the scope of this book. Advice of legal counsel should be sought regarding particulars to assure compliance with applicable state and local laws and fair housing requirements.) To dispel negative connotations, a residential lease is sometimes called an *occupancy agreement.* Whatever it is called, the document should be signed and legally binding on both parties.

To be legally binding, a lease must include certain provisions. It must name the parties to the agreement, describe the leased premises (apartment unit and address), and state the amount of rent and when it is due as well as any security deposit amounts to be paid up front. (NOTE: In some locales, *rent control laws* may set upper limits on rental rates.) All leases have a specified term or duration. Most residential leases are for one year only although actual practice varies from one market to another. The beginning and ending dates of the term as well as its length should be spelled out. If late fees or other charges can apply, these should be specified. Also, residents are usually prohibited from subleasing their premises to others without express written permission of the landlord. If residents are expected to abide by certain house rules and regulations, this is also typically indicated in the lease although the exact rules and regulations may not be spelled out. (These are subject to change, and it is often advisable to provide this information to the resident separately.)

Rules and regulations address such things as limitations on parking by residents and visitors, limitations on occupancy by visitors, and limitations on particular furnishings (e.g., waterbeds, pianos, or especially heavy items). Prompt payment of rent and any late charges are usually reiterated along with the purpose of the security deposit and conditions for its return. Use of the common amenities (e.g., laundry room, party room, recreational facilities) may be governed by specific rules. Fundamental upkeep and maintenance of the leased premises are often spelled out (residents may be required to replace lightbulbs, batteries in smoke detectors, etc.), as well as policies regarding move-in and move-out inspections and charges against the security deposit for cleaning and repairs.

Issues of residents' safety and self-protection in both apartment units and the common areas of the community are commonly addressed in rules and regulations. These may also specify unacceptable behaviors and requirements to control noise and other disturbances, especially during the late evening and overnight hours. A separate document provided at move-in is a good place to list emergency phone numbers for reaching the apartment manager and others, as well as spell out what steps residents should take in emergency situations (e.g., whom to call and types of information needed in fire, police, or weather emergencies).

In addition to the terms and conditions required to be documented in a lease agreement, a statement of condition of the premises, a pet clause, and responsibility for utilities are common inclusions. Other lease clauses typically address the duties and responsibilities of the landlord to the tenant and the rights and obligations of the tenant to the landlord, what constitutes default of the lease (by landlord and tenant) and the consequences of default, and provision for access to the leased premises by the landlord in case of an emergency and to make periodic inspections and effect repairs. Also, landlords today typically recommend that residents insure their belongings because the owner's insurance coverage on the building does not cover tenants' personal property.

The condition of the apartment should be established during a move-in inspection conducted by the landlord's representative (usually the apartment manager) in the presence of the new resident. A special inspection form may be used—ideally, it will be the basis for comparison to the condition of the apartment when the resident moves out so that charges for any excessive damage to the premises can be determined. The lease itself may simply state that the resident is expected to restore the premises to move-in condition when he or she vacates the apartment.

Pets are often a cause for concern in apartment leasing. The wisest position is to adopt a specific policy regarding pets and their activities on the property. These should be spelled out in a document provided to the residents. If pets are permitted, it is customary to require a separate pet deposit to cover repair of damage to the apartment by the animal. The specifics of your pet policy should reflect local ordinances regarding requirements for vaccinations and licenses as well as any laws regarding leashes and preventing a public nuisance. Handling of pet wastes should also be addressed.

It is common for residents to arrange and pay for their own utilities—e.g., electricity, cooking gas, and telephone services. Cable television may also be addressed in the context of utilities. If the resident is to provide heat for the apartment, that specific requirement should be spelled out in a separate lease clause. (Local ordinances may require that prospects be made aware of potential costs of heating and air conditioning their leased premises.)

Most importantly, whether you purchase preprinted leases that are approved by the municipality for use in your locale or create an original document, be sure the form you choose to use is reviewed and approved by legal counsel. Apart from addressing specific issues as required by local residential occupancy ordinances and state landlord-tenant laws, it is important to be certain that the lease is in compliance with all applicable fair housing laws—federal, state, and local. (NOTE: The Fair Housing Amendments Act of 1988 addresses occupancy by children and accommodation for physical handicaps.)

Lease forms should be prepared in duplicate with places for both lessor (landlord) and lessee (tenant) to sign and date them. Usually both copies are presented to the prospective resident for initial signing; they are then countersigned by the landlord (the property owner or the owner's authorized agent—e.g., the real estate manager), and one copy is returned to the resident.

Renewal Strategies

Many apartment managers announce renewals by sending completely new leases to their residents sixty to ninety days before their current ones expire. The new lease is usually identical with the current one except for the duration of the term and the rent amount—plus any amount to be added to the security deposit, if required. New rents are almost always higher. The actual amount depends on expected increases in operating expenses for the apartment community and may be limited by rent control laws. (Because rental income is used to pay for management services and staff salaries, utilities and maintenance of the property as a whole, real estate taxes, and debt service—among other expenses—rate increases must be factored into future rents to assure profitability.) In situations where the security deposit is equivalent to one month's rent, the resident is usually required to make up the difference in the deposit amount when a new lease at a higher rent is signed. As with the original lease, the renewal lease should be issued in duplicate.

Because the content of a standard lease form usually does not change from year to year, some apartment managers prefer to issue a lease renewal agreement that becomes an endorsement or addendum to the original lease. This short form states the extension of the lease term, the new rental amount, and the effective dates and may include specific additions or changes to the terms and conditions of the original lease. It should be prepared in duplicate and include places for landlord and resident signatures and dates.

Unless a resident has already signaled plans to move out at the end of the lease term, thoughts about moving are often deferred until a renewal lease is received. Because the amount of the rental increase may be a major factor in a decision to move, it is a good idea to send along a cover letter expressing the landlord's desire to continue the tenancy and explaining the increase in the rent. (Knowing that specific expense escalations necessitated the rent increase may make the higher rent of the renewal offer more acceptable.)

This is the point at which the resident's previously unexpressed dissatisfaction with the service received in exchange for his or her monthly rent may surface. Coupled with a large rental increase, general dissatisfaction with service may trigger a decision to move. Prior to lease renewal is thus an opportune time to survey residents with a questionnaire and follow up on specifics. This will avert a precipitate decision to move out and may help the apartment manager maintain and improve the services provided to residents.

In a soft market or when special inducements are being offered to *new residents,* consideration should be given to rewarding the current resident you want to retain. Such rewards are best indicated up front as an expression of appreciation for their continued long-term occupancy instead of being presented as an inducement to renew the lease. Minimally, prompt attention to any service issues identified in the resident survey mentioned earlier would be an aspect of the reward process.

Because apartment properties lose value with time and use, it is a good idea to have a program of planned improvements to individual units, especially when vacant units are being upgraded to entice new residents. The value of the award should be predicated on tenure, with those of greater value being given to longer-term residents. Thus, a resident renewing a lease might be offered some item of decorating (new wallpaper, a paint job) or an appliance upgrade or replacement. Not only does this say "thank you" and encourage the resident to stay, but it improves the individual unit and adds to the value of the property as a whole. These rewards to your best customers—your established residents—will be perceived as even more valuable if they are given at a different time altogether (rather than in conjunction with the renewal process).

Another option to consider is stepwise reduction of the security deposit with successive years' lease renewals or outright return after the first few years. This sends a message that the ownership and management trust the established resident and value his or her tenancy. It also reduces the impact of a rent increase. Note, too, that when interest must be paid to residents for security deposit funds held, the interest rate may be set by law, and often the payments must be made annually rather than when the deposit is refunded. In times when interest-bearing financial instruments are paying rates lower than the rate of interest ownership is required to pay to tenants, security deposit interest payments can be a hardship. The return of security deposits can reduce ownership's financial liability.

Caution: Early refund of a security deposit may be considered for residents who are consistently fulfilling their lease obligations—i.e., on-time payment of rent and appropriate care and upkeep of the leased premises (verified by inspection). Such a reward should *not* be considered if repeated late payments or other behaviors signal nonperformance. Also, extended terms of occupancy tend to increase the overall wear and tear on apartments, especially if maintenance inside them is deferred or not done at all. Part of the rationale for the security deposit is to defray the cost of any extraordinary repairs needed to restore the unit to rentability. To safeguard the protections afforded to the owner via the security deposit and to avert potential legal problems, advice of legal counsel should be sought before making such a change in your security deposit policies or practices.

Adjunct Issues

In the typical leasing office, there are usually a variety of printed materials that can be used to help the leasing agent acquire a signed lease. One that is particularly useful is the leasing brochure. The various forms used to collect prospect information are also resources for evaluating the current marketing effort and for planning future campaigns. Even if no lease resulted, guest cards and application forms qualify as marketing resources. They can be used to develop mailing lists and for follow-up of nonrenters.

Brochures. Leasing brochures may range from photocopied "flyers" to elaborate four-color booklets. Typically, they describe the types of apartments available (perhaps showing representative floor plans), the array of features and amenities in individual apartments and on the property, the lifestyle new residents can have there, and benefits they can derive from the surrounding neighborhood and the community at large (e.g., schools, shopping, churches, recreational facilities, transportation access, etc.), as well as whom to contact for rental information (company name and telephone number).

Whether you prepare something utilitarian or glossy, be sure to include the kinds of information that prospective renters in your market want. Also, design the piece so that it ties in with the image you want your property to project—i.e., the positioning statement for your advertising campaign or a unified graphics theme (as mentioned in an earlier chapter). Note that if rental rates are included, they should not be specific, otherwise the brochure will be outdated very quickly. (It is better to state, "one-bedroom apartments *from* the mid-$500s," than to say, "one-bedroom, $528.50.")

Because you will not be there when the prospect digs out the brochure to refresh his or her memory or to share with friends, it is imperative that your leasing brochure not leave a negative impression. Brochures should not be printed on cheap paper; print quality should be high, and information should be accurate. Something as small as a misspelled word can cancel the good intent of a brochure.

Brochures can be used in many ways. If one of your marketing strategies is to promote your apartments via direct mail, a brochure might be one of the components of a mailer package. Appropriately designed, a brochure can be a mailer by itself. Inclusion of floor plans in the brochure makes it a useful adjunct during prospect interviews, when the discussion of space requirements turns to particular layouts and rental rates.

Some leasing personnel use brochures as a way of escaping from a prospect—i.e., to avoid closing the sale. They will say, "Here's our brochure. Call me if you have any questions." As a result, the initiative is left to the prospect. We think it is better to hand prospects the leasing brochure after closing the sale—it can be viewed as a "receipt" for the rental application. In this way, it will serve as a reminder of the prospect's visit to your property and provide something the prospect can show proudly to friends and family after having rented an apartment: "Look where I'm going to live."

Despite your best efforts, not all prospects will become residents on the first visit to your apartment community. Some prospects may find it necessary to think about their rental decision and, possibly, to seek validation from friends and relatives before they make up their minds. For them, the leasing brochure will be a reminder of the information shared with them during the showing and a means of comparing the benefits of your apartment community with others they visit.

The point to remember is that brochures are just one of your leasing tools. They do not rent apartments—leasing agents do.

Marketing Resources. Information collected on *guest cards* can be useful market data even if the interviews do not result in showings or leases (see exhibit 6.1). In order to create and monitor your marketing campaign, it is essential to know certain things about your market area—e.g., where your prospects work, where they live now, some of their personal characteristics (age, gender, marital status, household size, income, and profession), and what stimulated their visit to your property (newspaper advertising, signage, etc.). Guest cards make these types of information accessible.

The prospect's current address is an indicator of the geographic reach of your market—you may want to concentrate your advertising in publications in that area if you do not do so already. The day of the week and the time of day when a prospect visited can help you establish adequate office coverage during peak traffic times.

Similarly, the apartment *rental application form* (see exhibit 7.1) has uses beyond qualifying prospective residents. Apart from providing information that will qualify applicants to become residents, your collection of application forms will ultimately become a storehouse of demographic data on your own residents and a resource for future marketing research.

Follow-Up of Nonrenters. Some prospects may choose not to sign a lease even though they qualified for it. Personal situations can change drastically in a very short time. Loss of a job, a broken engagement, and a death in the family are only a few examples of life-changing events that could preclude signing a lease. Some prospects may not even complete an application—they may not have liked any of the apartments they were shown, or they just may not be ready to make that kind of commitment. Regardless of the circumstances, not all prospective residents will be "sold" an apartment, and this eventuality must be considered at the beginning of the marketing effort.

The "golden rule" can be paraphrased to apply to leasing: Treat your prospects as you would want to be treated. In practical terms, this means you should practice some basic courtesies. Your relationship with an unsold prospect need not end with a door closing behind him or her. The nonrenter can be viewed as a temporarily unfinished sales opportunity. In chapter 3, we recommended use of a telephone survey as a form of market research on why prospects did not rent at your property. A simple "thank you"—whether as a phone call or a personal note—can generate immeasurable goodwill. Treating your nonrenters kindly is likely to lead them to say: "I didn't find an apartment at The Laurels, but they were so nice to me, I would like to live there someday."

CHAPTER

8

Market to Current Residents

Customer service was already recognized as a challenge more than 3,000 years ago. As noted in a papyrus found in the tomb of Tutankhamen (circa 1400 B.C.), "Good service is not hard to give; it is merely hard to get." Today, anyone browsing in a bookstore will find an impressive array of contemporary books on service, among them *Managing to Keep the Customer: How to Achieve and Maintain Superior Customer Service throughout the Organization* and *Customers for Life: How to Turn That One-Time Buyer into a Lifetime Customer*. There are literally dozens of such titles.

Characteristically, their tables of contents list numerous techniques for delivering quality service to customers, and they all predict dire consequences if the reader fails to follow the tips provided therein. The most popular books not only prescribe techniques for providing service, but also recommend procedures for monitoring service delivery and suggest ways to reward those who do the work.

Service and its delivery are fundamentals. In the multifamily housing industry, service is the wave of the future. Savvy real estate managers are already recognizing its importance—service can be just as important as price (and location) in motivating renting decisions. Service is the factor that determines the decision to renew.

Customer Service in the 1990s

Try to remember the last time you received what you considered to be acceptable service—say, for example, with an automobile repair. When you took your car in, was the repair handled adequately? Was the car returned when it was promised? Was the estimate accurate? Did the repair shop also wash and vacuum the car before it was returned to you? Did anyone follow up with you to find out whether you were satisfied with the repair? Most importantly, were you so satisfied with the results that you would return to that shop in the future rather than go to an equally convenient competitor? Chances are that one or more of these elements was omitted or mishandled. In fact, you may have become so accustomed to substandard service that you were surprised that some of these items can be part of a car repair shop's *routine* operations.

At one time or another, you may have received such poor service that you wanted to complain. Did you follow through on it or just let the incident pass? Have you ever felt so angry about mishandled service that you actually took the time to write a letter to someone influential to express your dissatisfaction? If you are like most consumers, you probably did not complain; more than likely you thought it would be a waste of time. If you did write, however, it is highly likely that you did not receive a satisfactory answer. In fact, you probably received no response at all, even though you might have been perfectly satisfied with a simple indication that somebody sincerely cared and would try to do better in the future.

Much aggravation in daily life is caused by frustration over poor service and the general lack of interest in improving it. (*Exhibit 8.1* shows some examples of service misdelivery.) Although most people eventually come to accept this situation as a fact of life, they are nonetheless aware that service is generally poor, and they may fervently wish that the situation were otherwise. In fact, while most consumers may fail to complain about poor service, they certainly do something about it: *They take their business somewhere else.* In *How to Win Customers and Keep Them for Life,* Michael LeBoeuf reported some findings from a study done for the White House Office of Consumer Affairs.

- A typical business receives complaints from only 4 percent of its dissatisfied customers—the other 96 percent just go elsewhere, and more than 90 percent will never return.
- A survey asking why customers quit revealed that 68 percent stopped being customers of a business because of the owner's, the manager's, or an employee's *attitude of indifference* toward them.
- Typically, a dissatisfied customer will tell 8–10 people about a problem—one in five will tell 20 people. (It takes 12 positive incidents to make up for one negative incident.)
- Among customers who do complain, 7 out of 20 (35 percent) will do business with a company again if the complaint is resolved in their favor—95 percent will return if their complaint is resolved on the spot. (Yet, a satisfied complainer will tell only 5 people, on average, about a problem resolved satisfactorily.)

EXHIBIT 8.1

Examples of Poor Service

Example #1
You return home with your dry cleaning only to find that someone else's overcoat has been included with your order. You return the coat to the shop, but the clerk is totally disinterested. In fact, you have to become fairly aggressive just to get a credit on the cleaning charge for the coat. You wonder why you are the only one who seems to care.

Example #2
You go to a major discount store looking for a stereo system that you had seen advertised in the morning newspaper. Six clerks are on duty, but only four are busy with customers—the other two are drinking coffee and chatting amiably. You approach them, but they ignore you. After waiting some ten minutes, you finally walk out. You wonder why the store bothers to advertise if customers cannot get waited on, and you decide never to go back there again.

Example #3
You are planning a weekend dinner party for several of your business associates. The garbage disposal in your apartment does not work even though you reported it to the manager a week ago and followed up on it twice since then. The manager told you that the maintenance man is on vacation and that the disposal will not be fixed until he returns. You arrange for the repair yourself and start making plans to look for another apartment next week.

A customer who received outstanding service would probably return to the same store again regardless of its pricing or convenience. It would seem possible, perhaps even probable, that really good (or even adequate) service, in an environment in which poor service is the norm, would make the recipient a lifetime customer. (*Exhibit 8.2* shows the examples in exhibit 8.1 as they might have been handled.)

We believe that the widespread failure of service delivery in contemporary society presents an extraordinary business opportunity, especially as it applies to apartment marketing. Those who understand this phenomenon know that promising service—and then actually delivering it—will absolutely distinguish their product from the competition and guarantee its success. This principle is fundamental.

The issue of service is exemplified by two trailblazers who have made their company names synonymous with service.

Trailblazers of Service. In *Total Customer Service: The Ultimate Weapon,* William H. Davidow and Bro Uttal cite Scandinavian Airlines System (SAS) and Nordstrom Department Stores as being particularly innovative with regard to customer service.

Like many other airline companies, SAS experienced a terrible year in 1981—they lost $8 million. Subsequently, the directors of SAS promoted

E X H I B I T   8.2

Examples of Better Approaches

Example #1
You return the overcoat to the dry cleaner. After you briefly explain the situation, the clerk thanks you sincerely for your thoughtfulness and asks you to accept a coupon for free dry cleaning. She excuses herself, and you overhear her telephoning the owner of the coat to arrange for a convenient time to drop it off at his home.

Example #2
You walk into the discount store. A clerk greets you at the door, welcomes you, and introduces the salesperson who will help you; you proceed with your selection. As you are leaving the store, the clerk warmly thanks you for your patronage, asks whether you are completely satisfied with the purchase, and invites you to return the following weekend for a "special sale" offered to "preferred customers."

Example #3
You see your resident manager in the hallway near your apartment. She greets you by name, asks whether there is anything she can do for you, and prepares a service request for repair of your garbage disposal. Ten minutes later, a friendly service technician knocks on your door, introduces himself to you, fixes the disposal, and explains how to prevent it from getting clogged in the future. As he is leaving, he notices a small crack in the living room ceiling and makes an appointment to fix it the next day.

Jan Carlzon (a 39-year-old marketing whiz) to the presidency, and he turned the company around. Within the next year or so, SAS posted a $71 million gross profit while the rest of the industry was losing nearly $2 billion a year. How Carlzon achieved this is crucial.

First of all, he decided to sell what the public wanted to buy. To learn what SAS customers wanted, he commissioned extensive customer research. Not surprisingly, he discovered that SAS customers expected more than mere transportation—in fact, they wanted SAS to serve an entire galaxy of travel needs. Among those "needs" were on-time departures and arrivals, greater attention to business executives (a large proportion of SAS customers), and better service at all points of contact between the airline's employees and its customers.

In Carlzon's view, these episodes of interaction between employee and customer constitute "moments of truth" during which the customer forms a lasting impression of the company and decides whether to continue to be its client. Because these moments of truth can and do occur at random, Carlzon decided to literally re-create SAS to make it totally customer-driven and service-oriented. His success in re-creating SAS is what turned the company around.

In contrast, Nordstrom is a chain of high-end retail fashion stores that originated in the Western states and has recently expanded to the Midwest and East Coast regions. Nordstrom has a long-standing reputation for and commitment to customer service. Examples of this exceptional service abound.

- The businessman who returned a pair of squeaky shoes purchased from Nordstrom a year earlier and, instead of a repair (which he expected), received a brand-new pair of shoes.
- The elderly woman who went shopping at Nordstrom for a shawl that would not get caught in the wheels of her wheelchair and the clerk who, after a fruitless search through Nordstrom's (and its competitors') stock, knitted a shawl and delivered it to the customer personally.
- The executive who ordered two suits just before leaving on a business trip and, when Nordstrom had not completed the alterations in time, was greeted upon arrival at his hotel by a Federal Express package containing the two suits and an apology letter—plus three new ties.

It is Nordstrom policy to accept returned merchandise and give an immediate refund or exchange (no questions asked and regardless of how used or worn the merchandise). As an accommodation to shut-ins and others who cannot come to their stores, Nordstrom will bring large selections of shoes and clothing to their homes. In addition, Nordstrom clerks keep extensive notes about the clothing preferences of repeat customers so they can be alerted when new goods that might please them arrive. They also send their customers a thank-you note with a personal message a few days after a sale.

As these examples demonstrate, Nordstrom employees are the superstars of service.

Service in the Apartment Industry

Most real estate managers and apartment marketers have the sources of prospect traffic at their properties literally at their fingertips. They know which of the newspaper advertisements they placed for a particular apartment community were most productive and how much all of the ads in their campaign cost. Because the numbers of telephone calls, visits to the property, and signed leases are routinely and carefully documented—along with the source of the traffic that produced each result—they can easily determine the cost of generating a single telephone call, visit, or lease at their properties. In general, property owners expect their managers to justify marketing efforts based on effectiveness, and the managers believe their jobs are dependent on delivering qualified prospects to their apartment communities. There may be other reasons as well, but whatever the rationale, the traffic log that is compiled, updated, and examined for trends is meant to be a test of the manager's ability to produce favorable occupancy percentages.

However, we believe that this tests management on the wrong subject and that passing this test may not even impact the bottom line. One of the most important lessons you should learn from this book is simply this: *Occupancy percentages are based on a combination of attracting new residents and retaining existing ones.* To the extent that current residents choose to remain where they are, apartment community owners and managers are correspondingly relieved of the expense, effort, and worry that accompany the task of securing new leases. Resident turnover batters the bottom line.

Considered solely in economic terms, part of the effort—and the budget—that is to be expended for advertising and marketing should be concentrated on retaining and cultivating your resident base. According to industry sources, attracting a new resident costs five times as much as keeping an existing one. Thus, it is essential for managers of multifamily housing to develop and implement a coherent strategy for resident retention based on service. The goal should be to continue doing business with residents who are doing business with you now. That is the strategy that worked for Jan Carlzon and SAS.

There is another lesson that can be learned from Jan Carlzon. When you are marketing a product that is fungible—i.e., generally indistinguishable from its competition—there has to be some feature of the product that makes it especially attractive to its potential customers so that it will stand out from the others. Otherwise, consumers will purchase products haphazardly, without giving much thought to the reasons for their choices. According to Karl Albrecht and Ron Zemke, in *Service America! Doing Business in the New Economy,* when Jan Carlzon became the president of SAS, he realized that it was just another airline. Unless he could make SAS unique in some way that would appeal to its customers, the company would continue to decline. What Carlzon did was change the company's focus from simply flying airplanes to serving the travel needs of its public. This is what *he* said about the change: "If we can [serve the air traveler] better than the other companies, we'll get the business. If we can't, we won't get the business, and we don't deserve to."

We believe the most effective apartment marketing strategy is to consider your product—and that of all of its competitors—as "four white walls and a rug." In other words, what you are taking to the marketplace every day is so similar to the "four white walls and a rug" offered by your competitors that there has to be something special about your apartments—something so unique and desirable that prospects will choose your community and reject all the other possibilities. Otherwise, decisions about renting and lease renewal are likely to be based solely on price or concessions or something else beyond your control.

Granted, this approach may be overly simplified. There certainly are distinguishing factors that make a particular building inherently appealing. Among them are lower rents than its competition, an indoor swimming pool compared to an exercise facility and a community room, and location closer to an attractive shopping center versus easier access to the freeway. The apartments in one building might be larger than those in another; the competition may have an attached garage while the first building does not. The differences are potentially infinite, and they are often important factors in a prospect's decision to rent. However, dispassionate analysis of a marketing grid that compares a property with its competition by attributing price differences to their various features and amenities will probably reaffirm the idea that apartments are essentially fungible. In other words, your apartment community is pretty much the same as your competitor's. Because of this, we believe that when it comes down to weighing the advantages and disadvantages of the various housing alternatives, the deciding factor will be how you serve the needs of your residents.

Motivators of Renters' Decisions. No doubt there are very specific reasons why your prospective residents have chosen to move from their current housing and why they are evaluating the possibility of renting in your apartment community. You can find out what motivates renters' decisions in your market, and your researches will likely yield interesting results. In fact, you may be more than a little impressed by the sophistication of your prospects. They are likely to be sensitive about pricing because they know about your competition, but they understand value as well. *Value* can be defined as the benefit that a customer receives from a product or service, minus the cost (money, time, effort) of purchasing it.

So many consumer goods are roughly comparable in terms of their price and quality that the distinguishing feature—the value portion of the equation—is service. Thus, the operative word in retailing for the 1990s is *service*. Service is also the single most important factor that will determine success in apartment marketing in the 1990s—and perhaps for decades to come. Your own particular environment will determine what constitutes value in rental apartments. Prospects will define it in several ways—possibly as amenities, probably as convenience, and undoubtedly as service. Taken together, these three factors will more than likely overwhelm price as the reason to rent.

If your residents believe they have received more value (apartment product plus its service component) in return for the amount of their investment (monthly rent payments), they will continue to pay their rent and will readily accept rent increases. In fact, your residents will constitute the most important—and least expensive—marketing base for your property. Furthermore, they will refer their friends, relatives, and business associates to your apartment community. All in all, they will guarantee your apartment community's success by building its occupancy levels in the short term and maintaining them over the long term.

Exhibit 8.3 illustrates what we believe motivates renters' decisions regarding move-in and move-out. While such charts are helpful, you need to find out in very specific terms:

EXHIBIT 8.3

Motivators of Renters

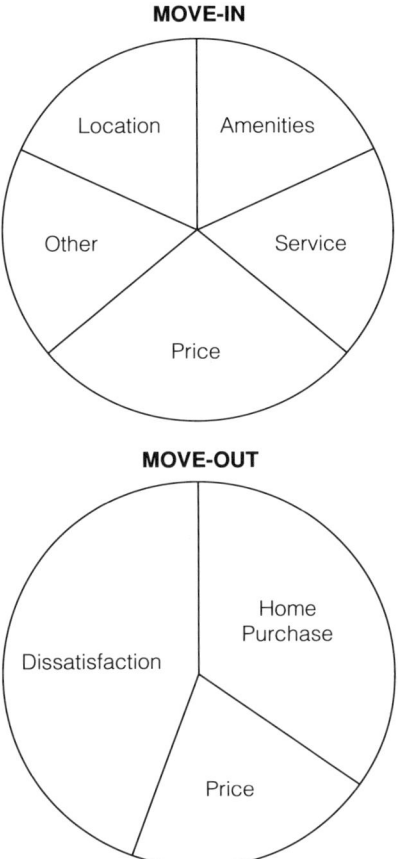

These pie charts reflect some of the factors the authors hypothesize are involved in a resident's decision to rent (or vacate) a particular apartment. The move-in diagram *(top)* indicates that location, amenities, service, price, and other ingredients (including word of mouth) combine to motivate the decision to rent, and they do so in different ways depending on the psychographic makeup of a particular resident. The move-out diagram *(bottom)* shows a home purchase, price, and dissatisfaction as motivators of the decision to leave.

It is likely that price will be a major force in the decision to rent—even more important than the potential service offered at the new location. All else being equal, price will be the strongest move-in motivator, especially in a slow economy. However, a renter's decision to move out is more likely to be related to dissatisfaction with poor service than to dissatisfaction with price. The authors' research indicates the following ratio: dissatisfaction > home purchase > price by approximately 3:2:1.

1. Why your residents choose to live in your property,
2. Why they continue to do so (i.e., renew their leases), and
3. Why they decide to move out.

We believe that the reasons residents move into or out of apartment communities—or stay where they are—are rarely obvious. As we demonstrated in an earlier chapter, real estate managers can utilize the techniques of market research to find out how they are perceived by their customers and to provide useful clues about how to improve their product. Questionnaires can be devised to determine why residents chose your apartment community, to measure residents' levels of satisfaction on an ongoing basis, and to ascertain why they moved out. Similarly, focus groups can be conducted and followed up with questionnaires to find out how your on-site management, maintenance, and housekeeping staff are performing; whether your residents are satisfied with the service they are receiving; and how you can improve your apartment community in general. (Application of market research techniques to the challenge of resident retention is discussed later in this chapter.)

Service and Profitability. Service is the key factor that will guarantee success and increase profit throughout the U.S. economy in the 1990s. Those in the apartment industry who know what service is, have a plan in place for its delivery, and then actually deliver it—day after day, for resident after resident—will prosper regardless of what happens to others in the industry. The relationship between service and profits in apartment management can be likened to a wheel rolling forward, gaining momentum with each successive resident-staff service interaction. *Exhibit 8.4* illustrates this idea.

There is also an important corollary to the service-profit relationship: If service is the way to guarantee success in the apartment business, and if you are the leader in your market in providing it, then your competition will be faced with trying to catch up with you. In effect, you will have established a reputation for delivering service, and that territory will be yours and yours alone. In this way, service will become a competitive weapon in the battle for apartment marketing and leasing success. Furthermore, because your service program will be well-established by that time—tested by your residents, fine-tuned and improved by you and your personnel, and judged by all to be unique—the competition's prospects for catching up will be very poor indeed. You will have a group of residents who could not imagine giving up the lifestyle you created for them. They will depend on you for service just as you depend on them for your success.

In a sense, renters are predisposed to becoming service-dependent simply because they choose to live in apartments. They have chosen that particular living environment at least in part because they prefer to have someone else handle the myriad tasks of single-family living, such as mowing the lawn, repairing the plumbing, washing the windows, and all the rest.

EXHIBIT 8.4

How Apartment Service Generates Management Profits

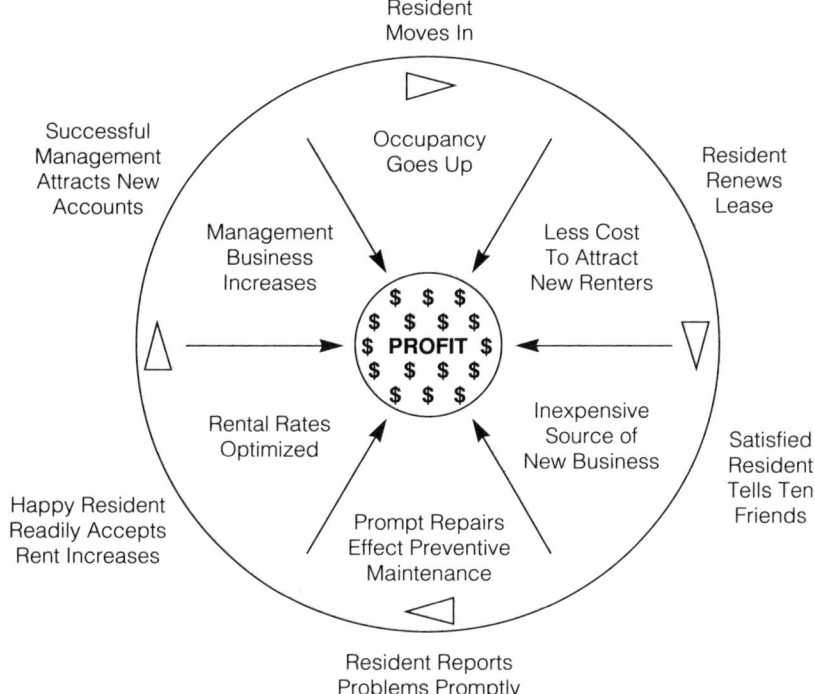

The relationship between service and management profit can be likened to a wheel. (1) When a resident moves into an apartment that delivers exceptional service value, occupancy goes up. (2) The resident renews the lease—having been treated very well, he or she would not consider moving. It takes less money and effort to maintain occupancy compared to attracting new residents. (3) The resident is very pleased with the apartment and tells an average of ten friends about it. This is an easy, inexpensive source of new business. (4) The resident realizes management is always responsive to requests for repairs—problems are reported quickly. Repairs are made before more expensive damage occurs. (5) The resident is so happy with the apartment that rent increases are accepted—rent concessions are not expected. As a result, rents are maintained at an optimum level. (6) The management company is successful—its impressive performance attracts additional management accounts for its portfolio. New business is generated. All six components increase profits. Then, as more new residents move in, the cycle repeats itself.

When they choose to rent in your apartment community, they are looking for a certain level of service. If you provide more and better service than they might expect, you will be providing extra value, and *value* is what will distinguish your product from all the others.

In truth, there are two different levels of service in the apartment business. Residents have both a baseline requirement and a service expectation. Residents buy housing with their rental dollars, and housing is one of their most fundamental needs (as we indicated in chapter 6). In exchange for their monthly payments, they expect to obtain "four white (freshly painted) walls and a (clean) rug." Included in this *baseline requirement* is the presumption that the kitchen and bathroom facilities will work—i.e., that the water will run, the refrigerator will keep food cold, the furnace will provide heat, and the ceiling fixtures will light. If the vertical blinds, in-sink garbage disposal, washer and dryer, dishwasher, and smoke detector are provided in the apartment, they are expected to perform their various functions flawlessly, too. Residents also expect that the windows will have been washed, the floors scrubbed and waxed, and all the appliances cleaned until they sparkle. Real estate managers use checklists to guarantee that the apartment will be rent-ready when residents move in. They want it to be as near to brand-new as it can possibly be made.

The only product you have to offer, and the one that your customers have a right to expect during their residency, is an apartment that *works*. However, some aspect of the apartment or the property as a whole will stop working sometime, and your residents assume that you will fix that, too. This is the resident's *service expectation*. Quite frankly, people who live in apartments expect that there will be temporary breakdowns of facilities. Garbage disposals become clogged, hallway lights burn out, folding doors slip off of their tracks. These are common occurrences and part of the reality of apartment living.

The question that arises, however, is how and how quickly does management respond to breakdowns when they occur. The answer probably depends on the nature of the problem, the time of day when it occurs, the availability of staff to handle it, and the danger it poses to the residents. Other factors are undoubtedly involved as well. Most likely the factors considered by the manager are those within his or her control. Except in an emergency, however, repairs are usually made when it is convenient for management rather than when the residents expect them to be done. The quality and timeliness of the management response are the measures of the residents' service expectations. The issue of quality concerns whether the problem was fixed or only temporarily repaired. That of timeliness concerns whether the work was done immediately or only when it could be fitted into an already crowded schedule.

In the area of service, the potential for dissatisfaction is defined by the difference between when your residents expect a response and when the response is actually made. The service expectations of your residents are also their way of defining value. Therefore, it is essential for you to know what their expectations are so that you can meet those expectations with the service-delivery systems you design and implement. You will do that successfully by managing the "moments of truth" at your apartment community better than anyone else in your market manages theirs.

"Moments of Truth" in Multifamily Housing

Earlier in this chapter, we introduced the concept of "moments of truth"—those instances of interaction between buyer and seller that influence (and may even determine) whether a customer decides to make a purchase. Moments of truth also motivate a customer to conclude that the purchase decision was a correct one so that he or she will either become a long-term client of the product (or the seller) or shop elsewhere. Such moments of truth are likely to occur randomly or unpredictably, but they have one trait in common: They are based on both the customer's opinions of the inherent quality of the product and his or her perceptions of the superiority of the service associated with it.

From the seller's perspective, the dispensation of service by his or her company might be termed "service-delivery." From the buyer's point of view, assessment of the quality of service will depend on whether he or she considers the business to be "customer-driven." While this distinction may appear to be only a matter of semantics, it has important consequences in the design of a service-delivery system for an apartment community.

In this section, we will explore some moments of truth in the apartment industry and discuss how these moments can arise and the impact they can have on your success. We believe that ignoring them may be dangerous (at the very least)—it may even turn out to be fatal. Organizations that are not fundamentally customer-oriented will be eaten alive by competitors that are. (This is really survival of the fittest. Those who do not recognize and act on their moments of truth will be left behind. The most successful enterprises are aware of this.)

The concept of service has two facets: (1) The quality of the contact between the customer and the service-provider leading up to the moment of sale and including the sales transaction and (2) the customer's assessments of the caliber of the continuing contacts that occur thereafter. In retailing, service involves isolated, productive incidents of contact between the owner of the goods (or his or her various agents) and the customer. Depending on the nature and volume of the business involved, there may be numerous episodes or only a few, but they are essentially repetitive. In the typical retail enterprise, we could say that these contacts are *discontinuous*—they are distinct, detached, and circumscribed. Consequently, they are rather easily taught, managed, and monitored because they are cookie-cutter transactions.

For example, in the milieu of airline travel, a moment of truth might be a purchase at a ticket counter, a baggage-handling episode, or a check-in encounter with an agent at the gate.

By contrast, the relationship between management employee and resident in the multifamily housing business is continuous and long-term. Some of the points of contact may be rather repetitious—e.g., the guest card phase of the leasing transaction or completion of the service request form. The lease sets out the terms of the association between the parties, which implies that there will be a series of contacts between buyer and seller that will be more or less ongoing, potentially endless, and certainly unpredictable. The continuity of these contacts is intensified by the fact that a part of these employees' compensation typically includes an apartment, which means that they literally live with the customers whom they serve. (Retailers can at least escape from even the most persistent customer by heading for home at the end of the day.)

Paradoxically, the ongoing relationship between apartment managers and their clients might be the envy of retailers who have to worry about whether their customers are satisfied enough to patronize them again. Apartment managers have the opportunity—and challenge—of pleasing their residents along a continuum of service interactions which can guarantee the residents' continued occupancy. To put it another way, because accumulated multiple beneficial moments of truth build and sustain value, apartment managers perpetually have opportunities to develop a bank of positive experiences.

Actually, there are several important differences between service in retailing and service in the housing industry. One of them is the fact that the delivery of service in the apartment business is primarily *contextual*. By this we mean that the quality of appropriate service at an apartment property depends on a variety of sometimes conflicting factors related to residents' expectations. Because of the nature of the property involved, these expectations are sometimes dissimilar. In comparing a 40-year-old three-story walkup building where apartment rents are in the $400–$500 range with a new 30-story high-rise where monthly rents are in excess of $1,500, it is obvious that the residents themselves will anticipate different types or levels of service at the two buildings. Both groups of residents will undoubtedly anticipate that their "four white walls and a rug" will work—i.e., that the various features of their apartments will function—or be fixed within a reasonable time when they need repair. However, the residents will rightly anticipate that the intensity of services will vary—they are living in different qualities of buildings, after all—and their specific expectations will remain a mystery until the managers ask direct questions about them.

What this means is that, compared to retailing, service in the apartment industry is inherently more difficult to describe, anticipate, deliver, and supervise. These tasks are profoundly complicated because, while service is what their customers increasingly consider to be the value of their rented apartments, awareness of this fact is only now becoming widespread among apartment managers.

While questionnaires (to be discussed later in this chapter) are very effective in finding out how residents define the moments of truth they experience with your personnel and your product and reporting how well these moments are being handled, there is an easier, faster, and less-expensive method of accomplishing the same goal, and that is *observation*.

One place to start looking for moments of truth is the management office of your property at the busiest time of the day. This may be when residents are leaving for work or arriving home in the evening. Perhaps they are picking up their mail or just stopping by to chat. Maybe they have a problem and have purposely come to see a member of your staff to get help. This is your opportunity to witness a moment of truth firsthand. (If you had the capability to do so, you would probably want to videotape what happens so that you could study and replay it frame-by-frame—for yourself and for the staff member involved.) The following is an example.

> Your assistant manager, busy with another resident on the telephone, greets a second resident with a snarl—instead of by name. *That is one moment of truth.* Furthermore, she fails to establish any rapport—she does *not* ask, "How are you doing this evening, Mr. Kimball? How was your day?" *That is another moment of truth.* Instead, she makes Mr. Kimball wait, his presence unacknowledged, until she has finished with the call. *Yet another moment of truth.*

The negative score mounts, minute by minute, until the manager discovers that the only attention Mr. Kimball required was the 45 seconds it would have taken to sell him a postage stamp or give him change for the washing machine or record his reservation for the community room the following week—or something equally simple. Your assistant manager has just transformed a momentary transaction into an unpleasant experience that she will probably forget immediately but Mr. Kimball will more than likely remember. He is also likely to communicate it in all of its negative impact to his wife, his dinner guests, and several other residents.

The following *positive* moments of truth were taken from tape recordings of actual interviews with residents.

> "When it was time to renew our lease, Kelly (the resident manager) asked if there was anything we wanted done to our apartment. Well, we had lived here for eight years, and the carpet was getting old. There were some places that were fraying and splitting apart. So I told her that we wanted new carpet, at least in the living room and the big bedroom. Kelly told me that she couldn't promise to replace

the carpeting, but she would have it shampooed and stitched. She did, and we signed the new lease. The carpet was better, but I was still kind of disappointed.

About three months later, right out of the blue, Kelly said that we could have new carpeting and that we could choose the color. She offered to let us use the apartment across the hall while it was being replaced. My husband is handicapped, you know, and Kelly said the maintenance technician would move the furniture.

Well, it turned out just great. They didn't have to give me the new carpeting, but they did. And because of that, I'll never move out. They'll have to take me out of here feet first!"

"I bought a new toilet seat for my bathroom. I was trying to put it in myself, but I wasn't having much luck. It was real hot that day, and I left the door open. Karen, our manager, was walking by on her way down to the office. She called out to me, and I yelled back to her to come on in.

She was all dressed up, you know. But she got right down on her hands and knees, grabbed the wrench, and just kept at it until she had it right. There was sweat dripping down her face, and her hair was a mess. I know she had to take a shower and change her clothes, and she was probably late for work. But I'll never forget how she helped me."

"My car was stolen six weeks ago from the parking lot at a nearby restaurant. The police came, and I filed a police report, but they still haven't found the car. What's worse is, I use the car to deliver newspapers in the morning and I also deliver packages during the day—my car is how I make my living.

Well, the day after it was stolen, my rent was due and I was really frantic. I called my manager, and she suggested that I call the management office to see what they could do. (She thought maybe I could pay my rent late or something.) I've lived here 12 years, and I have always paid on time. I really expected that they wouldn't help me out, but you know what they did? They applied some of my security deposit to my rent, and I made up the rest.

Don't tell me that landlords don't have a heart, or they wear black hats, or any of that. My landlord made it possible for me to pay my rent and keep a roof over my family's heads. That's really something, you know?"

The very best moments of truth are similar to these, although they may take many forms. They are satisfying for the parties involved, and they have tremendous impact over the long term. You can find moments of truth every day, as long as you pay close attention to what goes on around you. The pothole in the parking lot that your residents swerve to avoid every morning when they leave for work is a moment of truth. The service request that goes unattended (or unnoticed) for three days is a moment of truth. The smudged glass on the lobby windows and doors, the beer can tossed carelessly on the lawn, and the paint peeling off the shutters are all moments of truth.

Whenever current or prospective residents have opportunities to form impressions about how an apartment community cares for its residents, they will judge accordingly. Furthermore, their impressions do not distinguish between human action (such as the contact between the assistant manager and Mr. Kimball) and inaction (such as poor housekeeping and deferred maintenance). *They are all moments of truth.*

In a perfect world, real estate managers would try to document every potential moment of truth at the properties they manage. However, that is probably impossible or at least infeasible. Property managers and other professionals in the apartment industry simply have too many other pressing business concerns. They do not have time for what may seem to be an academic exercise. This is, unfortunately, the reality of the situation.

Fortunately, full-scale documentation is not an absolute necessity. You will serve yourself and your property well and sufficiently if you keep the concept of "moments of truth" in mind, if you are alert to such moments when you see them, and if you sensitize members of your staff to them as well.

Simply put, the notion of moments of truth is a powerful one. It is something everyone inevitably encounters as a consumer of service in a world in which service is a scarce commodity. Paradoxically, searching for positive moments of truth in everyday situations is likely to increase a manager's awareness of their absence. What is needed is a way to be innovative in managing the moments of truth at apartment properties.

First it is important to understand that moments of truth can be either passive or active. A passive moment of truth is one that is essentially inescapable, a situation inherent in the business of apartment management. On the other hand, an active moment of truth is one that is created intentionally.

Passive moments of truth are common to housekeeping, maintenance service requests, on-site marketing, and a host of other fairly routine tasks that include interactions between residents and staff. The fact that these tasks are routine does not mean that they are easy to perform, and it is the quality (and content) of these passive moments of truth that is responsible for the overall performance of an apartment community. Unfortunately, such interactions are often fumbled, or at least not handled effectively, despite the wealth of training and hands-on experience available to real estate management personnel. (People skills can be learned, but not all staff members may be provided opportunities for such training.)

That is why it is so important to create active moments of truth, intentional interactions among residents and staff that are designed to have positive outcomes. Newsletters and resident parties or other communal activities serve this purpose. Restriping the parking lot, building repairs, and other capital improvements also fall into this category. While some of these examples are rather ordinary, many of them provide opportunities for surprises. Suppose the resident manager were to cook chili and cornbread and, dressed in a chef's cap and apron, serve the residents dinner as they arrive home from work? That would be an active moment of truth. A flatbed truck loaded with beautiful evergreen trees residents can purchase for $20 apiece that arrived in the parking lot two weeks before Christmas would also be an active moment of truth. A midafternoon activity for senior citizen residents (e.g., a provocative guest speaker, a cooking demonstration, a drawing with door prizes) or a magic show on a Saturday morning for residents' children are other active moments of truth. Still another possibility is a large chalkboard installed next to the indoor swimming pool for listing the names of resident participants in a lap-swimming program (complete with their daily distance records) and a nutritious breakfast served to them at the end of their exercise program. The active moments of truth at your apartment community can be as ingenious as your imagination and your budget will allow, and they need not be all that expensive. For example, we did the chili and cornbread dinner at a 200-unit apartment community for around $1.00 per resident.

Instead of doing all the thinking yourself, you can challenge your site staff to brainstorm moments of truth they think will be especially effective. Reward the best ideas they come up with. If you manage several different communities, let their staffs compete with one another in designing winning moments. When we did this at properties we manage, participating staff members proposed a number of inexpensive active moments, and we implemented them. The following are some examples.

> *Send thank you notes.* We send out thank-you notes immediately after residents visit our management offices—even if they came by to complain. We do this to encourage the residents to contact our employees when they need help or want to improve their living situation. When we fix the problem, we cement our relationship with the resident. If we never even know that a problem exists, we have no chance to resolve it.

> *Acknowledge new and renewal leases.* We send a small plant to their home or office immediately after residents sign new leases or renew their current ones. This is done not only to express our appreciation for their choosing our property, but also to show them—and their fellow workers—just how we convey our thanks.

> *Welcome new residents.* We place a Mylar "Welcome Home" balloon on new residents' doors to greet them when they move in. This not only adds a cheery touch to their doorway, but also reinforces for

them and our existing residents the fact that they are living in a desirable apartment building.

Dinner on move-in day. We invite our new residents to select an entree from a local delicatessen or restaurant and have members of the leasing staff serve them dinner on move-in day (complete with linen tablecloth, crystal, and fine china). This provides an excellent opportunity for employees to help out with unforeseen problems and possibly relieve some of the stress of moving. (We also make it a habit to call on new residents the following day, and again 30 days after move-in, to make sure their expectations for their apartments have been fully met.)

In our experience, such active moments of truth are acts in a drama played before an appreciative audience. Usually apartment residents have never seen anything like it before.

We think the distinction between active and passive moments of truth is an important one. It highlights the fact that while some moments of truth are imposed on apartment marketers and managers simply because they are in the multifamily housing business, other moments of truth can be invented and controlled by them if they are at all imaginative. You can create your own moments of truth by providing opportunities for your residents to complain. The opportunities can be structured formally, using questionnaires, or they can be informal. Simply asking a resident, "How do you like living in your apartment?" is one way to invite complaints. If you then act on the resident's comments (i.e., resolve the complaint) with nothing more being said, the resident will surely remember and appreciate the prompt response.

Residents' comments and complaints are marketing opportunities. Like objections that must be overcome in a sales transaction, complaints may be the only clues to a resident's dissatisfaction with something in his or her apartment or the property as a whole. You cannot serve your residents well unless you know what they really want or expect. By mastering both passive and active moments of truth, apartment managers can meet their residents' baseline requirements and service expectations—and exceed them.

A Practical Example—
Market Research Applications

To demonstrate the benefits of market research in measuring service delivery and resident satisfaction, we conclude this chapter (and the book) with a few "moments of truth" from our own experience.

Market research techniques and the results obtained by using them can be vital components of a resident retention program. Focus group sessions and questionnaires document resident opinions; they also provide a basis for evaluating current service delivery and guide development of new strategies for improving it. We believe that efforts toward resident retention should be ongoing throughout the entire period of a resident's relationship with the apartment community. This means that resident retention should be considered in developing the annual budget and allocating funds for marketing and leasing activities.

As we indicated in an earlier chapter, we survey prospects who do not rent at our properties so that we can find out why they visited in the first place and why they decided to go elsewhere. Market research techniques are routinely utilized to evaluate our advertising campaigns before they are implemented. They are also used to evaluate competitors' promotions and to explore resident satisfaction in general.

Competitive Guarantees. Following the example set by properties in other parts of the United States, several apartment communities in our market area were offering a "living guarantee." Such a guarantee may take a variety of forms. The property may attract residents by advertising that they can move out (no questions asked) if they are dissatisfied for any reason. Alternatively, residents may receive one day of free rent for every day that a service problem goes uncorrected (i.e., a service request does not receive a response). It is possible that owners and managers of apartment communities will turn to such guarantees more and more as a way to demonstrate their confidence in their product and differentiate it from the competition. However, this tactic is risky on at least two grounds. In the first place, there are no parameters or limitations. If the guarantee means what it says, a disgruntled resident may attempt to enforce it regardless of whether a reasonable person would do so. Under such a guarantee, noisy neighbors, a squeaky bathroom fan motor, or some other minor annoyance could conceivably be cause for dissatisfaction, and residents might move out even though the landlord may have taken every precaution to assure their contentment.

On the other hand, prospective residents may react unfavorably to an apartment advertisement featuring the satisfaction guarantee. We tested the guarantee concept in several focus group sessions, and the following example is typical of the residents' responses.

> *Moderator:* "Suppose you read a newspaper advertisement that said something like this: 'After you move into our apartment building, if you are dissatisfied for any reason, you can move out, no questions asked.' How would you feel about it? Would you be inclined to move into that property because of the guarantee?"
>
> *Resident:* "I think that a guarantee like that would be a cop out. It would be just another way for the landlord to avoid responsibility

for fixing problems. After all, I wouldn't want to move out of my apartment just because I wasn't happy. Moving costs are outrageous! Landlords know that, too. It's basically an empty promise."

Resident Satisfaction. Another subject that is easily tested in a focus group session is resident satisfaction. In earlier discussions of market research and focus groups (see chapter 3), we recommended use of a disinterested outsider to conduct the session. In this particular application, however, the issue of self-interest is part of what you are testing. Therefore, you may find it more useful to have the property manager or building supervisor moderate the focus group. This will demonstrate to your residents that the landlord is vitally interested in their satisfaction and is aggressively involved in finding out whether they are comfortable with their living situation.

The following are some suggested questions for addressing issues of satisfaction in a focus group setting.

1. How satisfied are you with the communications you have with your management staff? Do you believe that your manager and the maintenance and housekeeping staff are doing a good job?
2. Have you ever asked for help with a repair in your apartment? How quickly did the staff respond? Were they friendly and helpful when you called? Were you satisfied with the quality of the service you received?
3. Do you believe that tenant screening is adequate in your apartment building? Are the rules and regulations enforced to your satisfaction? What about security in the building?
4. What improvements could be made that would increase your enjoyment of your apartment?
5. Do you believe that you get value in exchange for your monthly rent check? What do you consider to be "value"?

We can also provide an example from a focus group we conducted at one of the properties we manage.

Moderator: "What could the management or maintenance staff do to improve your enjoyment of your apartment?

Resident: "Well, the maintenance at my building is just outstanding. Every time I've needed the least little thing, somebody has been at my door in ten minutes or less. But you know, sometimes it's sort of embarrassing to ask for help. There are little problems that come up. A torn screen, a leaky faucet, or a closet door that comes off the track. Maybe we need some touch-up painting where we used to have a

EXHIBIT 8.5

Example Maintenance Cover Letter and Questionnaire

PERIODIC MAINTENANCE CHECK-UP

We try to provide the best possible maintenance at *[Name of Apartment Community]*. We are constantly working to improve the building itself, the common areas (such as the lobby and hallways), and the various amenities that you enjoy such as the exercise room, tennis courts and swimming pools.

Our goal is to keep all of the features of *[Name of Apartment Community]* brand-new—by providing quality maintenance we believe is *better* than that at any brand-new apartment building.

We understand that maintenance in your apartment is vitally important to you. The quality of maintenance is a major reason why you live at *[Name of Apartment Community]*, and we have tried to improve it, most recently by responding to your service requests within 20 minutes after you call them in to the office.

But we also realize that there may be maintenance problems in your apartment that you consider to be too insignificant to justify preparing a service request. These are some examples:

Drippy faucets
Torn screens
Noisy exhaust fans
Running toilets

We'd like to fix these problems for you, because they can be annoying.

Please complete the enclosed form, drop it off at the management office, and our service personnel will schedule a convenient time with you when we can do the work.

Thank you!

_____
Site Manager

---

picture hanging in the living room. Why don't you go around every six months or so and do a periodic maintenance check-up to fix these little annoyances? When I try to fix things, they just get worse!"

As we suggested previously (see chapter 3), whenever you conduct a focus group, be prepared to be surprised. You are very likely to find one or more participants who will make a remark or offer a suggestion that could change something significant about the way you do business. The preceding bit of dialog offers a prime example.

We responded to this resident's suggestion by developing a periodic maintenance checkup program. We circulate a memo to our residents describing the procedure and provide a form for listing the problems they are experiencing. Then, approximately 30 days before we send out lease renewal letters, our maintenance technician schedules an appointment with the resident. The checklist indicates the tools and equipment that are needed to complete the work, and the technician spends an average of 25 minutes doing

EXHIBIT 8.5 *(continued)*

PERIODIC MAINTENANCE CHECK-UP

Apartment Number _____
Resident's Name _____
Daytime Telephone Number _____

Maintenance Item　　If OK, check here:　　If not, please describe the problem:

Appliances:
  Refrigerator
  Stove
  Dishwasher
  Disposal
Plumbing:
  Kitchen sink
  Bathroom sink(s)
Heat/Air Conditioner:
  Thermostat
  Blower Unit
Miscellaneous:
  Doors/Locks
  Cupboards
  Closet Doors/Shelves
Windows:
  Torn Screens
Other Needs:

Date Completed: _____
Maintenance Technician: _____
　　　　　　　　　　　　　　　　(Signature)

---

the requested repairs or adjustments, most of which are minor. (*Exhibit 8.5* shows the format we used.)

This was such a terrific idea, we implemented the periodic maintenance checkup across our management portfolio, and the result has been a dramatically improved lease renewal ratio.

Written questionnaires are an especially productive means of exploring resident satisfaction. They can be used at any time during a resident's occupancy. A particularly advantageous time is several weeks before a lease renewal so that the resident's concerns can be addressed in advance. In the real world, residents move out of apartments, and a questionnaire is a good way to find out why—and whether you could have done something that would have altered their decision to move.

At Move-in. To determine whether new residents' apartments have met their expectations, a questionnaire can be administered shortly after move-in. *Exhibit 8.6* shows an example of a move-in questionnaire we developed.

EXHIBIT 8.6

Example Move-In Questionnaire

NEW RESIDENT QUESTIONNAIRE

YOUR OPINION IS IMPORTANT TO US! We want to make sure that living in your new apartment is as perfect as we can make it. Please take a few minutes to complete this questionnaire and return it in the enclosed, postage-paid envelope. **THANK YOU!**

1. The **attitude of our staff,** and how they treat you, is extremely important. Please CIRCLE the number that best describes how **friendly, prompt and respectful** they are. Please explain your answer in the COMMENTS section.

   ```
   1               2               3               4               5
   Attitude Needs Improvement                              Terrific Attitude
   ```
   COMMENTS: _____

2. We want to know how satisfied you were with the **condition of your apartment when you moved in.** Please CIRCLE the number that best describes whether it was **clean, freshly painted and in good repair.** In the COMMENTS section, tell us how we can make improvements.

   ```
   1               2               3               4               5
   Very Poor Condition                         Perfect Condition, No Complaints
   ```
   COMMENTS: _____

3. Tell us about how **comfortable you are with your apartment and your feelings about your building and grounds.** We're interested in knowing whether you have had problems with noisy neighbors (or other problems with residents/children), difficulties with the entry system, outside lighting, or other concerns about your well-being.

   ```
   1               2               3               4               5
   Serious Concerns About Well-Being           No Concerns About Well-Being
   ```
   COMMENTS: _____

4. **How responsive are we to your needs for maintenance** and other staff assistance? We'd like to know if our management and maintenance personnel respond *promptly* to your requests for work orders, if the work is completed to your satisfaction, and if our staff handle your other requests adequately.

   ```
   1               2               3               4               5
   Major Maintenance Problems                  Fast, Excellent Maintenance
   ```
   COMMENTS: _____

5. We hope that you are **proud of your apartment and your apartment community.** Are the "common areas" of the building (entryways, hall carpeting, elevators) clean and well maintained? Are the equipment and other facilities in good repair?

   ```
   1               2               3               4               5
   Poor Condition/Maintenance in Common Areas  Common Areas in Excellent Condition
   ```
   COMMENTS: _____

6. There are **"extras"** we provide that many of our residents enjoy. Have you had an opportunity to participate at resident parties or other apartment community activities? Have you read the newsletter? Please evaluate the "extras" below, and in the COMMENTS section, tell us how we could improve them.

   ```
   1               2               3               4               5
   Inadequate/Poor "Extras"                    "Extras" Just Right
   ```
   COMMENTS: _____

   Signature (Optional)

EXHIBIT 8.7

Example Resident Questionnaire

RESIDENT QUESTIONNAIRE

YOUR OPINION IS IMPORTANT TO US! We want to make sure that living in your apartment is as perfect as we can make it. Please take a few minutes to complete this questionnaire and return it in the enclosed, postage-paid envelope. WE WOULD APPRECIATE IT IF YOU WILL EXPLAIN YOUR ANSWERS ON THE BACK OF THIS SHEET. THANKS!

1. The **attitude of our staff,** and how they treat you, is extremely important. Please CIRCLE the number that best describes how **friendly, prompt and respectful** they are.

1	2	3	4	5
Attitude Needs Improvement				Terrific Attitude

2. We hope that you are **proud of the condition of your apartment and your apartment community.** Are the "common areas" of the building (entryways, hall carpeting, elevators) clean and well maintained? Are the equipment and other facilities in good repair?

1	2	3	4	5
Poor Condition/Maintenance in Common Areas				Common Areas in Excellent Condition

3. Tell us about how **comfortable you are with your apartment and your feelings about your building and grounds.** We're interested in knowing whether you have had problems with noisy neighbors (or other problems with residents/children), difficulties with the entry system, outside lighting, or other concerns about your well-being.

1	2	3	4	5
Serious Concerns About Well-Being				No Concerns About Well-Being

4. **How responsive are we to your needs for maintenance** and other staff assistance? We'd like to know if our management and maintenance personnel respond *promptly* to your requests for work orders, if the work is completed to your satisfaction, and if our staff handle your other requests adequately.

1	2	3	4	5
Major Maintenance Problems				Fast, Excellent Maintenance

5. Based upon your apartment living experience, **would you recommend us** to a friend, relative, or associate who might be considering living in an apartment?

1	2	3	4	5
Wouldn't Recommend				Would Recommend/No Hesitation

6. There are **"extras"** we provide that many of our residents enjoy. Have you had an opportunity to participate at resident parties or other apartment community activities? Have you read the newsletter? Please evaluate the "extras" below.

1	2	3	4	5
Inadequate/Poor "Extras"				"Extras" Just Right

Date: _____ Apartment Building: _____ Apartment No. _____
I HAVE MADE ADDITIONAL COMMENTS ON THE BACK OF THIS SHEET (Please check) _

Signature (Optional)

Note that the inclusion of rating scales provides numerical values which can be compiled and compared. Together with respondents' written comments, this type of questionnaire can yield a wealth of information.

Such a move-in questionnaire can also be used in conjunction with a service request form so that residents have an opportunity to indicate whether there are specific items that need improvement. Even better, introduce one of your maintenance personnel to the new resident during move-in. The maintenance worker can explain the service request procedure that is in effect in your community, attend to any problems the resident may have already identified, and leave behind a questionnaire to be completed at the new resident's convenience. This personal touch will establish a positive relationship between new residents and your staff.

During Residency. Residents' ongoing satisfaction with their apartments can be explored in a focus group session (such as the one we already described). However, a simple questionnaire can also be used. The questionnaire method allows you to collect information over a period of time and gather more data for your evaluations. *Exhibit 8.7* shows an example of a resident questionnaire we have used. Note that the questions and the rating scales are identical with those in exhibit 8.6. The principal difference is that respondents are asked to explain their answers on the back of the questionnaire. Here again, numerical ratings allow for realistic comparisons, and respondents' specific comments guide our approach to a response so that we do the right thing. Their comments may also suggest modifications to our service strategies.

After Move-out. The owners of a group of six suburban apartment properties were perplexed by excessive move-outs at their properties. The move-out numbers for part of one year exceeded by more than 100 the numbers for the corresponding period in the previous year—a period when move-outs had reached an all-time high. Rents had been raised slightly but no more than previously, and the same personnel had been in place at the site throughout the past two years (at least in key positions). The owners asked us a simple question: What was wrong at these properties?

There were, of course, a number of ways to find answers to this question. We could have telephoned some former residents and asked for their opinions, and we could have met with the management and maintenance staffs and asked what they thought. However, the situation appeared to be so unexpected and so serious that we believed a comprehensive survey was needed to obtain a response from virtually every resident who had moved out within the last six months or who was planning to do so within the next sixty days. When we added up the figures, we found that we were dealing with the residents of more than 300 apartments. It was obvious that we could not speak with each of them individually and that sampling only some of them might yield misleading results. The need for immediate information from such a large number of respondents required the use of a written instrument.

We devised a simple, two-page questionnaire which, together with a cover letter and a postage-paid return envelope, was sent to the residents and former residents on lists provided by the owners. The questionnaire was specifically designed to uncover every negative feature these current and former residents could identify as having influenced their decision to move. *Exhibit 8.8* shows the questionnaire. (It is similar to the ones retailers use to measure customer satisfaction—especially satisfaction with service.)

When you prepare a questionnaire, remember that the instrument itself should be short and have a substantial amount of white space. This is to minimize the impression that the questionnaire is overwhelming and that it might require too much time to complete. The length of a questionnaire (i.e., the number of answers required) poses a similar problem whether it is administered by mail, in person, or over the telephone—respondents generally need assurance that their participation will require only a limited amount of time. Also, provision of a postage-paid return envelope reinforces for them your desire for a response and your intent to minimize the inconvenience to the respondent (both cost and time). The questions themselves should be stated to maximize the information obtained in reply. The content and intent of the questions in exhibit 8.8 is as follows.

- *Question 1* was designed to determine whether the respondent moved to another apartment community or a single-family home. The answers would also reveal which local apartment buildings were particularly competitive and whether price was a significant factor in determining the respondent's housing choice.
- *Question 2* was designed to elicit as many different responses as possible. Being open-ended, it conveys the idea that the respondent should think through all possible—and subjective—reasons for his or her opinion or an action taken and then list the one that is most important. As might be expected, the answers to an open-ended question are likely to be extremely varied and therefore difficult to categorize, but they tend to be illuminating.
- *Question 3,* by contrast, suggests the most apparent likely responses; it was designed to explore move-out reasons that we had hypothesized. (The open-ended question contains no such suggestions.) Note that respondents were asked to spell out "problems with management or maintenance" (the open-ended question at the top of the second page). We considered this item to be the heart of the questionnaire.

EXHIBIT 8.8

Example Move-Out Questionnaire

FORMER RESIDENT QUESTIONNAIRE

1. When you moved from your apartment, did you choose
   _____ Another apartment community? If so, which one?

                      (Property Name)   (City)

   _____ A single-family home/townhouse/condominium?
   Renting _____ Buying _____
   _____ Something else (please specify) _____
   I'm spending approximately $_____.00 per month on my new rent/mortgage payment.

2. Please complete this sentence: "What I disliked most about my apartment was
   _____
   _____."

3. Why did you decide to move out of your apartment? (Please check all reasons that apply)
   _____ Too expensive
   _____ Problems with management
   _____ Problems with maintenance
   _____ Buying a home/condominium/townhouse
   _____ Work reasons (job transfer, lost job, decided to move closer to work, had to move out of the area)
   _____ Personal reasons (problems with roommate, divorce, etc.)
   _____ Other reasons (please list them):

- *Question 4* was a different way of framing Question 2. We wanted to know whether there was anything—other than not raising the rent—that would have kept the respondent from moving out. This, too, is an open-ended question.

Note that the questionnaire concluded with the option for direct follow-up. We wanted to know whether some residents were willing to discuss their responses—we hoped to be able to explore in detail any answers that were unclear to us or to learn more about what the respondents thought.

So that we could determine the number of responses related to each apartment community (move-out location), we coded the return envelopes. However, the questionnaire itself had no identifier. If we did not receive a response after ten days, a duplicate questionnaire package was sent. Within a month and a half, we had received completed questionnaires from more than 50 percent of our sample. This is what we learned from the exercise:

EXHIBIT 8.8 *(continued)*

If you checked "problems with management" or "problems with maintenance" in question 3, please write down what the problems were:

_____
_____
_____

4. This is the last question. Aside from the amount of rent you would have paid if you had signed a new lease, was there **any one thing** that the owner or manager of your apartment community could have done that would have convinced you to continue living where you were? What would that one thing have been?

_____
_____
_____

Please return the questionnaire in the enclosed stamped, self-addressed envelope to *[Management Company Name and Address]*. If you would be willing to discuss your answers to the questionnaire in more detail, please sign the form and provide your telephone number. Otherwise, you will remain completely anonymous.

_____   _____
(Signature)   (Telephone Number)

Thank you for your help.

---

1. The written questionnaire method of collecting data can be effective, and the response rate may be higher than anticipated—even when respondents do not benefit directly from their participation. In this case, the request for participation was predicated on the stated willingness of our client—the owners of an apartment building—to improve conditions for residents in the future, a situation that does not provide any measurable benefits for the respondents to the questionnaire. Nonetheless, we verified our supposition that many people are willing to participate in a survey simply because they are asked to do so when it can be made apparent and believable to them that their answers will be helpful to someone else.
2. The "open-ended" questions elicited the types of responses that we had anticipated—i.e., mentions of subjects that were not contained elsewhere in the questionnaire. Several of the survey responses were actually typewritten, and many respondents wrote extensive answers to the open-ended questions using the backs of the pages of the survey. In addition, perhaps because we had invited telephone contact, we received at least ten phone calls—many of them from very angry people whose participation was extremely helpful for that reason alone.

3. Much to our surprise (and the owners' amazement) these residents' decisions to move out had *not* been motivated primarily by job relocations, price considerations, or even the desire to purchase single-family housing—only about 10 percent of the respondents cited these reasons. We found, instead, that slightly more than 90 percent had moved out of their apartments (or were planning to do so) because they were fundamentally dissatisfied with the service they were receiving in their apartment community. They considered that their apartment living experience had failed in numerous critical ways to meet both their "baseline requirements" *and* their "service expectations."

One conclusion we reached was that the overwhelming majority of former residents we surveyed felt that they had not been treated fairly by the site personnel at the property. They had complaints about poor treatment from their resident managers, inadequate tenant screening, lack of parking, poor appliances and carpeting, and much more. However, the most significant common complaint involved what residents considered to be shabby service from the site staff.

> "When I asked my resident manager whether the washers and dryers could be replaced or fixed (they didn't work for at least two months), he laughed at me. But the real reason I decided to move out was that the manager laughed at me when I made a reasonable request."

This former resident's comment was typical of the responses we received. It was indeed a "moment of truth."

In conclusion, we suggest that you think seriously about whether any of the examples of poor service and management neglect and ineptitude presented here could happen at one of your properties. Do you know for certain that this sort of thing—or something similar or even worse—could never happen there? How do you know that? Do you have a reliable system in place that guarantees the quality of the moments of truth at your properties?

Furthermore, can you imagine any of these types of incidents happening at Scandinavian Airlines or a Nordstrom Department Store?

The conventional wisdom about apartment marketing is that the most productive source of advertising is word-of-mouth. As we noted at the beginning of this chapter, customers tend to tell others about their dissatisfaction—rather than complain to the source. The same thing happens in apartment management. You cannot respond to residents' complaints if you do not know what they are. However, you can actively manage *all* of the moments of truth at your apartment community, and the active moments of truth you create can be the *value* that will differentiate your "four white walls and a rug" from all the other, similar apartments in your neighborhood. This will be true for your own residents and for every single person to whom your residents brag about their experiences—and they will brag about them!

Index

A

Absorption, 12–13
Ad copy. *See* Advertisements; Advertising
Adjunct leasing activities, 176–195
Adjusted rent, calculating, 21
Adjusted rent per square foot, 21–22
Adjustments, making specific, 20–21
Advertisements, contents, 91, 93, 94, 96
Advertising, 87–119.
    billboards, 94, 114–115, 116
    brochures, 193–194
    budget considerations, 94–97
    bus stop enclosures, 117
    classified, 92, 94
    costs, 96, 101
    creating effective, 93
    developing, 103
    direct mail, 115, 117, 194
    display, 92, 94, 110
    employment, leasing personnel, 126, 127
    evaluation, 108–109
    illustrations, 108
    magazines, 111–112
    market research, 91–92
    media selection, 104–108
    miscellaneous media, 117–118
    newspapers, 110–111
    nondiscriminatory, 185–186, 187
    objectives, 88–90
    outdoor, 117–118
    print, 95, 107–108
    radio, 94, 112–113
    staff requirements, 97–104
    strategies, 90–92, 94
    television, 94, 113–114
    word-of-mouth, 52, 82, 85, 197, 209, 224
Advertising agency, 67, 71, 97, 98–102, 109, 113
    client relations, 102
    cost containment, 101
    exclusivity of category, 100
    fees, 100–101
    selection, 99–100
Advertising budget, 93–97. *See also* Marketing budget
Advertising campaign, 46, 95
Advertising costs, 94–96, 99, 104–105, 111, 112, 113
    agency fees, 100–101

225

Advertising media, 31, 46, 94–95, 110–118
Advertorial, 111
Affordability, rent, 13, 93, 107, 147, 171, 176–177, 179, 183, 184
Age discrimination, 185–186. *See also* Fair housing laws
Alaskan winter marketing, 30, 34
Amenities, 202–204. *See also* Buy factors
  objections, 156–157
Americans with Disabilities Act, 186
Apartment industry, service, 200–202
Apartment management, objectives, 2–3
Apartment marketing, retailing comparison, 34, 162, 164–175, 202–213, 221
Application form
  employment, 127
  rental, 178–182, 195
Appointment-setting example, 142
Audience, advertising media, 95, 96, 104–106, 113

B

Baseline requirement, 206–208, 213, 224
Base unit of value, calculating, 21–22
Basic selling techniques, 163
Bathtub analogy, 33
Behavior, resident, 177, 183, 184, 189, 190, 193
Benefit selling, 145–146, 150–151
Billboards, 41, 46–47, 94, 114–115, 116
  location, 94
Blue suit purchase scenario, 164–165, 168–169, 172–173
Broadcast advertising. *See* Electronic media
Brochures, 193–194
Budget, 26, 27, 31, 212
  advertising, 93–97
  marketing, 31, 32–33, 41–53, 63, 93, 95–97, 104, 109, 132, 201, 214
  pro forma, 27
  staff compensation, 124–125
Building types, 14
Bus stop enclosures, 117

Buy factors, comparing, 19–23, 91
By the Numbers: Using Demographics and Psychographics for Business Growth in the 90's (Nichols), 9

C

Capitalization rate, 27
Carlzon, Jan, 199, 201
CERTIFIED PROPERTY MANAGER® (CPM®), 126
Children, minor, 178, 184. *See also* Fair housing laws
Civil rights. *See* Fair housing laws; Equal employment opportunity
Classified advertisements, 93, 94
  example, 92
Closing, 141–143, 158–163, 194
  avoiding, 194
  comparison with retailing, 162, 164–175
  examples, 159–161
  strategies, 158–162
Closing ratio, 58
Cohorts, 35
Competition, 15–23, 54, 59–60, 109, 120, 155, 189, 201–202, 204, 214
  buy factors, 19–23
  evaluation, 15, 17
  marketing grid, 15–17
  rents, 17–19
Competitive guarantees, 214–215
Computers, record keeping, 52, 57
  leasing agent performance, 137
Concessions, competing against, 28–29
Consolidated MSA (CMSA), 5
Contextual service, 208
Contract. *See* Residential lease
Contract rent, 17
Conversion ratios, 52, 55, 57–58
Costs per rental, 52. *See also* Traffic logs
Count data, 5–6
Credit bureau, 183, 188
Credit references, verifying, 179, 183
Curb appeal, 24–25, 42, 148
Current residents
  demographics, 39, 58, 104, 105, 195
  psychographics, 91
Customer service, 167, 168–171,

192–193, 196–200, 202. *See also* Resident retention; Resident satisfaction
   apartment industry applications, 200–202
   importance, 168–171
   market research, 213–224
   moments of truth, 207–213
   profitability, 204–207
   renter motivation, 202–204
   resident satisfaction, 201, 215–224
   retailing, 196–200
Customers, understanding, 62
Customers for Life: How to Turn That One-Time Buyer into a Lifetime Customer, 196
Cycle of yeses, 172–175
   hidden negatives, 174–175

D

Decorating, lease renewal strategy, 192–193
Demand. *See* Supply and demand
Demographic data, 4–9, 10
   counts, 5–6
   how to use, 10
   periodic measures, 8
   proportions, 7–8
   rates, 6
   ratios, 6–7
   sources, 9, 104
   supply, demand, and absorption, 10–13
   types of data, 5–9
Demographics, 35, 39, 45, 54, 58, 60, 71, 89, 95, 104. *See also* Marketing research
   audience, advertising media, 95, 104–106, 113
   current residents, 39, 58, 104, 105, 195
   defined, 63
   media selection, 104–105
   versus psychographics, 63–64
Demography, defined, 4
Desirability factors, 26. *See also* Buy factors
Desirability issues, 171–172

Directive listening, 121, 123
Direct mail advertising, 115, 117, 194
   brochures, 194
Discontinuous contact, 207
Discrimination, 184, 185, 187. *See also* Equal employment opportunity; Fair housing laws
   interviewing job applicants, 127
   lawsuits, 185
   types, 186
Display advertisements, 93, 110
   example, 92
Disposable income, 11

E

Economics, apartment marketing, 26–28, 54–55
Economic vacancies, 12
Economy
   local, 55–56, 59
   national, 59
Effective gross income, 26
Effective rent, 18–19
Electronic media, 46, 94–95, 96, 105, 109. *See also* Advertising media; Radio; Television
Employees. *See also* Hiring practices; Leasing personnel; Marketing personnel
   feedback, 133, 135, 137
   maintaining morale, 136–138
   motivating, 132–134
Employment agency, 126–127
Employment application, 127
Equal employment opportunity, 126, 127
Ergonomics, 44
Evaluating competition, 15–23, 35–39
Eviction, 55, 58
Exclusivity of category, 100
Exit interview, 58

F

Face rent, 17
Fair employment practices, 127
Fair Housing Amendments Act (1988), 186, 191

Fair housing laws, 177, 178, 189, 191
    compliance requirements, 184–188
Familial status, 184
Families, defined, 10
Features, apartment. *See* Buy factors
Floor plans, leasing strategy, 150, 169–171, 194
Focus groups, 71–72, 77–79, 103, 213, 214–217, 220
    competitive guarantees, 214–215
    marketing strategies, 71–72, 75–79
    moderator's role, 72, 80, 215
    practical example, 79–86
    resident satisfaction, 215–217, 220
    versus questionnaires, 77–79
Focusing on the property, 23–26, 57–59
    curb appeal, 24–25
    shopping, 24–25
    unit readiness, 25–26
Former residents, follow-up, 58–59, 222–223
Form stage, team-building, 135
Forms, examples. *See also* Questionnaires
    guest card, 143–144
    marketing grid, 16
    rental application, 180–182
    traffic logs, 48–51
Four white walls and a rug, 1, 201, 206, 208, 224
Frequency, advertising, 96, 105, 106–107, 109

G

Gross potential income, 26
Guest card, 137, 143–147, 149, 169, 194–195, 208
    completing, 144–146
    example, 143–144
    information resource, 149, 194–195
    leasing use, 146–147
Guest card as sales tool, 145

H

Handicapped people, 144, 184, 186
Haverhill marketing grid example, 36–38

Head-to-head price correlation, 18
Hiring practices, 119–129
    defining the job, 120–121
    developing interview questions, 122, 124
    identifying prospective employees, 125–127
    identifying skills, 121–122
    interviewing applicants, 127–129
    networking, 125–127
Hot buttons. *See* Buy factors
Households, defined, 10–11
Housing demand, 10–11
Housing market, 13
Housing ordinances, local, 179, 184, 189, 191
How to Win Customers and Keep Them for Life (LeBoeuf), 197

I

Income capitalization approach to value, 27
Insertion, print advertising, 105. *See also* Advertising costs
Insider's Guide to Demographic Know-How: Everything You Need to Find, Analyze, and Use Information About Your Customers (Crispell), 9
Insider's Guide to Demographic Know-How: Everything Marketers Need to Know About How to Find, Analyze and Use Information About Their Customers (Wickham), 9
Inspection
    leased premises, 190, 191, 193
    property, 25, 148, 190, 191
Institute of Real Estate Management (IREM), 61, 126
Intangibles, renting decision, 1
Interviewing job applicants, 127–129
Inventory of vacancies, 25–26

L

Landlord-tenant laws, 179, 191
Laurels, The, example, 67, 68–70, 73–75, 79–87, 195
    display ad, 69
    focus session, 79–87

nonrenter survey, 74–75, 195
positioning statement, 68
resident questionnaire, 73
Law of supply and demand, 12, 66
Lawsuits, civil, 185, 188
Lease. *See* Residential lease
Leasing adjuncts, 176–196
 documenting the lease, 189–191
 marketing resources, 194–195
 qualifying prospects, 177–189
 renewal strategies, 191–193
 rental application form, 178–182
 security deposits, 177, 188–189, 190, 192
Leasing brochures, 193–194
Leasing center, 23, 44–46, 53, 149, 171
Leasing office. *See* Leasing center
Leasing performance, evaluation, 57–61
Leasing personnel, 119–138, 148, 185, 208
 compensation, 124–125, 131, 132, 133–134, 137
 employee feedback, 133, 135, 137
 hiring, 119–129
 interviewing applicants, 123, 127–129, 133
 interview question development, 122–124
 job definition, 120–121, 129–130, 131–132
 motivating, 132–134
 performance evaluation, 132, 137–138
 productivity, 53, 132, 137–138, 149, 178–179
 prospecting for applicants, 124–127
 qualifying applicants, 107
 skill requirements, 121–122
 staff morale, 136–138
 team-building, 134–136
 training, 129–132
Leasing plan, 31. *See also* Marketing plan
Leasing strategies, 139–175
 basic selling techniques, 163
 closing, 141–143, 158–163
 concept of need, 164–167
 customer service, 167, 168–171

cycle of yeses, 172–175
floor plans, 150, 169–171, 194
getting acquainted, 140–147
guest card, 137, 143–147, 149, 169
issues of desirability, 171–172
issues of value, 167–168
nature of objections, 172–174
overcoming objections, 152–158, 172–175
personalized selling, 151–152
practical example, 162, 164–175
preparing to sell, 149–150
retailing comparison, 162, 164–175
selling benefits, 146, 150–151
showing apartments, 148–158, 171–175
soft markets, 139, 163
telephone techniques, 140–143
Leasing team, 134–136
 form stage, 135
 norm phase, 135–136
 perform phase, 136
 storm phase, 135
Listening skills, 121–123, 130, 136–137, 147, 149, 153
Local economy, 55–56, 59
Local market, 15–23
Location, 14, 38, 91, 201

M
Magazines, advertising, 111–112
Maintenance checkup program, 216–217
Management office, 45–46, 209. *See also* Leasing center
Management profit, service-generated, 205
Management strategies
 defining the market, 3–15
 owner's objectives, 2–3
Managing to Keep the Customer: How to Achieve and Maintain Superior Customer Service throughout the Organization, 196
Market, target, 35, 39
Market analysis
 competing against concessions, 28–29

Market analysis (*continued*)
  defining the market, 3–15
  economics, 26–28
  evaluating competition, 15–23
  focusing on the property, 23–26
Market conditions, 52, 53–62
  impact, 53–56
  soft markets, 2, 12, 54–61, 66, 162, 192
Marketing
  defined, 63
  visual theme, 43
Marketing budget, 31, 32–33, 41–53, 63, 94–97, 104, 109, 132, 201, 214
Marketing grid, 15–23, 35, 36–38, 39–40, 60, 202
  calculating adjusted rents, 20–22
  comparing buy factors, 19–23
  comparing rents, 17–19
  completed example, 36–38
  evaluating competition, 15–23
  head-to-head rent comparison, 18–19
  objective effort, 17
  sample form, 16
  setting rent, 17, 22–23, 26
  subjective nature, 17
Marketing opportunities, 35, 213
Marketing personnel, 31, 56, 97, 102–104, 107, 109, 148. *See also* Leasing personnel
Marketing plan, 29
  defined, 31
  development, 34–53
Marketing planning, 30–61
  adjusting for market conditions, 53–61
  advertising media, 31, 46
  budgeting, 31, 32–34, 41, 53
  focusing on the property, 23–26, 57–59
  marketing opportunities, 35
  marketing programs, 46–47
  marketing strategies, 39–46
  media selection, 46, 53
  monitoring results, 47, 52–53
  owner's objectives, 31, 39
  personnel, 31, 56
  positioning statement, 31, 46
  soft markets, 54–61
  target markets, 35, 39
Marketing process, 34–35
Marketing programs, 46–47
Marketing research, 3–15, 41, 103, 104. *See also* Demographics
  neighborhood, 13–15
  region, 3, 4–13
Marketing resources, 41–46, 194–195
  guest cards, 194–195
  rental application forms, 195
Marketing strategies, 1–2, 39–46, 189, 193–194, 213. *See also* Leasing strategies
  comparing buy factors, 19–23
  comparing rents, 17–19
  competing against concessions, 28–29
  economics, 26–28
  evaluating competition, 15, 17
  follow-up of nonrenters, 195
  guest cards, 194–195
  leasing brochure, 193–194
  security deposit, 189
  soft markets, 2, 12, 192
  strengths, 39–40
  understanding management objectives, 2–3
  weaknesses/solutions, 40–41
Market rent, 17–18, 66, 90
Market research, 3, 43, 62–86, 91, 103, 104, 113, 194–195, 204, 213–224
  ad develpoment, 91–92, 103
  application to resident retention, 215–224
  choosing methodology, 77–79
  customer service, 213–224
  defined, 63
  focus groups, 71–72, 75–79, 103, 213
  methodologies compared, 77–79
  questionnaires, 72–79, 103, 213
  rationale, apartment marketing, 65–68, 70–71
  sampling, 77, 79
  types of data, 63–64
Market research applications
  move-in, 217–220

move-out, 220–224
nonrenters, 74–77, 79, 195
retailing, 64–65
resident satisfaction, 215–224
Mean, 18
Media buying, 104
Median, 18
Media selection, 46, 53, 94, 104–108, 109. *See also* Advertising
effectiveness of print media, 107–108, 109
frequency, 105, 106–107, 109
reach, 105–106
Metropolitan statistical area (MSA), 4–5
Minimum standards for resident selection, 184
Minorities. *See* Protected classes
Minors, 179, 183
Mode, 18
Model apartments, 32, 43–44
Moments of truth, 199, 207–213
active, 211–213
examples, 209–210, 212–213
passive, 211, 213
Monitoring marketing results, 47, 52–53, 195. *See also* Traffic logs
Motivation
employees, 132–134
renting decisions, 196, 202–204
Move-in, questionnaires, 217–220
Move-out, questionnaires, 221–224

N

National economy, 59
Need, concept in selling, 164–167
Neighborhood, 3, 13–15, 54, 59, 91
Net operating income, 26–27, 56–57, 66, 90, 177
Networking, 125, 126
Newspapers, advertising, 110–111
prospecting for employees, 126
Nonrenters, follow-up, 47, 57, 58, 76–77, 193, 195, 214
questionnaire example, 74–75
Nordstrom Department Stores, 199–200, 224
Norm phase, team-building, 135–136

O

Objections, 152–158, 172–175
amenities, 156–157
decision-making process, 157–158
nature, 172–174
overcoming, 152–158
price, 155–156, 170
sales tool, 153
Observation, 209
Occupancy agreement, 189. *See also* Residential lease
Occupancy limits, 183, 184
Occupancy rate, 201–202. *See also* Vacancy rate
Outdoor advertising, 117–118
Oversupply of apartments, 12, 54–55, 65–67, 139, 162
Owner's objectives, 2–3, 31, 39, 177

P

Perform phase, team-building, 136
Periodic measures, 8
Personalized selling, 151–152
Personnel, 148. *See also* Employees; Leasing personnel; Marketing personnel
Pets, 178, 191
Physical vacancies, 12
Poor service, 197–198, 224
better approaches, 199
examples, 198
Positioning statement, 31, 46, 68, 108, 194
Practical examples
competing against concessions, 28–29
experiments with media, 110–118
focus group session, 79–86
market research applications to resident retention, 213–224
retailing comparison, 162, 164–175
Preparation, 149–150
Prequalifying prospective residents, 93, 107, 176, 177–178, 179
Presentation, 148–149
Preventive maintenance, 88
Price, 14. *See also* Rent

Price (*continued*)
  head-to-head correlation, 18
  objections, 155–156
Price points, 27–28
Pride, 148
Primary MSA (PMSA), 5
Print media, 46, 94–95, 96, 109. *See also* Advertising media; Magazines; Newspapers
  effectiveness, 107–108, 109
Product, 148
Productivity, 149
  leasing agents, 53, 132, 137–138, 149, 178–179
Product presentation, 42
Professional organizations, 126
  Institute of Real Estate Management, 126
Professionalism, 60–61, 109, 136
Profitability and customer service, 204–207
Pro forma budget, 27
Property
  curb appeal, 24–25, 42
  desirability factors, 26–27
  focus on in soft market, 57–59
  gross income, 2
  inspection, 25, 148, 190, 191, 193
  leasing center, 44–46
  model apartments, 43–44
  quality, 23–24
  signage, 42–43
  unit readiness, 25–26
Property managers, professional, 2, 14–15, 60–61
Property value, 27, 66, 90, 193
Proportion data, 7–8
Prospects. *See also* Residents
  compliance with fair housing laws, 184–188
  follow-up of nonrenters, 47, 57, 58, 74–77, 193, 195, 214
  motivators of renters, 202–204
  qualifying, 177–178
  reasons for not renting, 58
  rental application form, 178–182
  resident selection standards, 179, 183–184
  security deposits, 188–189
  soft market, 192
Protected classes, 126, 178, 184, 189. *See also* Equal employment opportunity; Fair housing laws
Psychographics, 35, 63–64, 71, 72, 89, 104. *See also* Market research
  advertising audience, 104
  current residents, 91
  defined, 63
Psychology, sales transaction, 151, 153, 157, 160–161, 164, 165, 167, 169, 171–174

Q

Qualification standards, 176
Qualifying job applicants, 107
Qualifying prospective residents, 169–172, 177–189
  application form, 178–179, 180–182
  compliance with fair housing laws, 184–188
  income requirements, 13, 147, 171, 177, 179, 183
  security deposits, 188–189
  selection standards, 179, 183–184
Quality, property, 14, 23–24
Questionnaires, 72–79, 103, 209, 213, 216–224
  developing questions, 76, 221–222
  follow-up of nonrenters, 74–77, 193, 195
  market research, 72–79
  rating scales, 220
  resident satisfaction, 217–224
  versus focus groups, 76–79
Questionnaires, examples
  former resident, 222–223
  maintenance survey, 216–217
  new resident, 218
  nonrenter, 74–75
  resident, 73, 219
Quoted rent, 17

R

Radio, advertising, 94, 112–113
Range, 18
Rate data, 6

Ratio data, 6–7
Reach, advertising, 105–106
Region, 3, 4–13, 54, 59
Renewal lease, 188, 191–193
Renewal strategies, 191–193
Rent
    adjustments, 20–21
    affordability, 13, 93, 107, 147, 171, 176–177, 179, 183, 184
    collecting, 179
    comparison, 17–19
    concessions, 18, 28–29, 33, 55, 56, 59, 66, 90, 155, 178, 201
    economics, 26–28
    method of analysis, 18
    structure, 26
Rental application form, 39, 58, 178–179, 195
    example, 180–182
Rent concessions, 18, 28–29, 33, 55, 56, 59, 66, 90, 155, 178, 201
Rent control laws, 190
Renter motivation, 202–204
Residential lease, 189–191
    renewal strategies, 191–193
    rent control laws, 190, 192
Resident retention, 196–224. *See also* Customer service; Resident satisfaction
    apartment industry service, 200
    moments of truth, 207–213
    practical example, 213–224
Resident retention programs, 1, 33, 86
    costs, 33
Resident satisfaction, 58–59, 73, 84, 192, 215–224
    focus group, 215–227
    maintenance survey, 216–217
    move-in questionnaire, 217–218, 220
    move-out questionnaire, 220–224
    resident questionnaire, 219, 220
Resident selection standards, 179, 183–184. *See also* Fair housing laws; Tenant screening
Residents. *See also* Prospects
    acknowledging, 212
    baseline requirements, 206–208
    current, service, 201
    occupancy limits, 184
    retention costs, 33
    service expectations, 206–207, 208. 213, 224
    welcoming new, 212–213
Resident turnover, 33, 58, 120, 121, 201
Results, monitoring, 47, 52–53
Retailing
    customer service, 196–200
    leasing strategies comparison, 163–175
    market research applications, 64–65
Risk, 177
Role-play scenarios, examples, 123
Rules and regulations, 177, 190, 215

S

Sales techniques. *See also* Leasing strategies
    basic, 163
    benefit selling, 146, 150–151
    closing, 141, 158–162, 174–175
    concept of need, 164–167
    cycle of yeses, 174–175
    importance of service, 168–171
    issues of desirability, 171–172
    issues of value, 167–168
    moments of truth, 207–213
    nature of objections, 172–174
    objections, 152–158, 172–175
    psychology, 151, 153, 157, 160–161, 164, 165, 167, 169, 171–174
    retailing comparison, 162, 164–175
    strategies for closing, 158–162, 174–175
    targeted benefit selling, 146, 148–149, 150–151
    telephone, 140–143
Sampling, 77, 79
Scandinavian Airlines System (SAS), 198–199, 201, 224
Security deposit, 177, 188–189, 190, 192
    amount, 188–189, 192
    discrimination, 186, 189
    interest, 189, 193
    lease renewal, 193
    marketing strategy, 189
Self-service, 167, 169

Selling techniques, basic, 163
Senior citizens, 185–186. *See also* Fair housing laws
Service. *See* Customer service; Resident retention; Resident satisfaction
Service America! Doing Business in the New Economy (Albrecht and Zemke), 201
Service expectations, 206–207, 208, 213, 224
Service-profit relationship, 204–207
Shoppers, role, 24–25, 137
Shopping a property, 24–25
Showing apartments, 148–158
  leasing strategies, 148–149
  overcoming prospects' objections, 152–158
  personalized selling, 151–152
  preparation, 149–150
  selling benefits, 150–151
  versus a tour, 146–147, 148–149, 152, 153, 154, 172
Signage, 32, 42–43, 44, 109. *See also* Billboards
  directional, 41, 44, 46, 114, 117
Soft markets, 2, 12, 33, 54–61, 66, 163, 192
  defined, 12, 54
  oversupply of apartments, 12, 54–55, 65–67, 139, 163
  recommended approaches, 57–61
  rent concessions, 33, 66
  rewarding current residents, 192
  typical reactions of ownership, 56–57
Spots, advertising, 94, 96. *See also* Electronic media; Radio; Television
Standard deviation, 18
Standard metropolitan statistical area (SMSA), 4–5
Standards, resident selection, 179, 183–184
Statistical calculations, 18
Statistical units, 4–5
Steeplechase example, 28–29
Step theory of selling, 163
Storm phase, team-building, 135
Street rent, 17
Supply and demand, 10–13, 59

T

Targeted benefit selling, 146, 148–149, 150–151
  examples, 150, 151–152
Targeted marketing, 35–44, 60, 95, 113. *See also* Media selection
Target markets, 35, 39
Telephone, leasing strategies, 140–143
Television, advertising, 94, 113–114
Tenant screening, 81–82, 83, 177–179, 183–184, 215, 224
Thank you notes, 212
Theme, 43, 194. *See also* Positioning statement
Time, broadcast advertising, 92, 94. *See also* Advertising costs
Total Customer Service: The Ultimate Weapon (Davidow and Uttal), 198
Traffic, monitoring, 57–61
Traffic logs, 47–53, 102, 103, 106, 137, 200
  monthly analysis, 51
  phone calls, daily, 50
  showings, daily, 48
  weekly, 49
Traffic reports. *See* Traffic logs
Trailblazers of service, 198–200
Training, employee, 129–132
  alternatives, 131
  individualized learning, 130–131
  job parameters, 131–132
  motivation, 132–134

U

Unified graphic theme, 43, 194
Unit readiness, 25–26, 148, 206
Urbanized area (UA), 4–5

V

Vacancies
  adjusting marketing grid, 21
  economic, 12
  physical, 11–12
Vacancy rate, 11, 58, 59, 110
  analyzing, 8
Valuation, income capitalization approach, 27
Value, perceived, 14, 18–19, 26, 29, 35,

60, 66, 155–156, 167–168,
202–207, 209, 215, 224
defining, 14, 202, 206
issues, 167–168
key to leasing success, 60, 224
techniques for selling, 29
Voice, sales tool, 140

W

Word-of-mouth advertising, 52, 82, 85, 197, 209, 224
Wrong carpeting example, 174
Wrong location example, 175

About the Institute of Real Estate Management

The Institute of Real Estate Management (IREM) was founded in 1933 with the goals of establishing a Code of Ethics and standards of practice in real estate management as well as fostering knowledge, integrity, and efficiency among its practitioners. The Institute confers the CERTIFIED PROPERTY MANAGER® (CPM®) designation on individuals who meet specified criteria of education and experience in real estate management and subscribe to an established Code of Ethics. Similar criteria have been established for real estate management firms that are awarded the ACCREDITED MANAGEMENT ORGANIZATION® (AMO®) designation. The ACCREDITED RESIDENTIAL MANAGER (ARM®) service award is presented to individuals who meet specified educational and professional requirements in residential site management and subscribe to a Code of Ethics.

The Institute's membership includes more than 8,900 CPM® members, 3,000 ARM® participants, and 635 AMO® firms. CPM members manage all types of investment real estate properties in the United States, including nearly 30% of all the multifamily rental housing.

For sixty years, IREM has been enhancing the prestige of property management through its activities and publications. The Institute offers a wide selection of courses, seminars, periodicals, books, and other materials about real estate management and related topics. To obtain a current catalog, write to: Institute of Real Estate Management, 430 North Michigan Avenue, P.O. Box 109025, Chicago, Illinois 60610-9025, or telephone (312) 661-1953.